15.39

OCEAN

Writer – Warren Ellis
Penciler – Chris Sprouse
Inker – Karl Story

Colorist – Randy Mayor (1-4)
Randy Mayor & Wendy Broome (5)
WildStorm FX with Tony Aviña (6)
Letters – Jared K. Fletcher

Original Series Covers - Michael Golden
OCEAN Created by Warren Ellis and Chris Sprouse

Jim Lee, Editorial Director
John Nee, VP—Business Development
Scott Dunbier, Executive Editor
Kristy Quinn, Assistant Editor
Robbin Brosterman, Senior Art Director
Ed Roeder, Art Director
Paul Levitz, President & Publisher
Georg Brewer, VP—Design & DC Direct Creative
Richard Bruning, Senior VP—Creative Director
Patrick Caldon, Senior VP—Finance & Operations
Chris Caramalis, VP—Finance
Terri Cunningham, VP—Managing Editor
Stephanie Fierman, Senior VP—Sales & Marketing
Alison Gill, VP—Manufacturing
Rich Johnson, VP—Book Trade Sales
Hank Kanalz, VP—General Manager, WildStorm
Lillian Laserson, Senior VP & General Counsel
Paula Lowitt, Senior VP—Business & Legal Affairs
David McKillips, VP—Advertising & Custom Publishing
Gregory Noveck, Senior VP—Creative Affairs
Cheryl Rubin, Senior VP—Brand Management
Jeff Trojan, VP—Business Development, DC Direct
Bob Wayne, VP—Sales

APR 4 2007

OCEAN published by WildStorm Productions. 888 Prospect St. #240, La Jolla, CA 92037. Compilation © 2006 Warren Ellis and Chris Sprouse. All Rights Reserved. OCEAN is ™ Warren Ellis and Chris Sprouse.
WildStorm Signature Series and its logo are trademarks of DC Comics. Originally published in single magazine form as OCEAN #1-6 copyright © 2004, 2005.
The stories, characters, and incidents mentioned in this magazine are entirely fictional. Printed on recyclable paper. WildStorm does not read or accept unsolicited submissions of ideas, stories or artwork. Printed in Canada.

DC Comics, a Warner Bros. Entertainment Company.

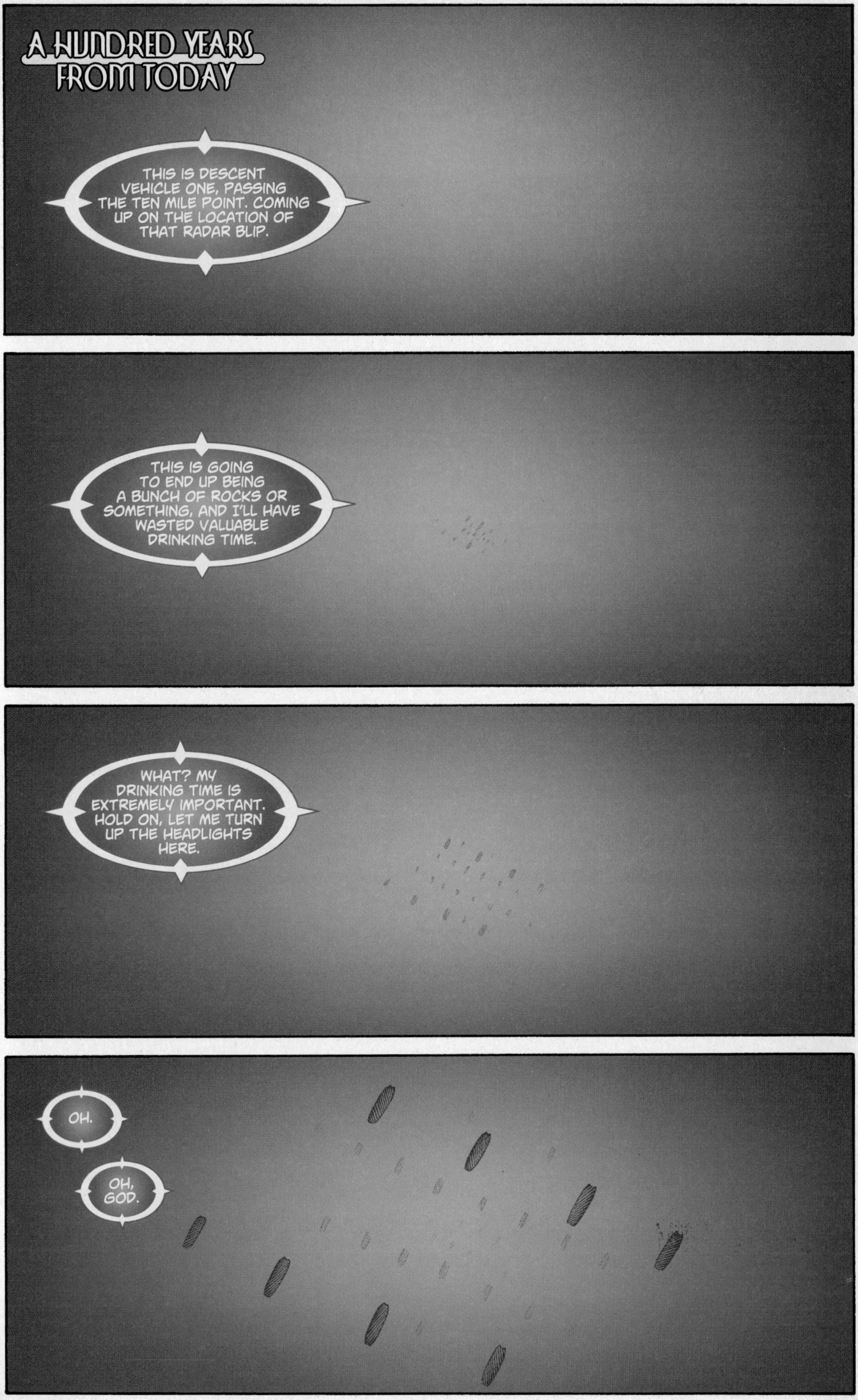
A HUNDRED YEARS FROM TODAY
THIS IS DESCENT VEHICLE ONE, PASSING THE TEN MILE POINT. COMING UP ON THE LOCATION OF THAT RADAR BLIP.
THIS IS GOING TO END UP BEING A BUNCH OF ROCKS OR SOMETHING, AND I'LL HAVE WASTED VALUABLE DRINKING TIME.
WHAT? MY DRINKING TIME IS EXTREMELY IMPORTANT. HOLD ON, LET ME TURN UP THE HEADLIGHTS HERE.
OH.
OH, GOD.

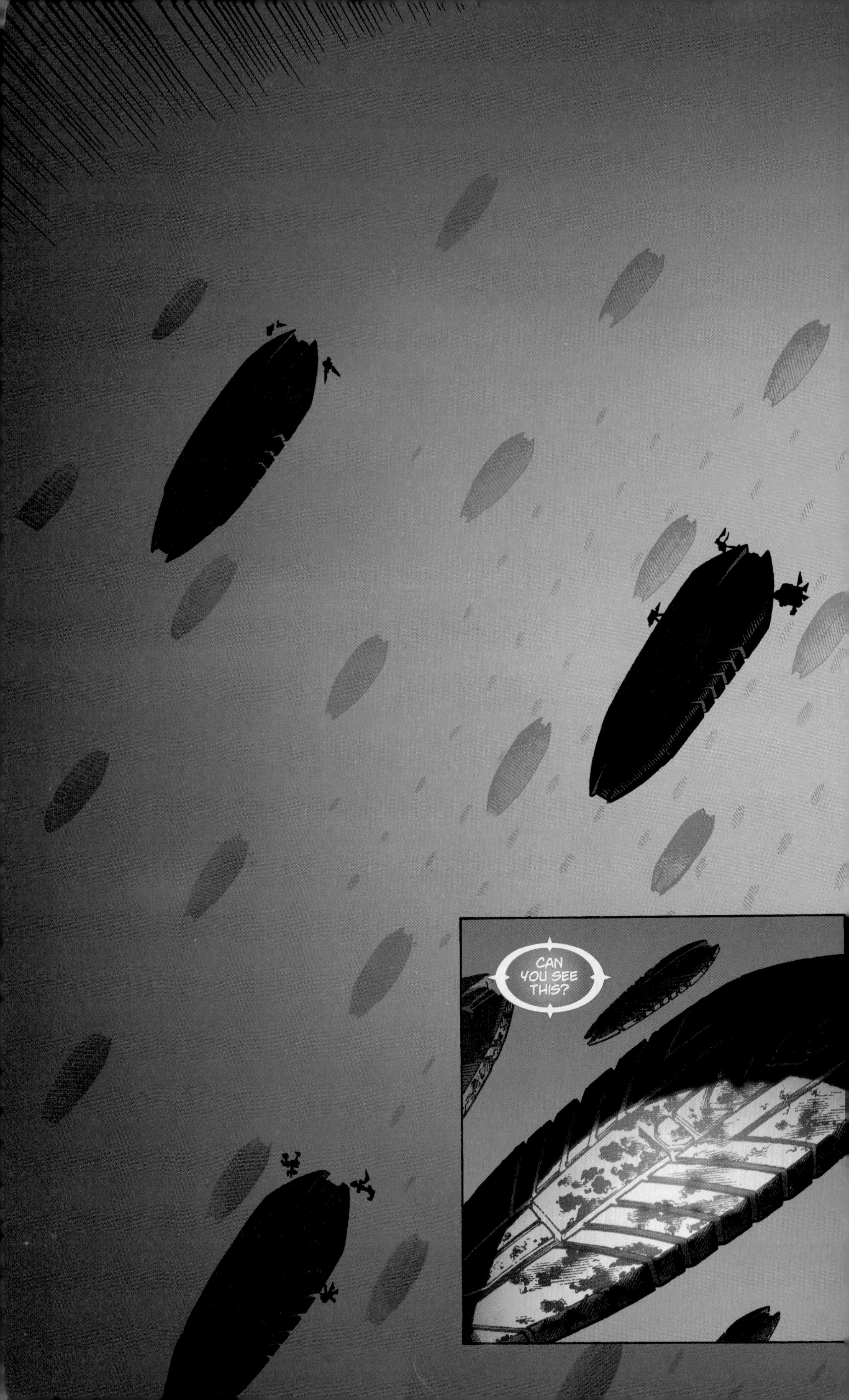
CAN YOU SEE THIS?

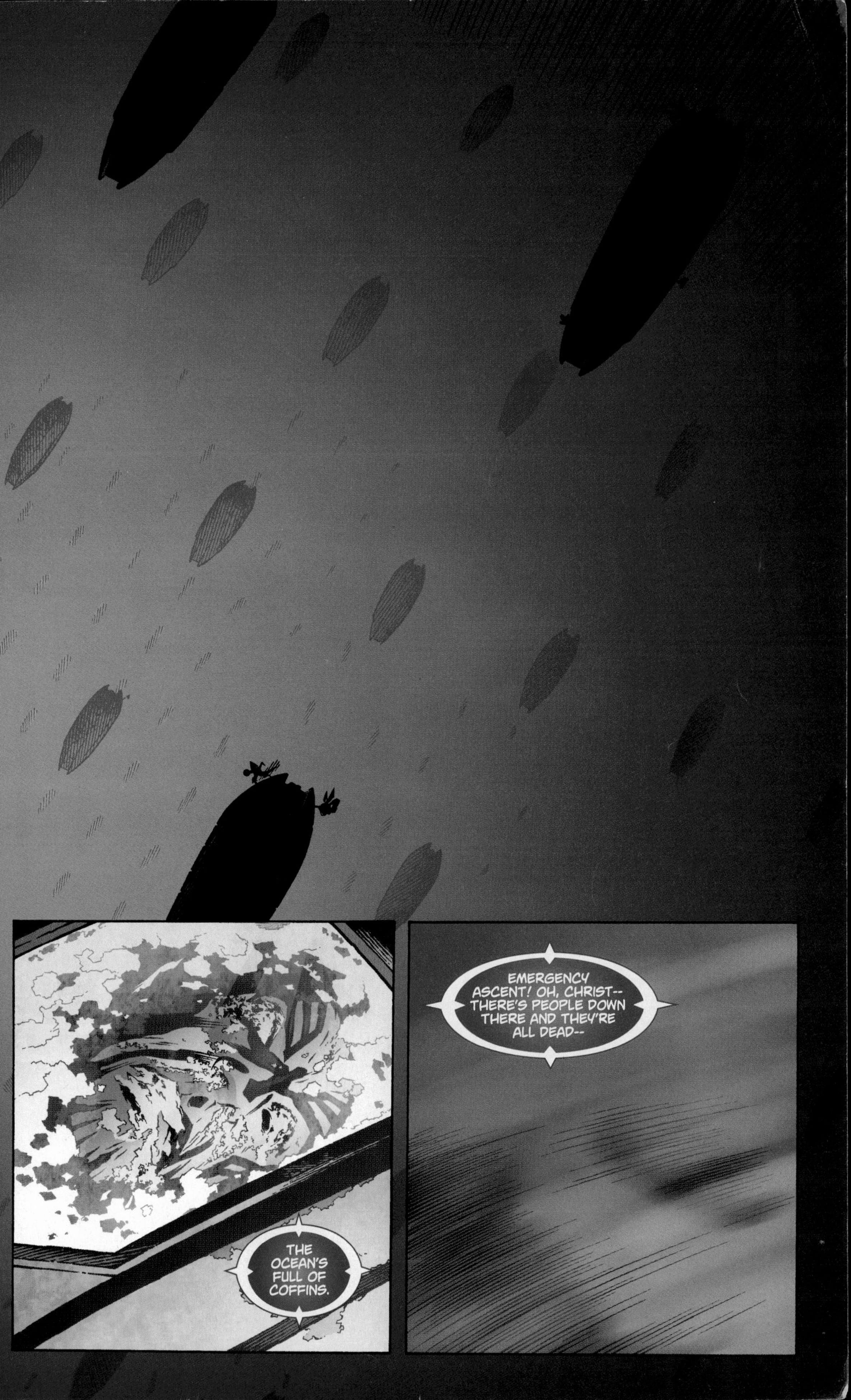
THE OCEAN'S FULL OF COFFINS.
EMERGENCY ASCENT! OH, CHRIST-- THERE'S PEOPLE DOWN THERE AND THEY'RE ALL DEAD--

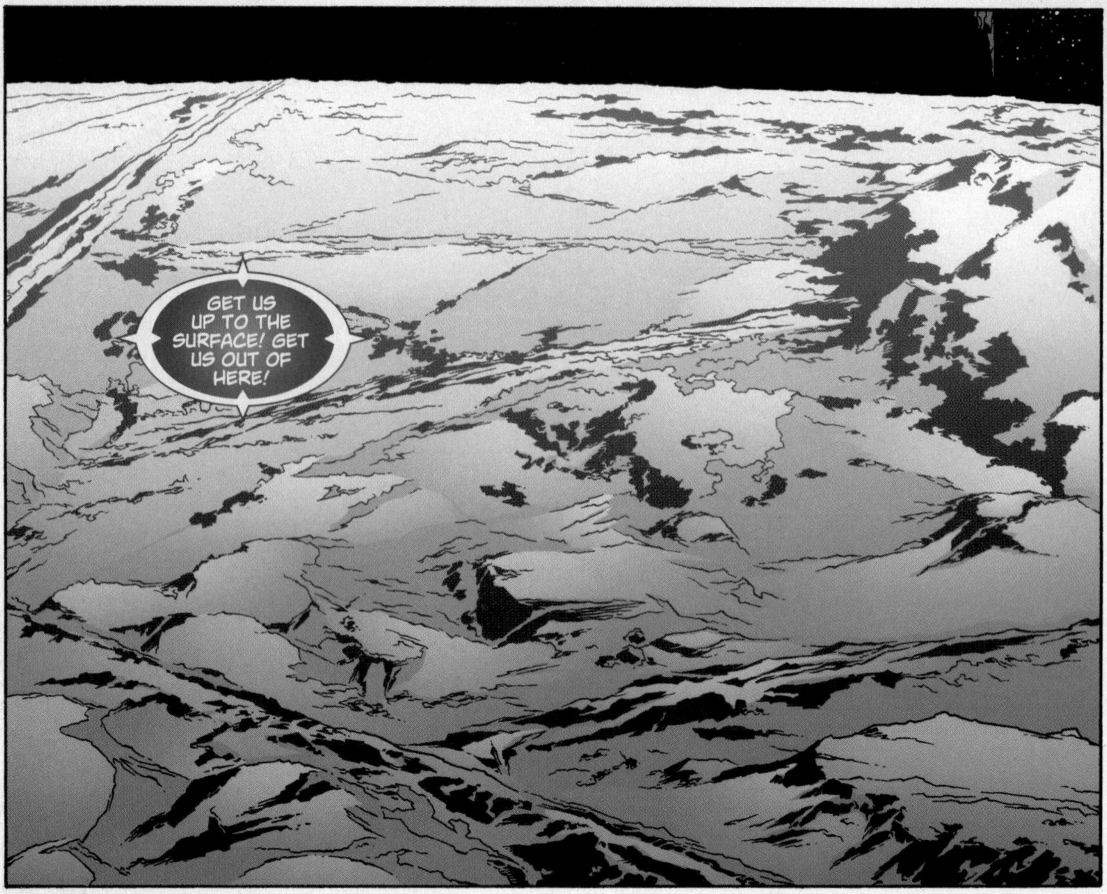
GET US UP TO THE SURFACE! GET US OUT OF HERE!

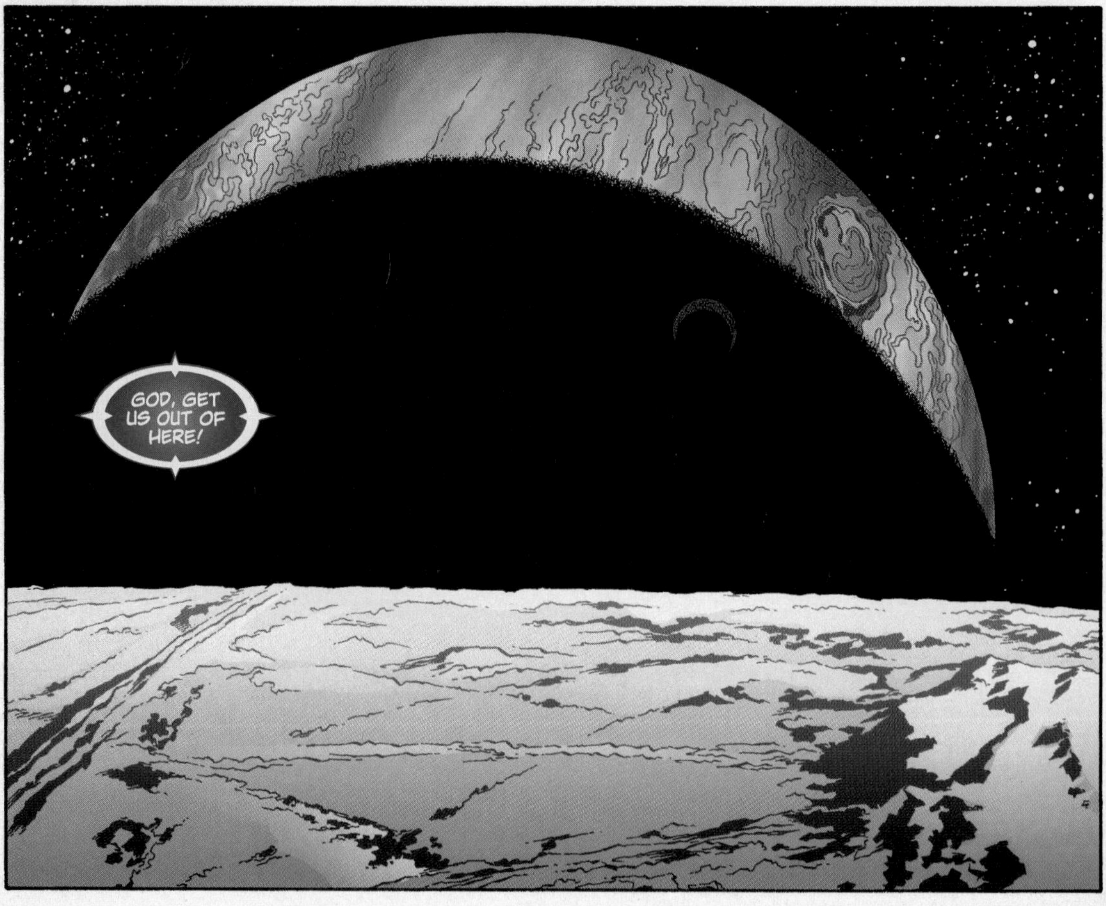
GOD, GET US OUT OF HERE!

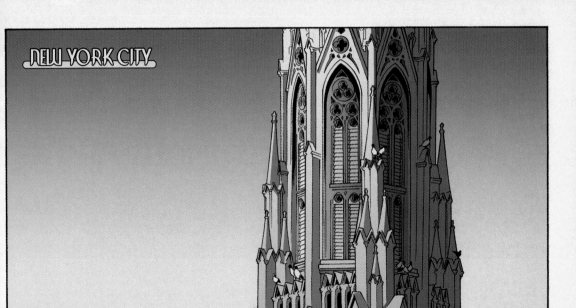

NEW YORK CITY

ONE WEEK LATER

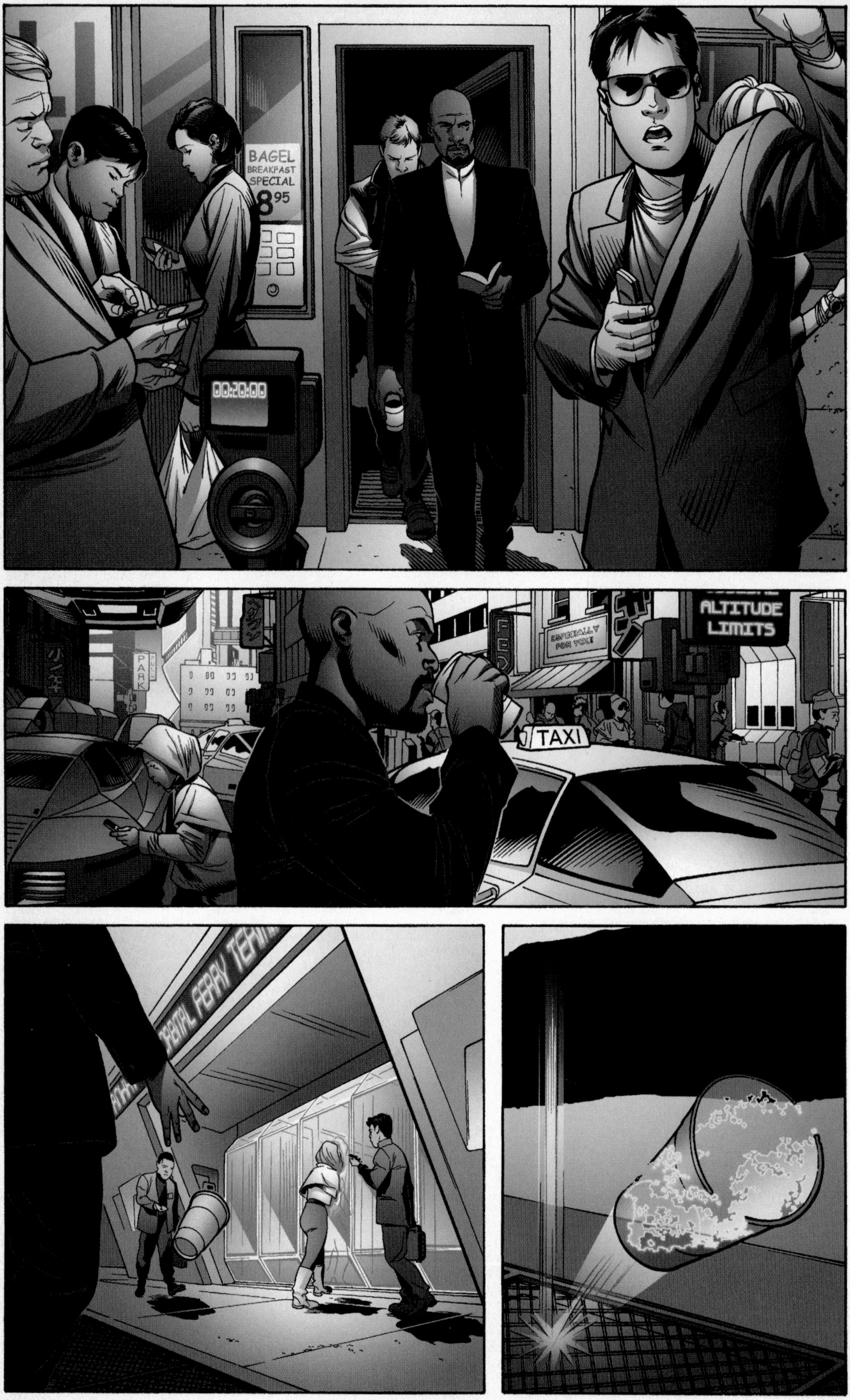

BAGEL
BREAKFAST
SPECIAL
8.95
00:20:00
PARK
ESPECIALLY FOR YOU!
ALTITUDE LIMITS
TAXI

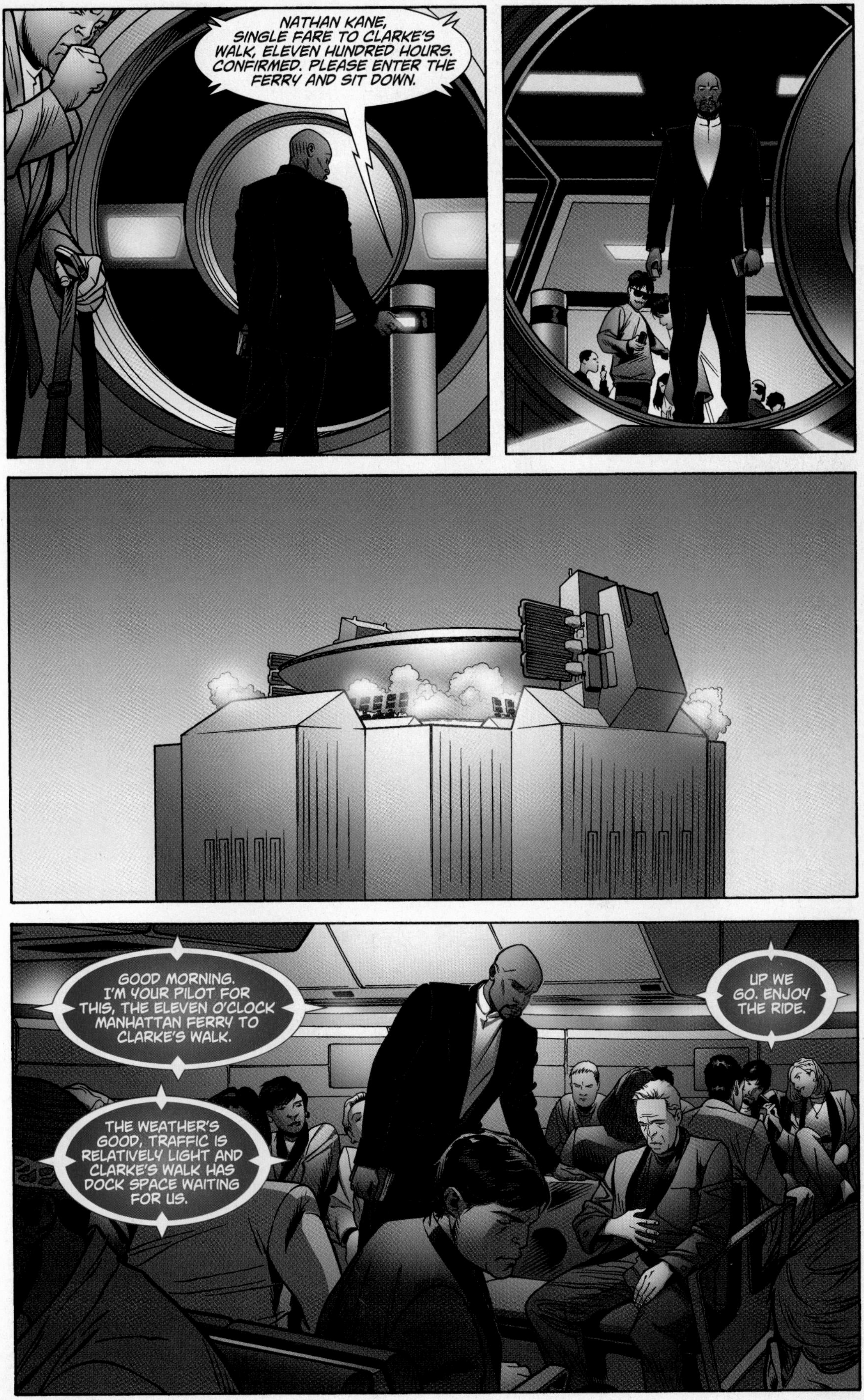
NATHAN KANE, SINGLE FARE TO CLARKE'S WALK, ELEVEN HUNDRED HOURS. CONFIRMED. PLEASE ENTER THE FERRY AND SIT DOWN.
GOOD MORNING. I'M YOUR PILOT FOR THIS, THE ELEVEN O'CLOCK MANHATTAN FERRY TO CLARKE'S WALK.
THE WEATHER'S GOOD, TRAFFIC IS RELATIVELY LIGHT AND CLARKE'S WALK HAS DOCK SPACE WAITING FOR US.
UP WE GO. ENJOY THE RIDE.

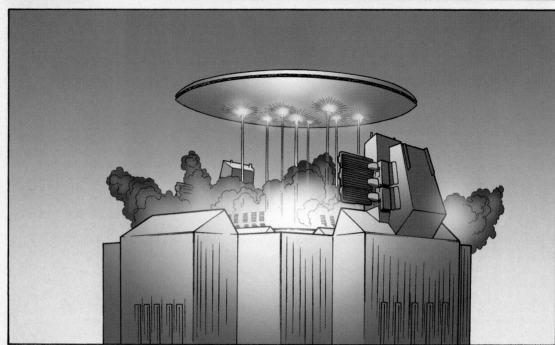

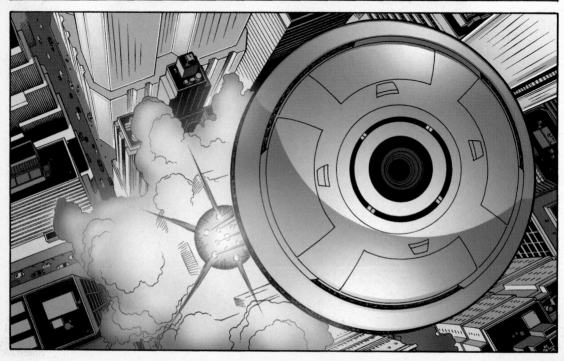

YOU KNOW HOW PEOPLE USED TO GO UP? ON TOP OF SOMETHING THE SIZE OF AN OFFICE BLOCK, FULL OF CHEMICAL EXPLOSIVES.

IS THAT BERSERK OR WHAT? RIDING A BOMB TO ORBIT.

YEAH. LISTEN, I DON'T TRAVEL TOO WELL--

NO, LISTEN, IT GETS WORSE. I MEAN, THIS FERRY HERE? IT'S GOING TO JUST DRIFT BACK SLOWLY ON A REDUCED LASER PULSE.

BACK IN THE OLD DAYS? THEY DID BALLISTIC RE-ENTRY. JUST AIMED AT THE PLANET LIKE A BULLET OUT OF A GUN, IN A LITTLE CAPSULE WITH A FAT BASE.

HEAT SHIELD, YOU SEE? TO STOP 'EM ROASTING ON THE WAY IN.

FIRST STEP TO SPACE

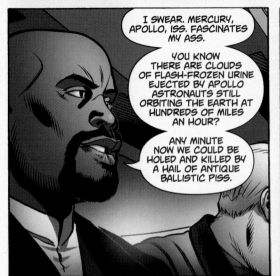

I SWEAR. MERCURY, APOLLO, ISS. FASCINATES MY ASS.

YOU KNOW THERE ARE CLOUDS OF FLASH-FROZEN URINE EJECTED BY APOLLO ASTRONAUTS STILL ORBITING THE EARTH AT HUNDREDS OF MILES AN HOUR?

ANY MINUTE NOW WE COULD BE HOLED AND KILLED BY A HAIL OF ANTIQUE BALLISTIC PISS.

LITTLE SPACESHIPS THE SIZE OF YOUR BATHROOM, JUST DROPPING ON EARTH FROM SPACE, CATCHING FIRE AND DROPPING IN THE OCEAN...

HORK

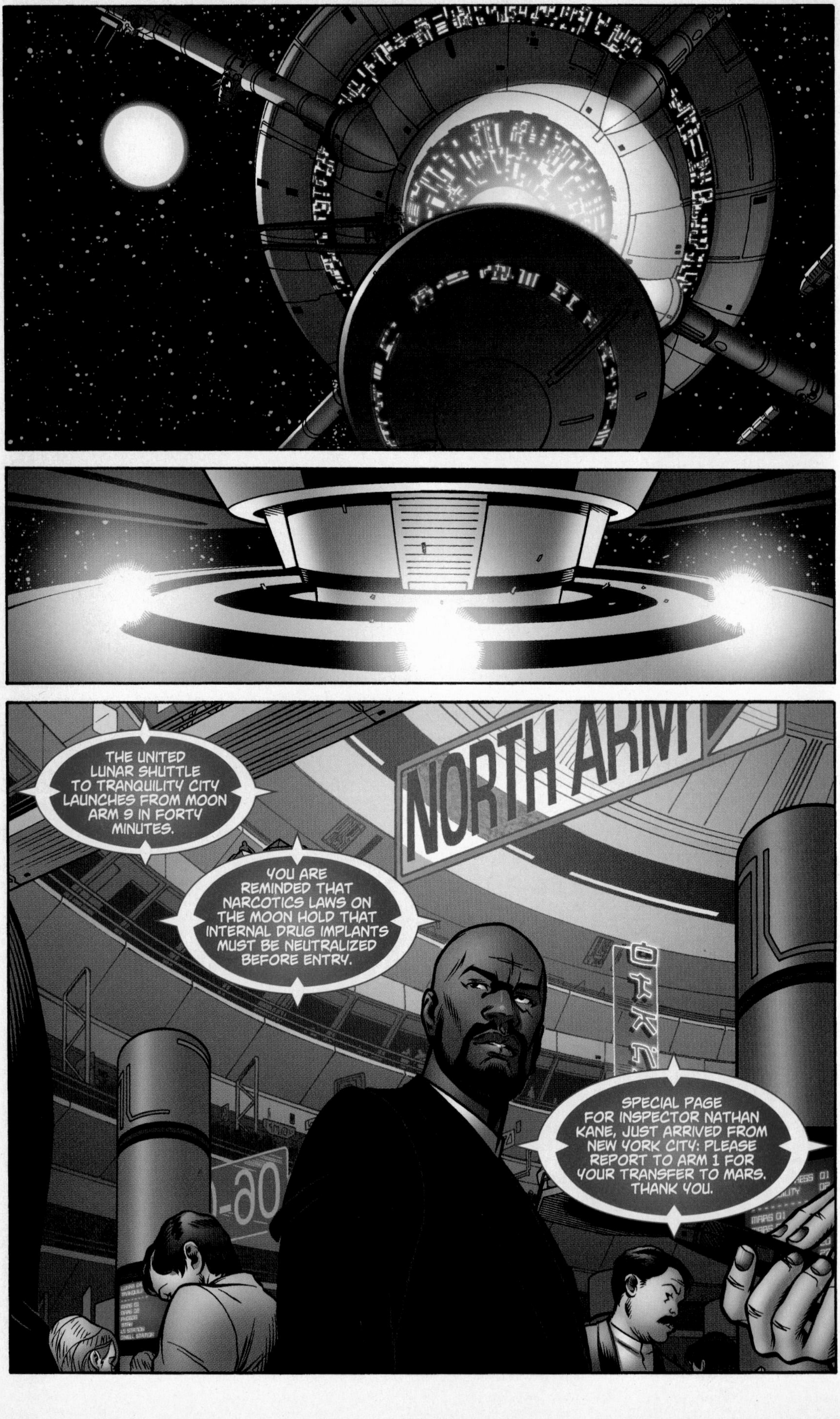
NORTH ARM
THE UNITED LUNAR SHUTTLE TO TRANQUILITY CITY LAUNCHES FROM MOON ARM 9 IN FORTY MINUTES.
YOU ARE REMINDED THAT NARCOTICS LAWS ON THE MOON HOLD THAT INTERNAL DRUG IMPLANTS MUST BE NEUTRALIZED BEFORE ENTRY.
SPECIAL PAGE FOR INSPECTOR NATHAN KANE, JUST ARRIVED FROM NEW YORK CITY: PLEASE REPORT TO ARM 1 FOR YOUR TRANSFER TO MARS. THANK YOU.

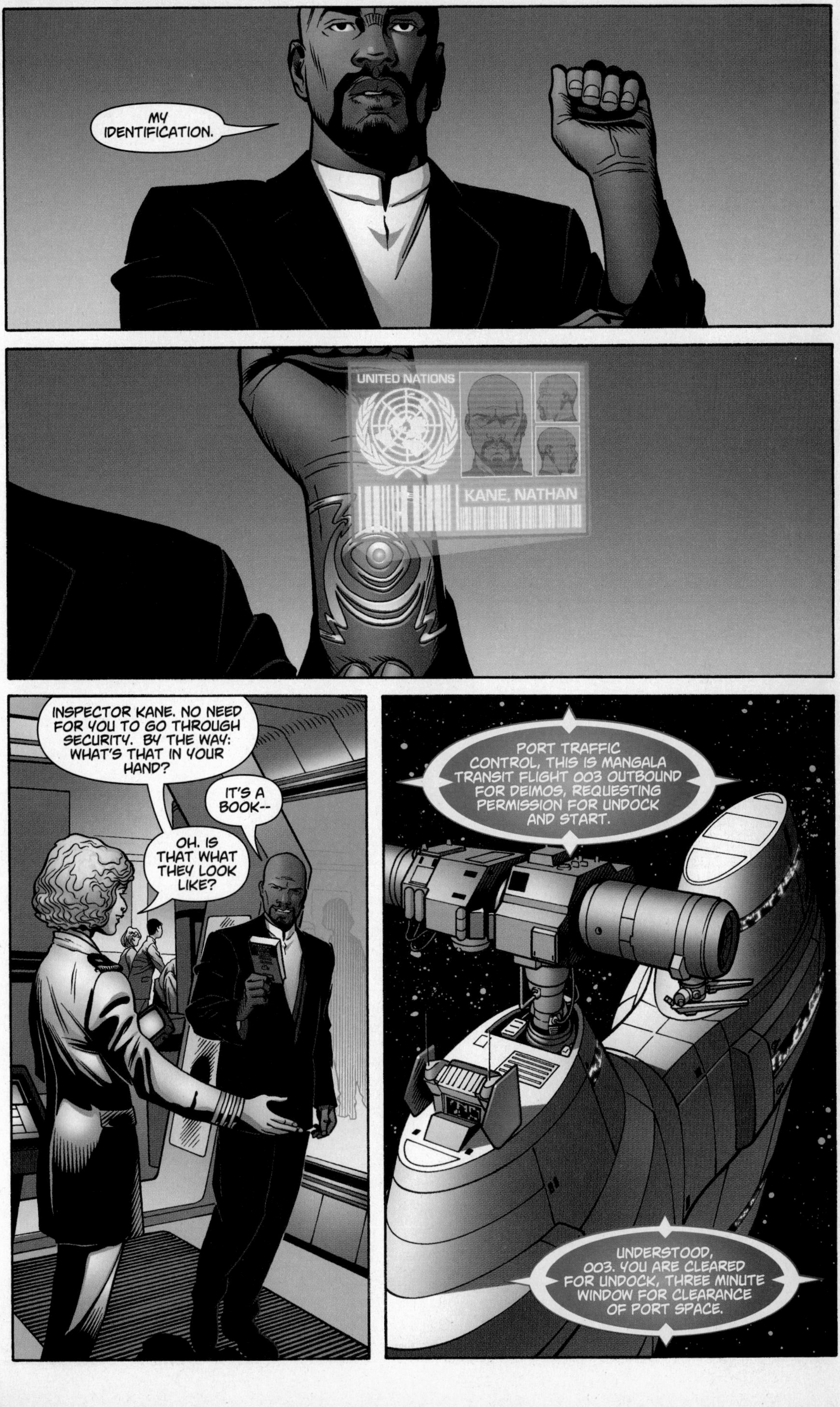
MY IDENTIFICATION.
UNITED NATIONS
KANE, NATHAN
INSPECTOR KANE. NO NEED FOR YOU TO GO THROUGH SECURITY. BY THE WAY: WHAT'S THAT IN YOUR HAND?
IT'S A BOOK--
OH. IS THAT WHAT THEY LOOK LIKE?
PORT TRAFFIC CONTROL, THIS IS MANGALA TRANSIT FLIGHT 003 OUTBOUND FOR DEIMOS, REQUESTING PERMISSION FOR UNDOCK AND START.
UNDERSTOOD, 003. YOU ARE CLEARED FOR UNDOCK, THREE MINUTE WINDOW FOR CLEARANCE OF PORT SPACE.

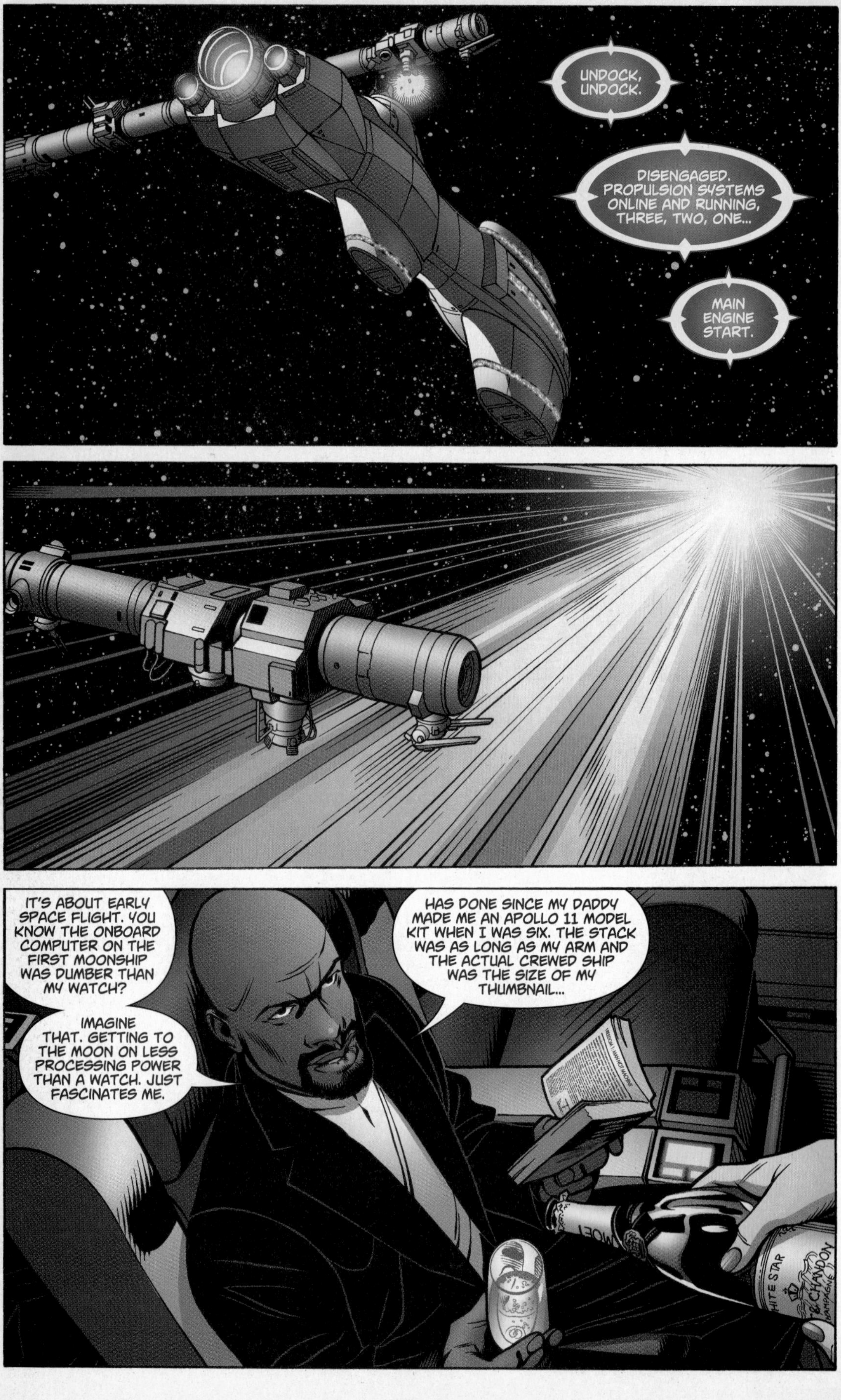

UNDOCK, UNDOCK.
DISENGAGED. PROPULSION SYSTEMS ONLINE AND RUNNING, THREE, TWO, ONE...
MAIN ENGINE START.
IT'S ABOUT EARLY SPACE FLIGHT. YOU KNOW THE ONBOARD COMPUTER ON THE FIRST MOONSHIP WAS DUMBER THAN MY WATCH?
IMAGINE THAT. GETTING TO THE MOON ON LESS PROCESSING POWER THAN A WATCH. JUST FASCINATES ME.
HAS DONE SINCE MY DADDY MADE ME AN APOLLO 11 MODEL KIT WHEN I WAS SIX. THE STACK WAS AS LONG AS MY ARM AND THE ACTUAL CREWED SHIP WAS THE SIZE OF MY THUMBNAIL...

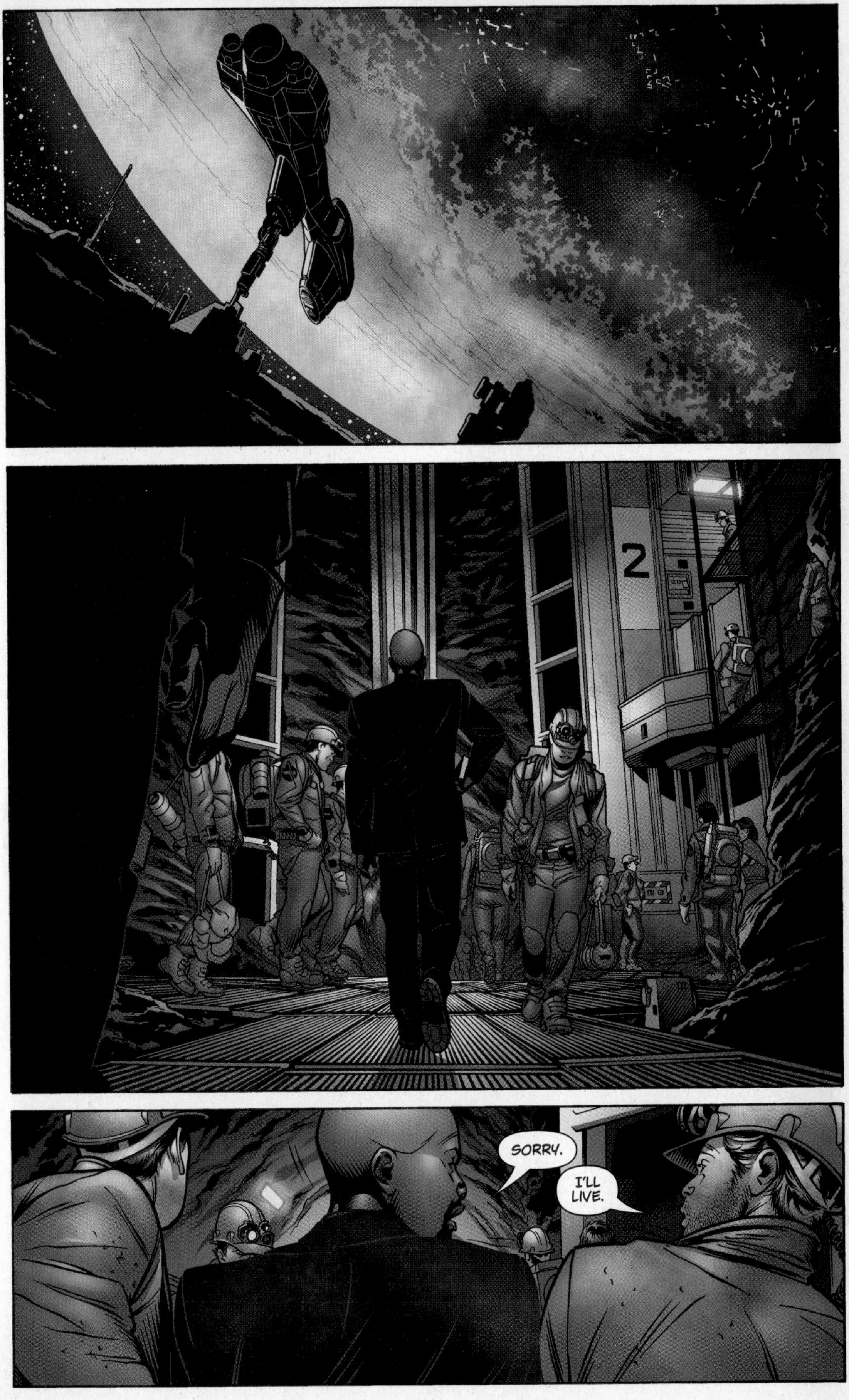
SORRY.
I'LL LIVE.

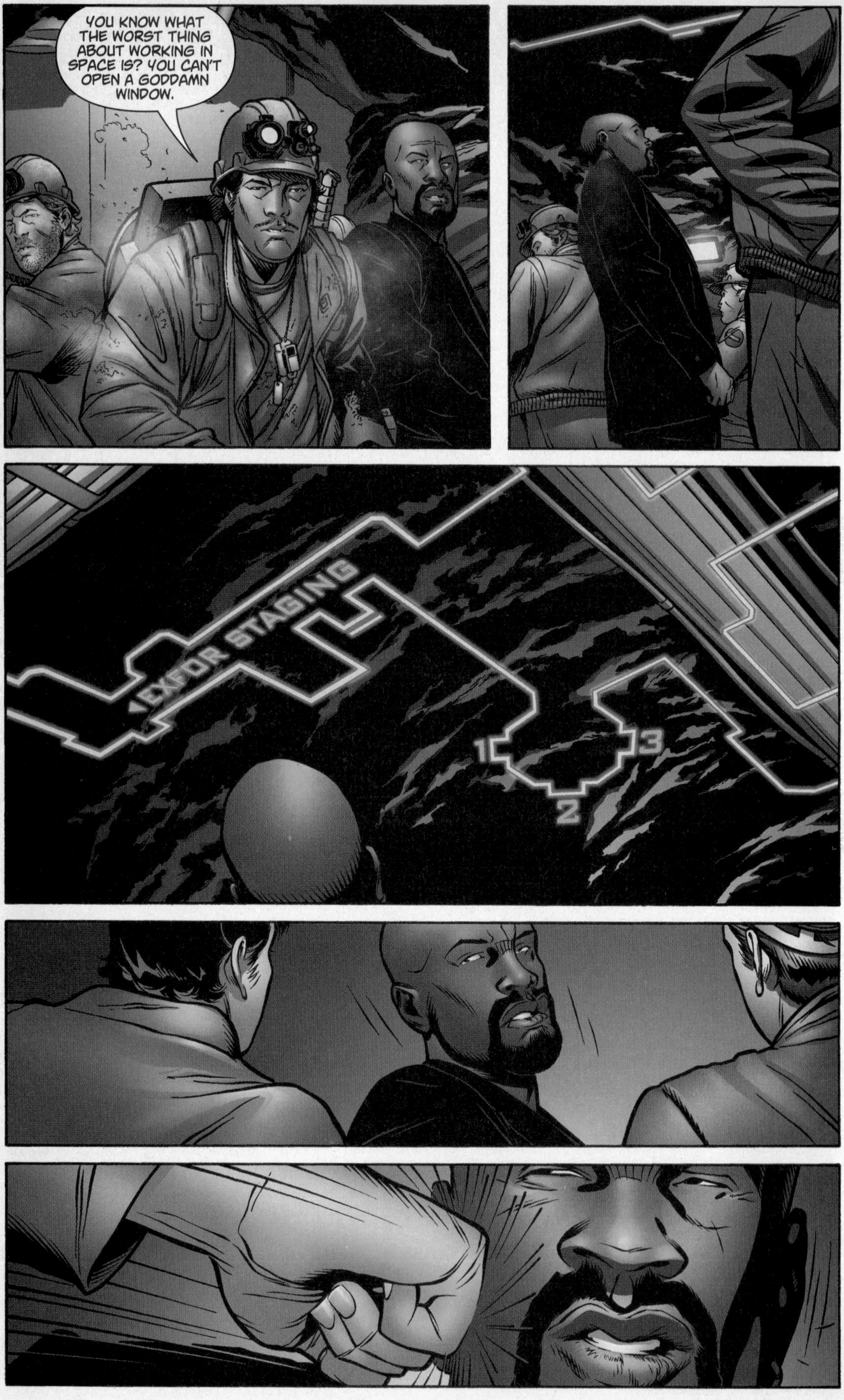
YOU KNOW WHAT THE WORST THING ABOUT WORKING IN SPACE IS? YOU CAN'T OPEN A GODDAMN WINDOW.
EXFOR STAGING
1
2
3

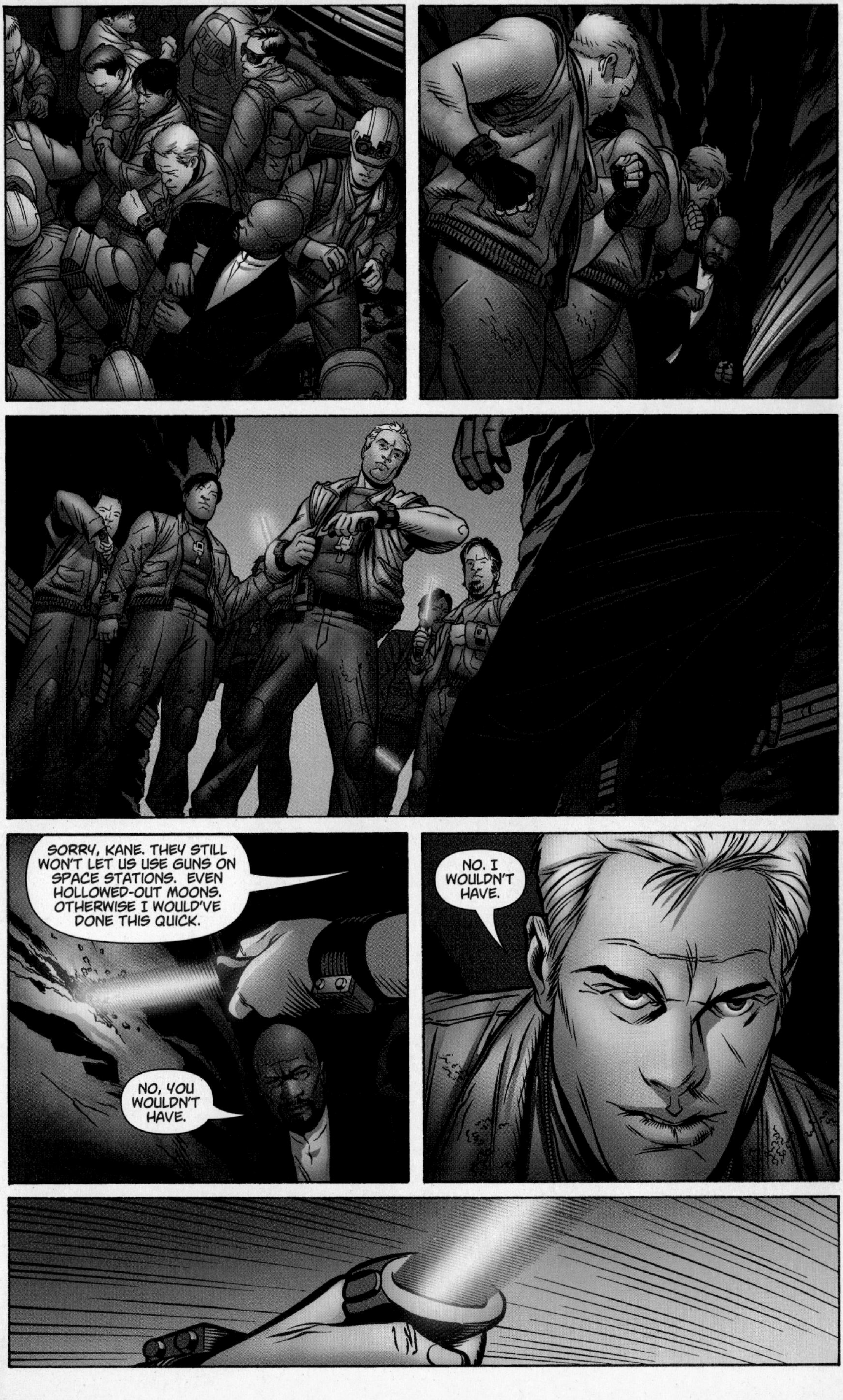
SORRY, KANE. THEY STILL WON'T LET US USE GUNS ON SPACE STATIONS. EVEN HOLLOWED-OUT MOONS. OTHERWISE I WOULD'VE DONE THIS QUICK.
NO, YOU WOULDN'T HAVE.
NO. I WOULDN'T HAVE.

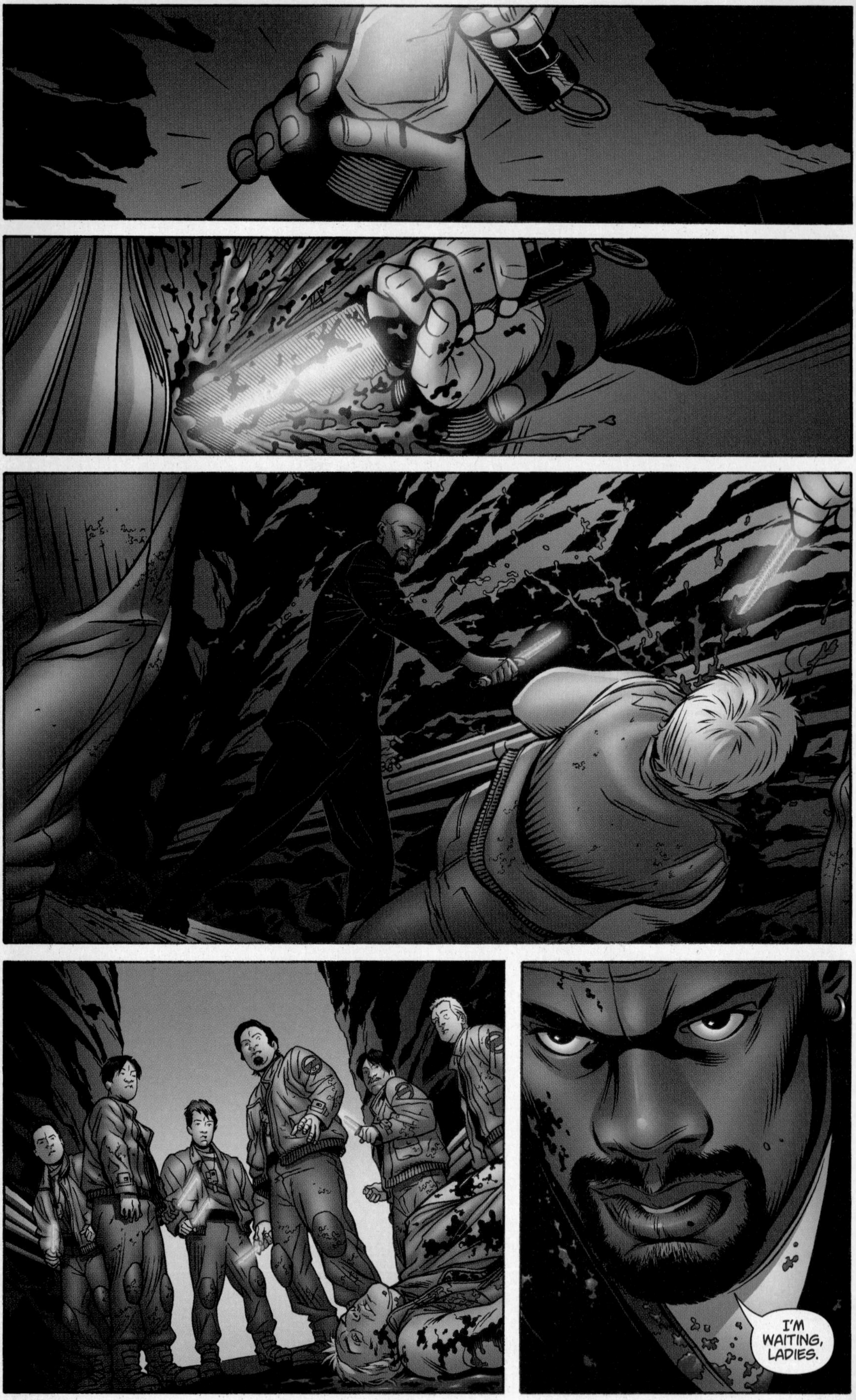
I'M WAITING, LADIES.

CAN I PLEASE GET CHANGED?

YOU LOOK GOOD IN RED. SHUT UP.

TAKE OFF, ROSEWOOD. TAKE PATROL NINE. FORGET EVER SEEING THIS GUY.

I WAS NEVER HERE. SPOOOOOOKY.

NATHAN KANE. SPECIAL WEAPONS INSPECTOR, UNITED NATIONS. COOPERATION FROM ALL POLICE SERVICES MANDATORY. ALL APPLICABLE IMMUNITIES.

WHAT'S THE STORY HERE, INSPECTOR KANE?

STORY IS, I WAS JUMPED.

STEAMER GANG. HAPPENS ALL THE TIME.

WORKERS MUG PEOPLE, EITHER BECAUSE THEY'RE UNDERPAID AND LOOKING FOR CASH, OR BECAUSE THEY'RE OFF THEIR TITS ON SPEED AND LOOKING FOR SOMEONE TO HURT.

WEREN'T WORKERS. CLEAN HANDS, SMOOTH NAILS.

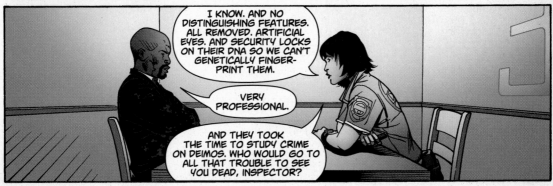

I KNOW. AND NO DISTINGUISHING FEATURES. ALL REMOVED. ARTIFICIAL EYES. AND SECURITY LOCKS ON THEIR DNA SO WE CAN'T GENETICALLY FINGERPRINT THEM.

VERY PROFESSIONAL.

AND THEY TOOK THE TIME TO STUDY CRIME ON DEIMOS. WHO WOULD GO TO ALL THAT TROUBLE TO SEE YOU DEAD, INSPECTOR?

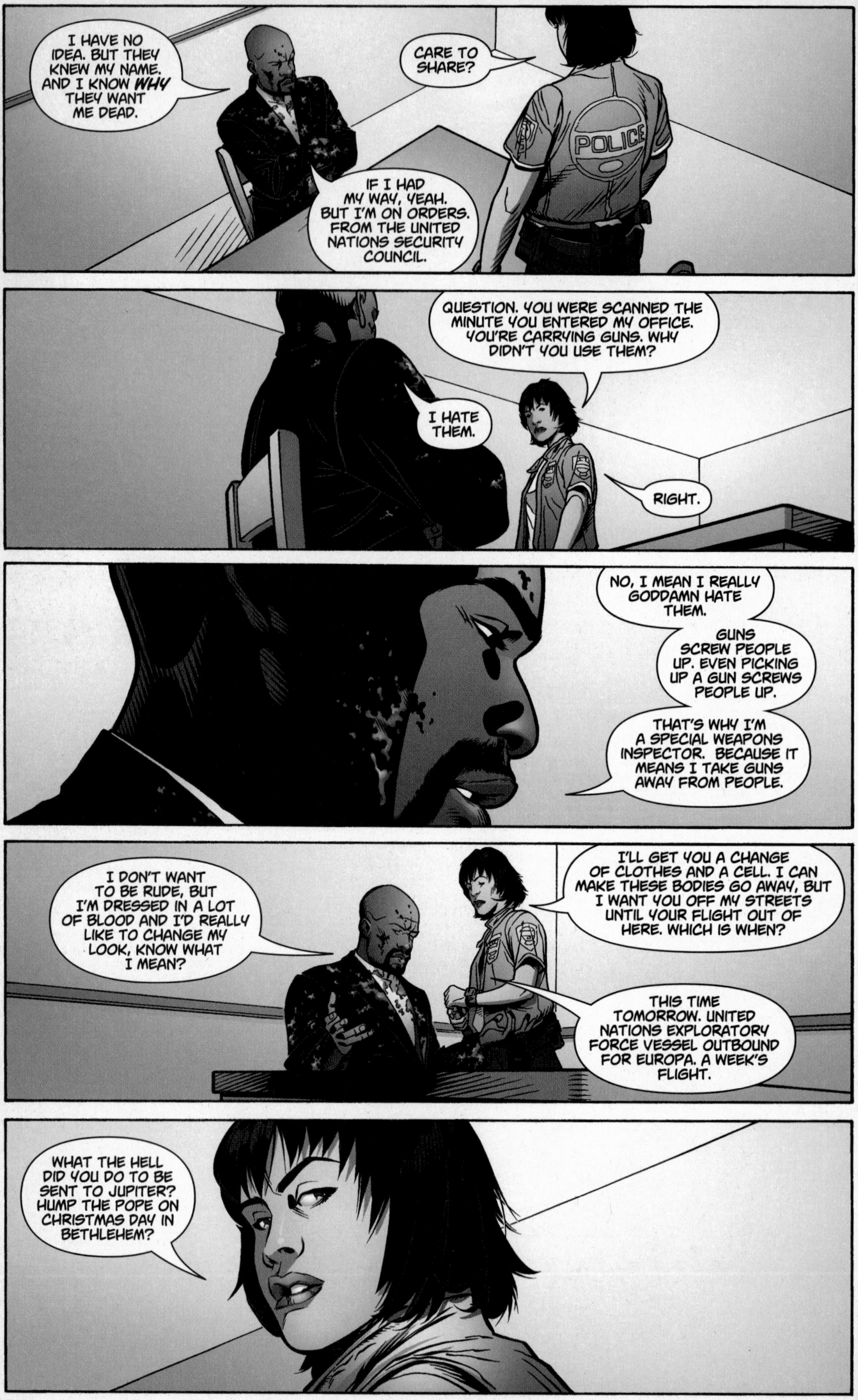
I HAVE NO IDEA. BUT THEY KNEW MY NAME. AND I KNOW WHY THEY WANT ME DEAD.
CARE TO SHARE?
IF I HAD MY WAY, YEAH. BUT I'M ON ORDERS. FROM THE UNITED NATIONS SECURITY COUNCIL.
POLICE
QUESTION. YOU WERE SCANNED THE MINUTE YOU ENTERED MY OFFICE. YOU'RE CARRYING GUNS. WHY DIDN'T YOU USE THEM?
I HATE THEM.
RIGHT.
NO, I MEAN I REALLY GODDAMN HATE THEM.
GUNS SCREW PEOPLE UP. EVEN PICKING UP A GUN SCREWS PEOPLE UP.
THAT'S WHY I'M A SPECIAL WEAPONS INSPECTOR. BECAUSE IT MEANS I TAKE GUNS AWAY FROM PEOPLE.
I DON'T WANT TO BE RUDE, BUT I'M DRESSED IN A LOT OF BLOOD AND I'D REALLY LIKE TO CHANGE MY LOOK, KNOW WHAT I MEAN?
I'LL GET YOU A CHANGE OF CLOTHES AND A CELL. I CAN MAKE THESE BODIES GO AWAY, BUT I WANT YOU OFF MY STREETS UNTIL YOUR FLIGHT OUT OF HERE. WHICH IS WHEN?
THIS TIME TOMORROW. UNITED NATIONS EXPLORATORY FORCE VESSEL OUTBOUND FOR EUROPA. A WEEK'S FLIGHT.
WHAT THE HELL DID YOU DO TO BE SENT TO JUPITER? HUMP THE POPE ON CHRISTMAS DAY IN BETHLEHEM?

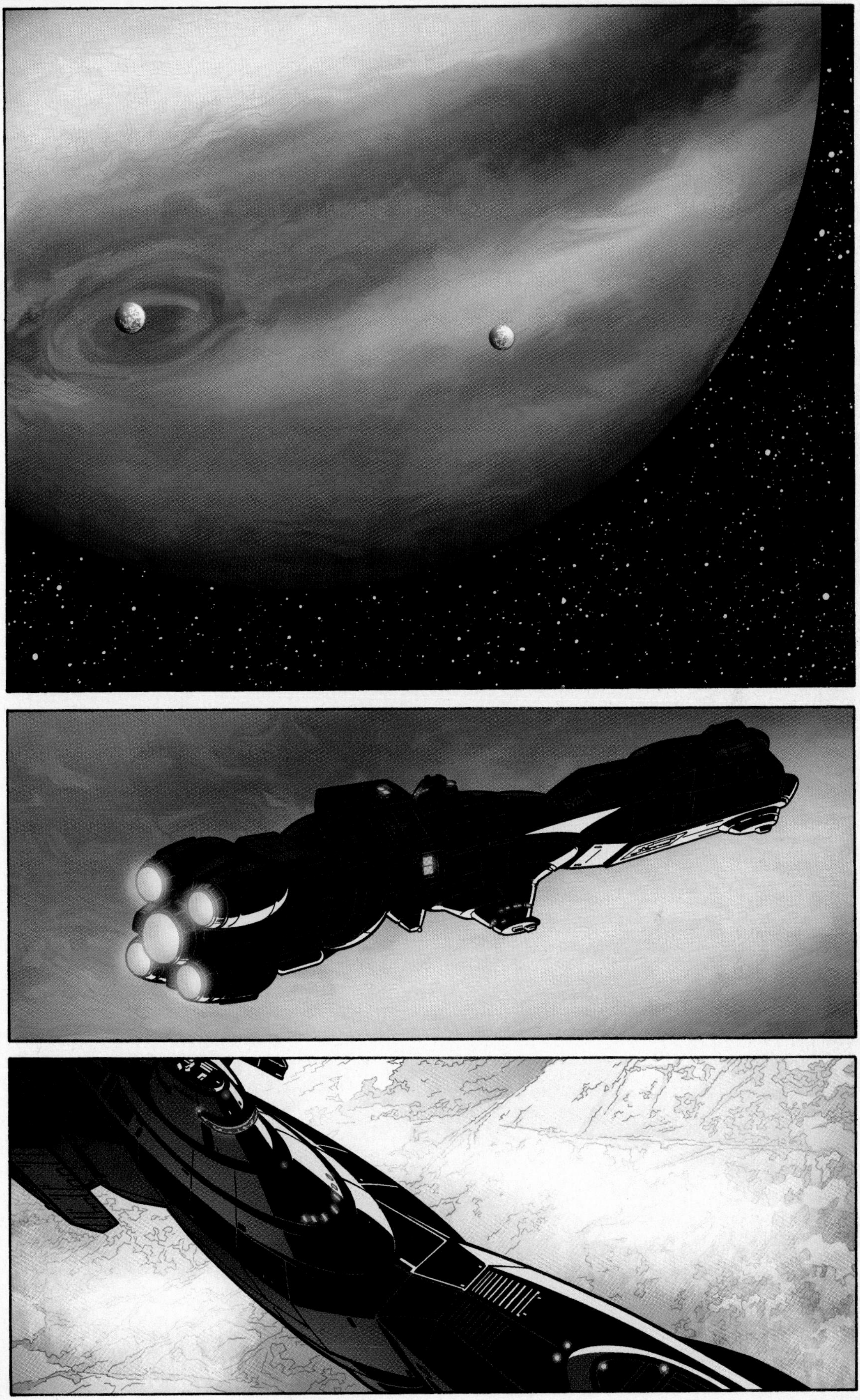

WOULD YOU LOOK AT THAT.

EUROPA. ONLY GENUINE OCEAN PLANET WE KNOW OF. IF IT WERE ANYWHERE ELSE, IT *WOULD* BE A PLANET.

BUT NEXT TO JUPITER, IT'S JUST A MOON. HELL, NEXT TO THAT, *EARTH* WOULD BE A MOON.

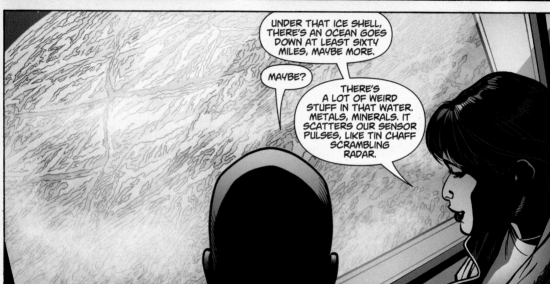

UNDER THAT ICE SHELL, THERE'S AN OCEAN GOES DOWN AT LEAST SIXTY MILES, MAYBE MORE.

MAYBE?

THERE'S A LOT OF WEIRD STUFF IN THAT WATER. METALS, MINERALS. IT SCATTERS OUR SENSOR PULSES, LIKE TIN CHAFF SCRAMBLING RADAR.

THAT'S THE EXPLORATORY FORCE'S PERMANENT EUROPA STATION: COLD HARBOR.

BEEN HERE THREE YEARS. FIRST MAJOR STATION WE'VE HAD IN THE JUPITER SYSTEM.

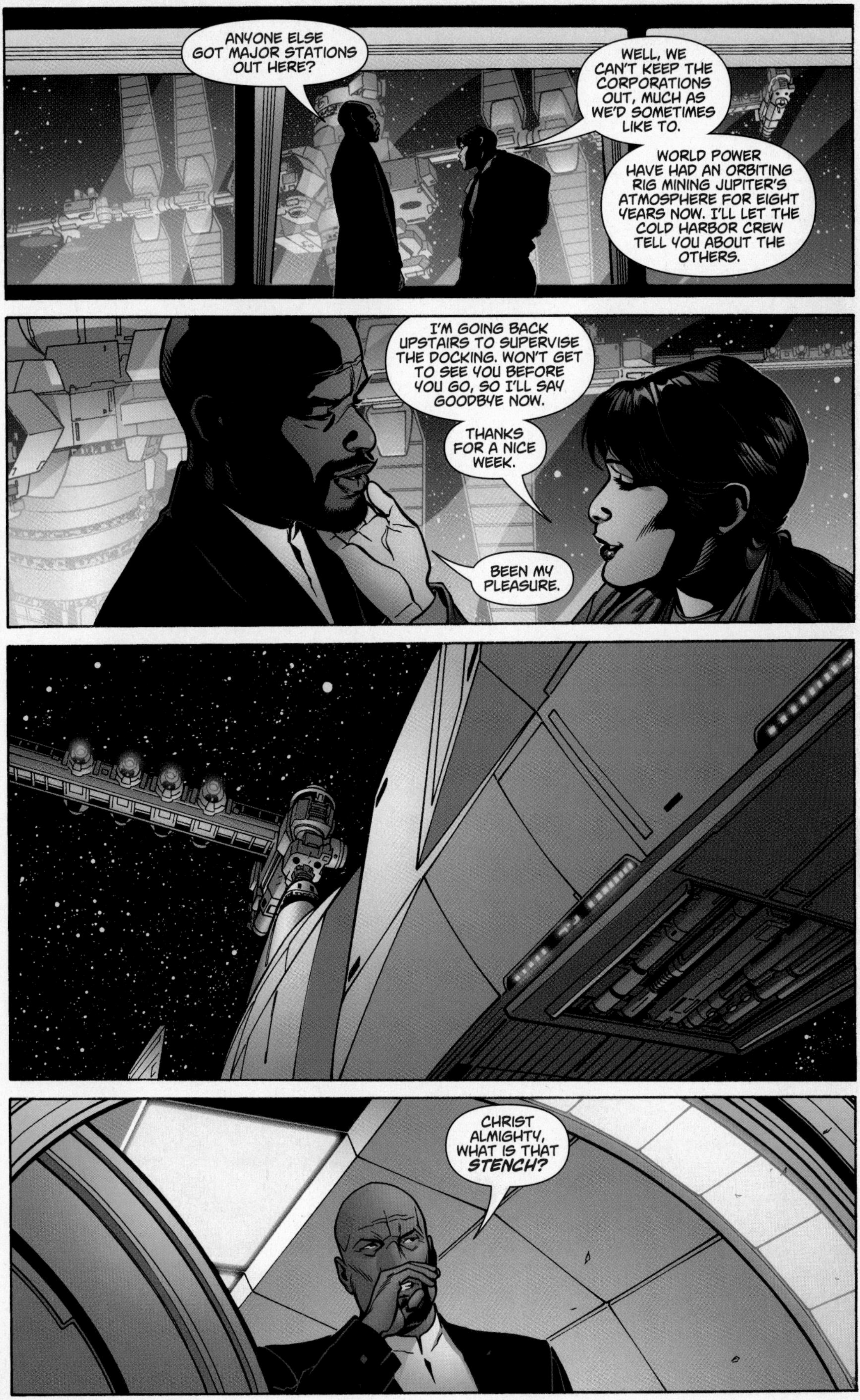
ANYONE ELSE GOT MAJOR STATIONS OUT HERE?
WELL, WE CAN'T KEEP THE CORPORATIONS OUT, MUCH AS WE'D SOMETIMES LIKE TO.
WORLD POWER HAVE HAD AN ORBITING RIG MINING JUPITER'S ATMOSPHERE FOR EIGHT YEARS NOW. I'LL LET THE COLD HARBOR CREW TELL YOU ABOUT THE OTHERS.
I'M GOING BACK UPSTAIRS TO SUPERVISE THE DOCKING. WON'T GET TO SEE YOU BEFORE YOU GO, SO I'LL SAY GOODBYE NOW.
THANKS FOR A NICE WEEK.
BEEN MY PLEASURE.
CHRIST ALMIGHTY, WHAT IS THAT *STENCH*?

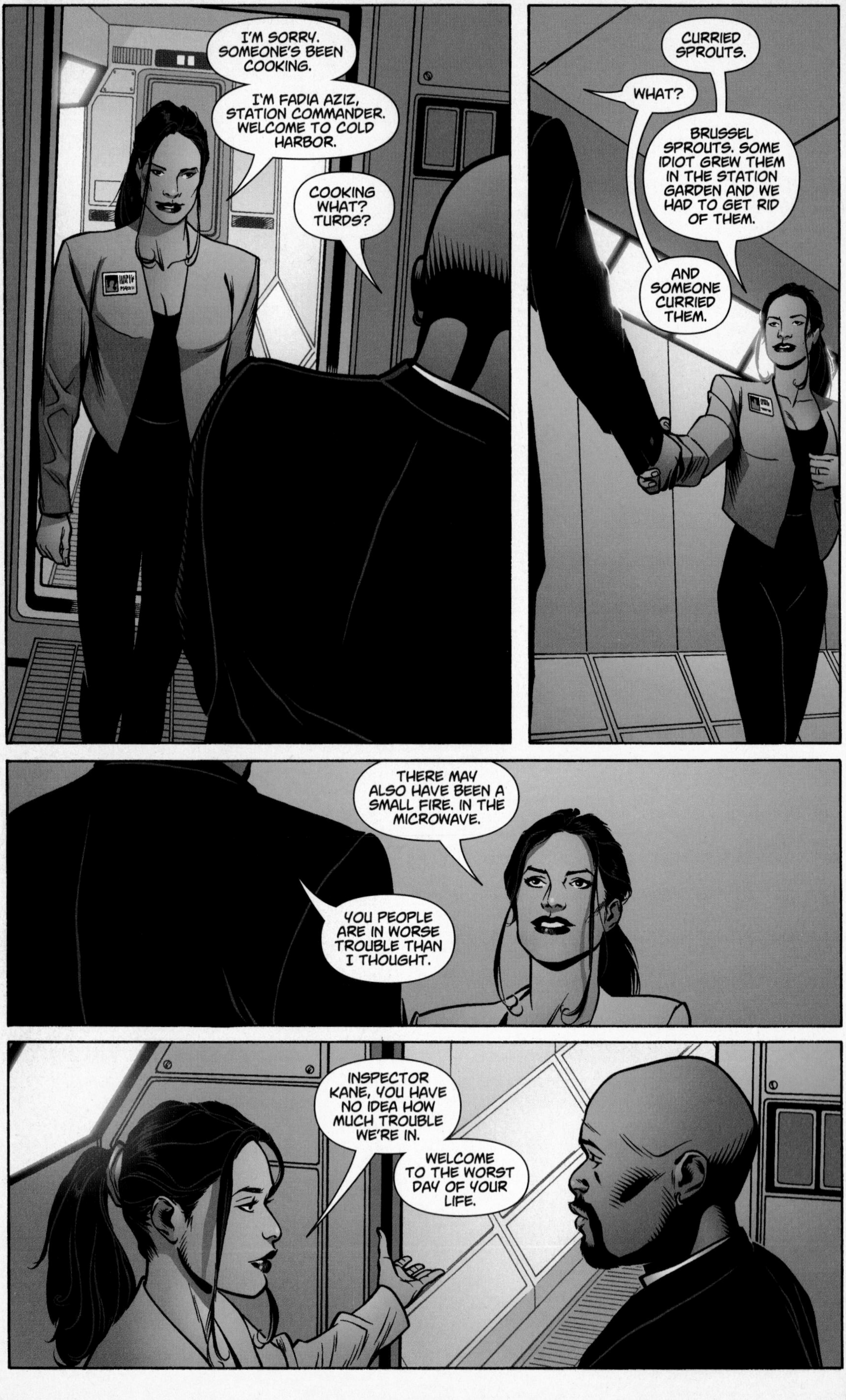
I'M SORRY. SOMEONE'S BEEN COOKING.
I'M FADIA AZIZ, STATION COMMANDER. WELCOME TO COLD HARBOR.
COOKING WHAT? TURDS?
CURRIED SPROUTS.
WHAT?
BRUSSEL SPROUTS. SOME IDIOT GREW THEM IN THE STATION GARDEN AND WE HAD TO GET RID OF THEM.
AND SOMEONE CURRIED THEM.
THERE MAY ALSO HAVE BEEN A SMALL FIRE. IN THE MICROWAVE.
YOU PEOPLE ARE IN WORSE TROUBLE THAN I THOUGHT.
INSPECTOR KANE, YOU HAVE NO IDEA HOW MUCH TROUBLE WE'RE IN.
WELCOME TO THE WORST DAY OF YOUR LIFE.

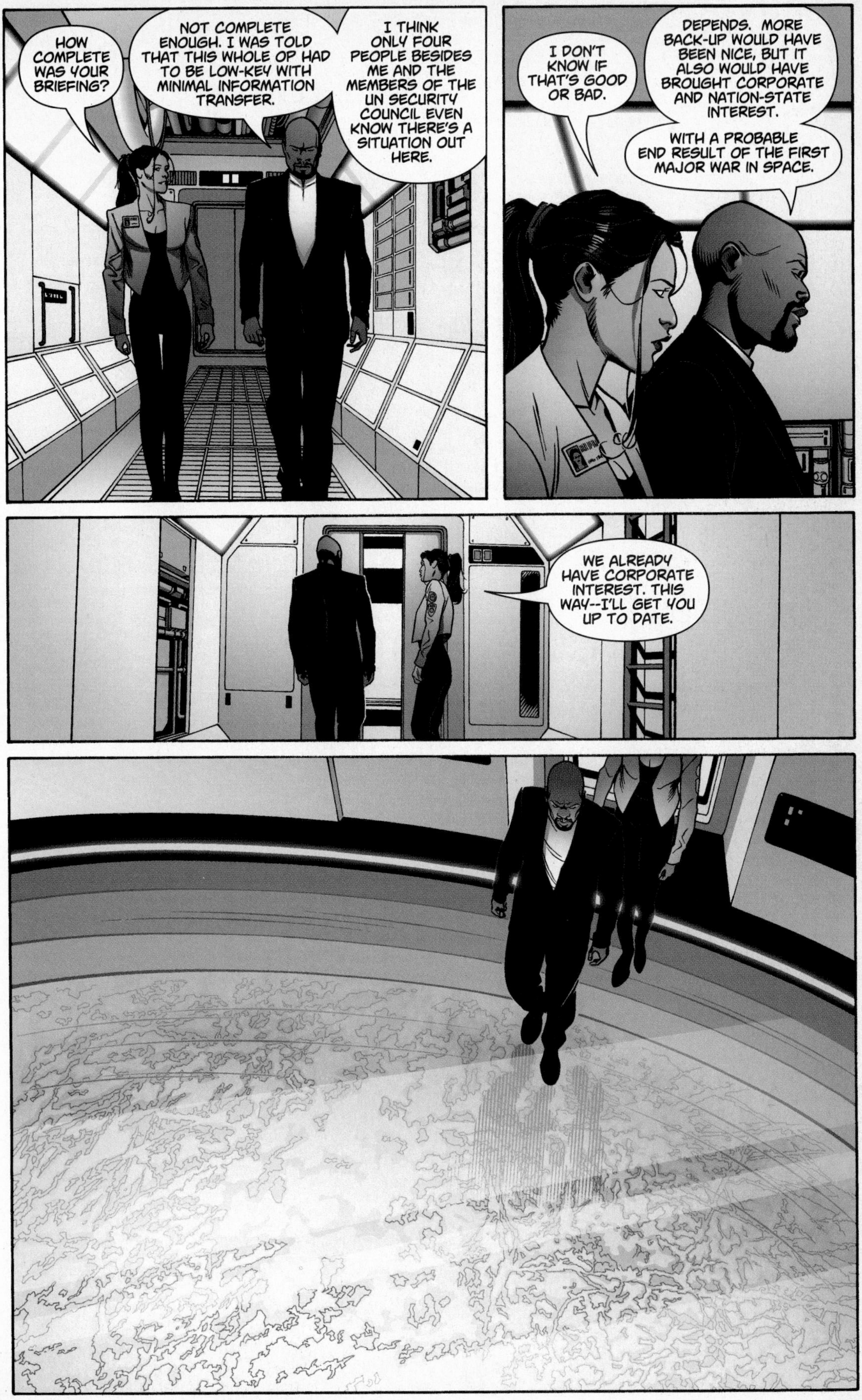
HOW COMPLETE WAS YOUR BRIEFING?
NOT COMPLETE ENOUGH. I WAS TOLD THAT THIS WHOLE OP HAD TO BE LOW-KEY WITH MINIMAL INFORMATION TRANSFER.
I THINK ONLY FOUR PEOPLE BESIDES ME AND THE MEMBERS OF THE UN SECURITY COUNCIL EVEN KNOW THERE'S A SITUATION OUT HERE.
I DON'T KNOW IF THAT'S GOOD OR BAD.
DEPENDS. MORE BACK-UP WOULD HAVE BEEN NICE, BUT IT ALSO WOULD HAVE BROUGHT CORPORATE AND NATION-STATE INTEREST.
WITH A PROBABLE END RESULT OF THE FIRST MAJOR WAR IN SPACE.
WE ALREADY HAVE CORPORATE INTEREST. THIS WAY--I'LL GET YOU UP TO DATE.

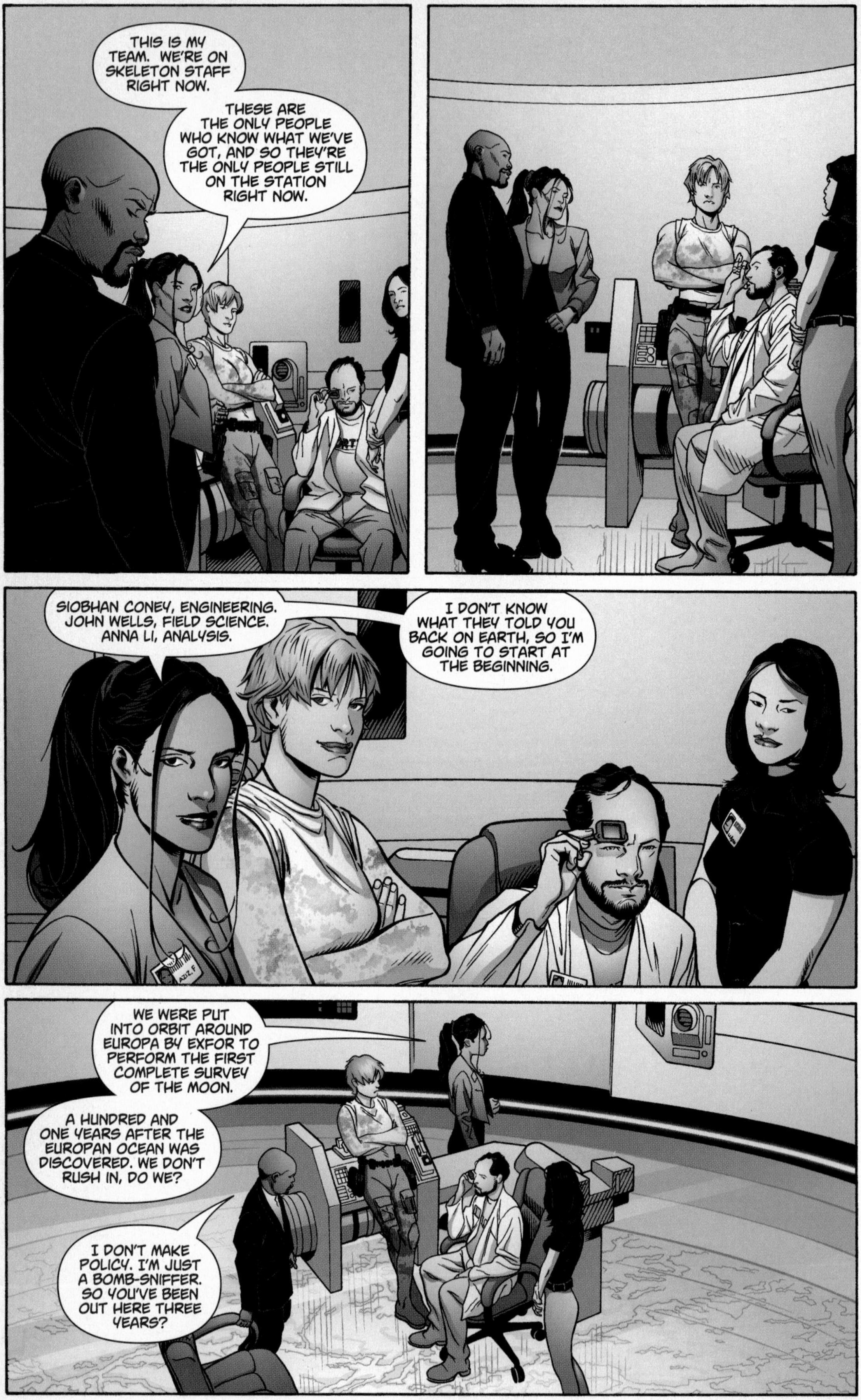
THIS IS MY TEAM. WE'RE ON SKELETON STAFF RIGHT NOW.
THESE ARE THE ONLY PEOPLE WHO KNOW WHAT WE'VE GOT, AND SO THEY'RE THE ONLY PEOPLE STILL ON THE STATION RIGHT NOW.
SIOBHAN CONEY, ENGINEERING. JOHN WELLS, FIELD SCIENCE. ANNA LI, ANALYSIS.
I DON'T KNOW WHAT THEY TOLD YOU BACK ON EARTH, SO I'M GOING TO START AT THE BEGINNING.
WE WERE PUT INTO ORBIT AROUND EUROPA BY EXFOR TO PERFORM THE FIRST COMPLETE SURVEY OF THE MOON.
A HUNDRED AND ONE YEARS AFTER THE EUROPAN OCEAN WAS DISCOVERED. WE DON'T RUSH IN, DO WE?
I DON'T MAKE POLICY. I'M JUST A BOMB-SNIFFER. SO YOU'VE BEEN OUT HERE THREE YEARS?

RIGHT. THE FIRST TWO AND A HALF YEARS WE SPENT UP HERE, WE GOT NOWHERE. WE ESTABLISHED THE PRESENCE OF ACTUAL WATER UNDER THE ICE.

WAS THAT EVER IN QUESTION?

HEY, JUST BECAUSE SOMETHING COMES OUT OF OUR GALLEY ON A PLATE, DOESN'T MEAN IT'S FOOD.

CURRYING THE SPROUTS SEEMED LIKE A GOOD IDEA AT THE TIME. I SAID I WAS SORRY.

NO APOLOGY COVERS THE DAMAGE YOU DID TO OUR ENVIRONMENT.

I'M GOING TO HAVE TO HAVE NEW LUNGS GROWN WHEN WE GET HOME.

IF WE GET HOME.

POINT BEING-- ONCE YOU'RE OFF EARTH, YOU CAN'T MAKE ASSUMPTIONS ABOUT ANYTHING.

SO. WATER. DOES THAT MEAN THERE'S LIFE OUT HERE?

HELL, THREE WEEKS AGO I COULDN'T HAVE TOLD YOU HOW DEEP THE OCEAN IS. ALL THE CRAP IN THE WATER WAS SCATTERING OUR DETECTION PULSES.

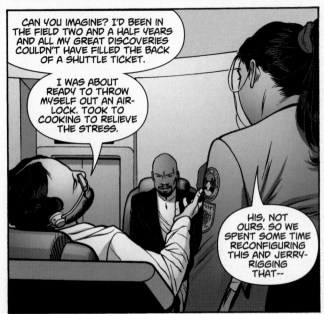

CAN YOU IMAGINE? I'D BEEN IN THE FIELD TWO AND A HALF YEARS AND ALL MY GREAT DISCOVERIES COULDN'T HAVE FILLED THE BACK OF A SHUTTLE TICKET.

I WAS ABOUT READY TO THROW MYSELF OUT AN AIR-LOCK. TOOK TO COOKING TO RELIEVE THE STRESS.

HIS, NOT OURS. SO WE SPENT SOME TIME RECONFIGURING THIS AND JERRY-RIGGING THAT--

"WE?"

--AND THEN SENT DOWN A NEW DETECTION ARRAY THAT WOULD DO THE JOB.

AND OUR FIRST PROPER LOOK AT THE OCEAN DEPTHS, WELL...

LOOK AT THIS. SIOBHAN, SWITCH THE FLOOR TO REMOTE DISPLAY. HOOK INTO OCEAN CAM 01.

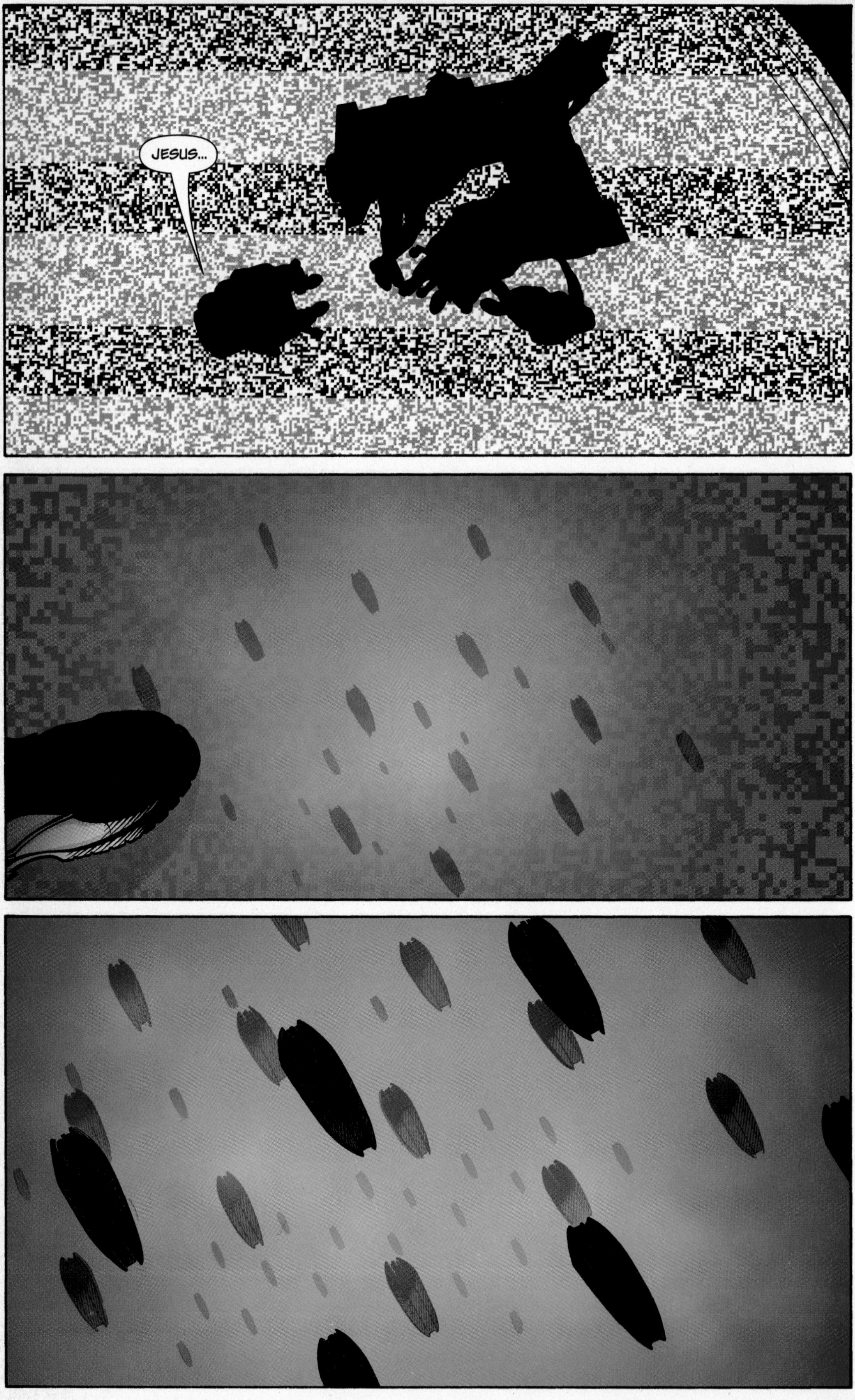
JESUS...

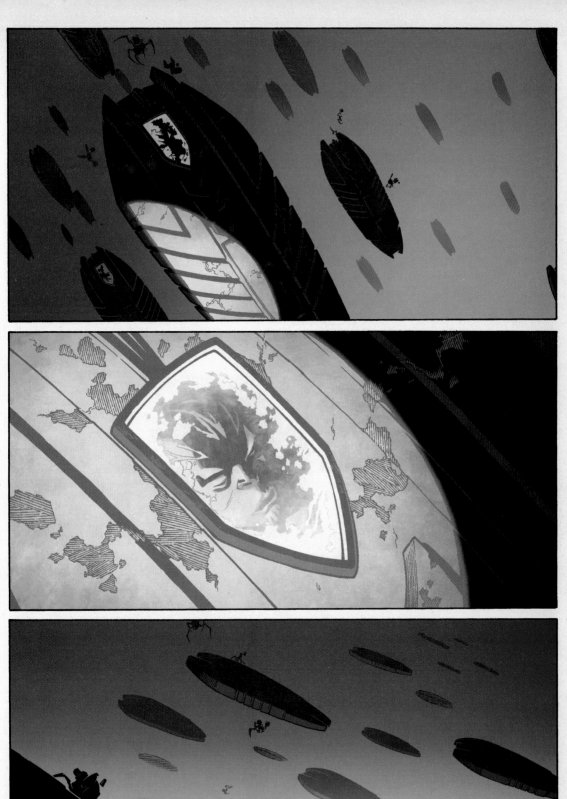

GO TO CAM 089.

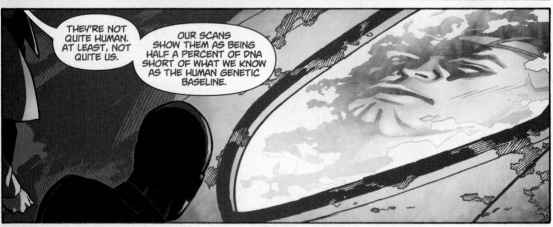

THEY'RE NOT QUITE HUMAN. AT LEAST, NOT QUITE US.

OUR SCANS SHOW THEM AS BEING HALF A PERCENT OF DNA SHORT OF WHAT WE KNOW AS THE HUMAN GENETIC BASELINE.

WE'VE DATED THOSE... SARCOPHAGI THEY'RE IN. WE'VE GOT IT TO WITHIN A FEW THOUSAND YEARS, BUT THE FIELD OF ERROR DOESN'T REALLY MATTER.

CAM 066.

THEY'RE ABOUT A BILLION YEARS OLD.

YOU DON'T CURRY THE COFFEE TOO, DO YOU?

RELAX. I TOLD JOHN THAT IF HE COMES IN HERE WITH INTENT TO COMMIT FOOD CRIME AGAIN I'M GOING TO STRAP HIM TO A DESCENT DISK AND DROP HIM.

HE MIGHT THANK YOU FOR THAT. WHERE IS HE?

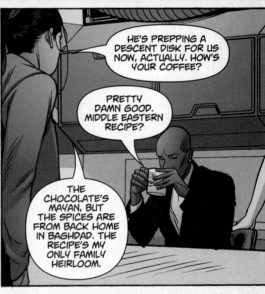

HE'S PREPPING A DESCENT DISK FOR US NOW, ACTUALLY. HOW'S YOUR COFFEE?

PRETTY DAMN GOOD. MIDDLE EASTERN RECIPE?

THE CHOCOLATE'S MAYAN, BUT THE SPICES ARE FROM BACK HOME IN BAGHDAD. THE RECIPE'S MY ONLY FAMILY HEIRLOOM.

CONSIDER YOURSELF HONORED. WE PRACTICALLY HAVE TO DRUG HER TO GET HER TO MAKE IT FOR US.

I SPAT IN THAT.

I DON'T CARE. IT'S THE FIRST DECENT COFFEE I'VE HAD SINCE I LEFT MANHATTAN AND I AIN'T GIVING IT UP. YOU'LL JUST HAVE TO DRUG HER.

I PEED IN IT TOO.

YOU PEOPLE HAVE BEEN OUT HERE WAY TOO LONG.

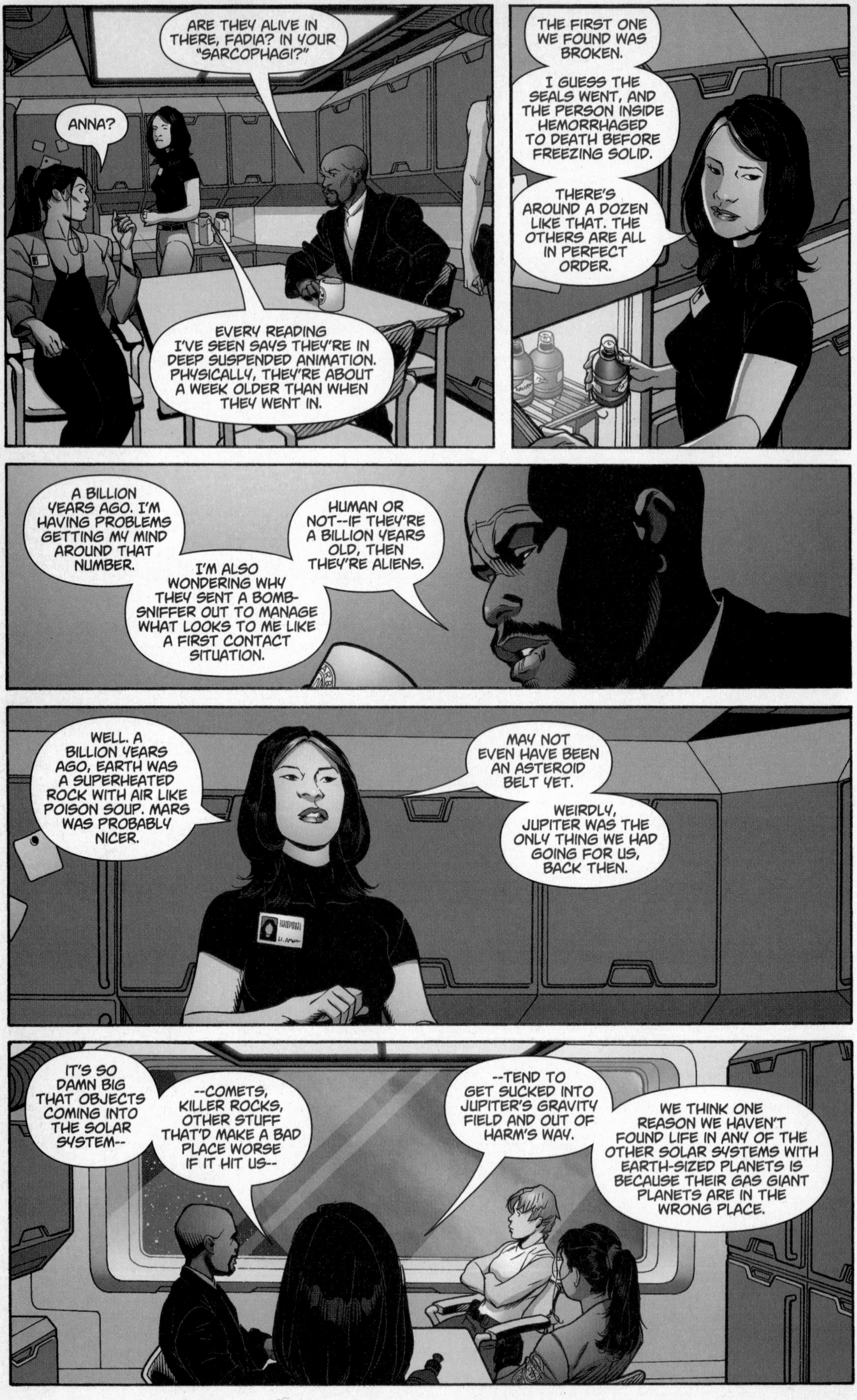
ARE THEY ALIVE IN THERE, FADIA? IN YOUR "SARCOPHAGI?"
ANNA?
EVERY READING I'VE SEEN SAYS THEY'RE IN DEEP SUSPENDED ANIMATION. PHYSICALLY, THEY'RE ABOUT A WEEK OLDER THAN WHEN THEY WENT IN.
THE FIRST ONE WE FOUND WAS BROKEN.
I GUESS THE SEALS WENT, AND THE PERSON INSIDE HEMORRHAGED TO DEATH BEFORE FREEZING SOLID.
THERE'S AROUND A DOZEN LIKE THAT. THE OTHERS ARE ALL IN PERFECT ORDER.
A BILLION YEARS AGO. I'M HAVING PROBLEMS GETTING MY MIND AROUND THAT NUMBER.
HUMAN OR NOT--IF THEY'RE A BILLION YEARS OLD, THEN THEY'RE ALIENS.
I'M ALSO WONDERING WHY THEY SENT A BOMB-SNIFFER OUT TO MANAGE WHAT LOOKS TO ME LIKE A FIRST CONTACT SITUATION.
WELL. A BILLION YEARS AGO, EARTH WAS A SUPERHEATED ROCK WITH AIR LIKE POISON SOUP. MARS WAS PROBABLY NICER.
MAY NOT EVEN HAVE BEEN AN ASTEROID BELT YET.
WEIRDLY, JUPITER WAS THE ONLY THING WE HAD GOING FOR US, BACK THEN.
IT'S SO DAMN BIG THAT OBJECTS COMING INTO THE SOLAR SYSTEM--
--COMETS, KILLER ROCKS, OTHER STUFF THAT'D MAKE A BAD PLACE WORSE IF IT HIT US--
--TEND TO GET SUCKED INTO JUPITER'S GRAVITY FIELD AND OUT OF HARM'S WAY.
WE THINK ONE REASON WE HAVEN'T FOUND LIFE IN ANY OF THE OTHER SOLAR SYSTEMS WITH EARTH-SIZED PLANETS IS BECAUSE THEIR GAS GIANT PLANETS ARE IN THE WRONG PLACE.

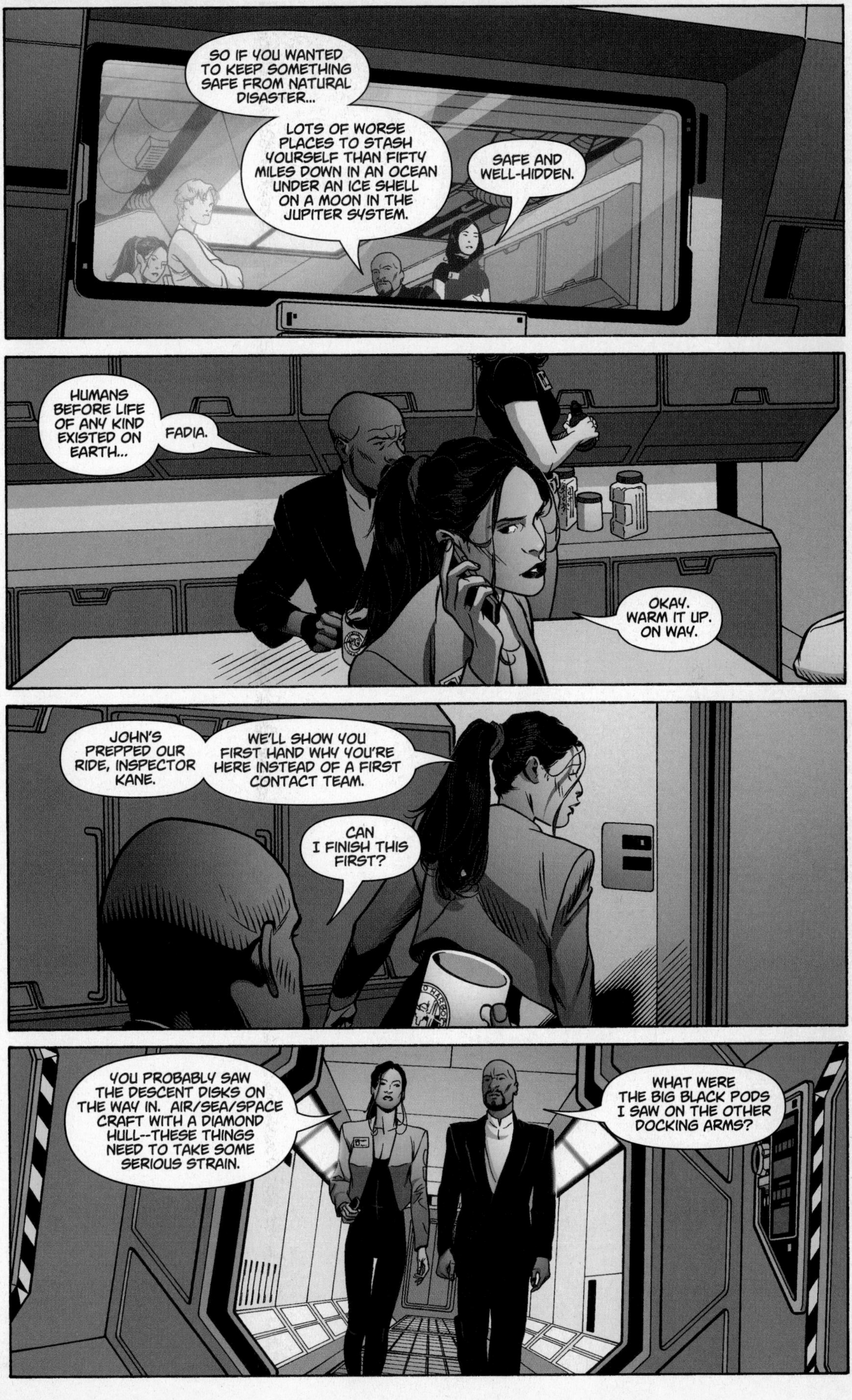
SO IF YOU WANTED TO KEEP SOMETHING SAFE FROM NATURAL DISASTER...
LOTS OF WORSE PLACES TO STASH YOURSELF THAN FIFTY MILES DOWN IN AN OCEAN UNDER AN ICE SHELL ON A MOON IN THE JUPITER SYSTEM.
SAFE AND WELL-HIDDEN.
HUMANS BEFORE LIFE OF ANY KIND EXISTED ON EARTH...
FADIA.
OKAY. WARM IT UP. ON WAY.
JOHN'S PREPPED OUR RIDE, INSPECTOR KANE.
WE'LL SHOW YOU FIRST HAND WHY YOU'RE HERE INSTEAD OF A FIRST CONTACT TEAM.
CAN I FINISH THIS FIRST?
YOU PROBABLY SAW THE DESCENT DISKS ON THE WAY IN. AIR/SEA/SPACE CRAFT WITH A DIAMOND HULL--THESE THINGS NEED TO TAKE SOME SERIOUS STRAIN.
WHAT WERE THE BIG BLACK PODS I SAW ON THE OTHER DOCKING ARMS?

ESCAPE CAPSULES. THEY'VE GOT ENOUGH OOMPH TO SHUNT US THROUGH THE MOON SYSTEM AND INTO A RESCUE ORBIT AROUND JUPITER.

WE HAVE A FINANCIAL DEAL WITH THE MINING RIG, THEY'LL PICK US UP AND CALL HOME.

SIOBHAN, YOU WITH ME?

RIGHT HERE. YOU ARE GO FOR UNDOCK IN YOUR OWN TIME, FADIA.

YOU LOCKED DOWN?

ALL READY FOR MY MAGICAL MYSTERY TOUR.

UNDOCK.

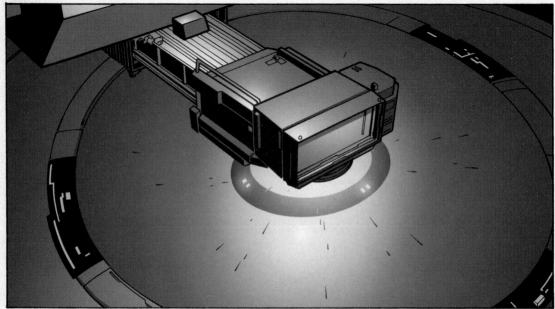

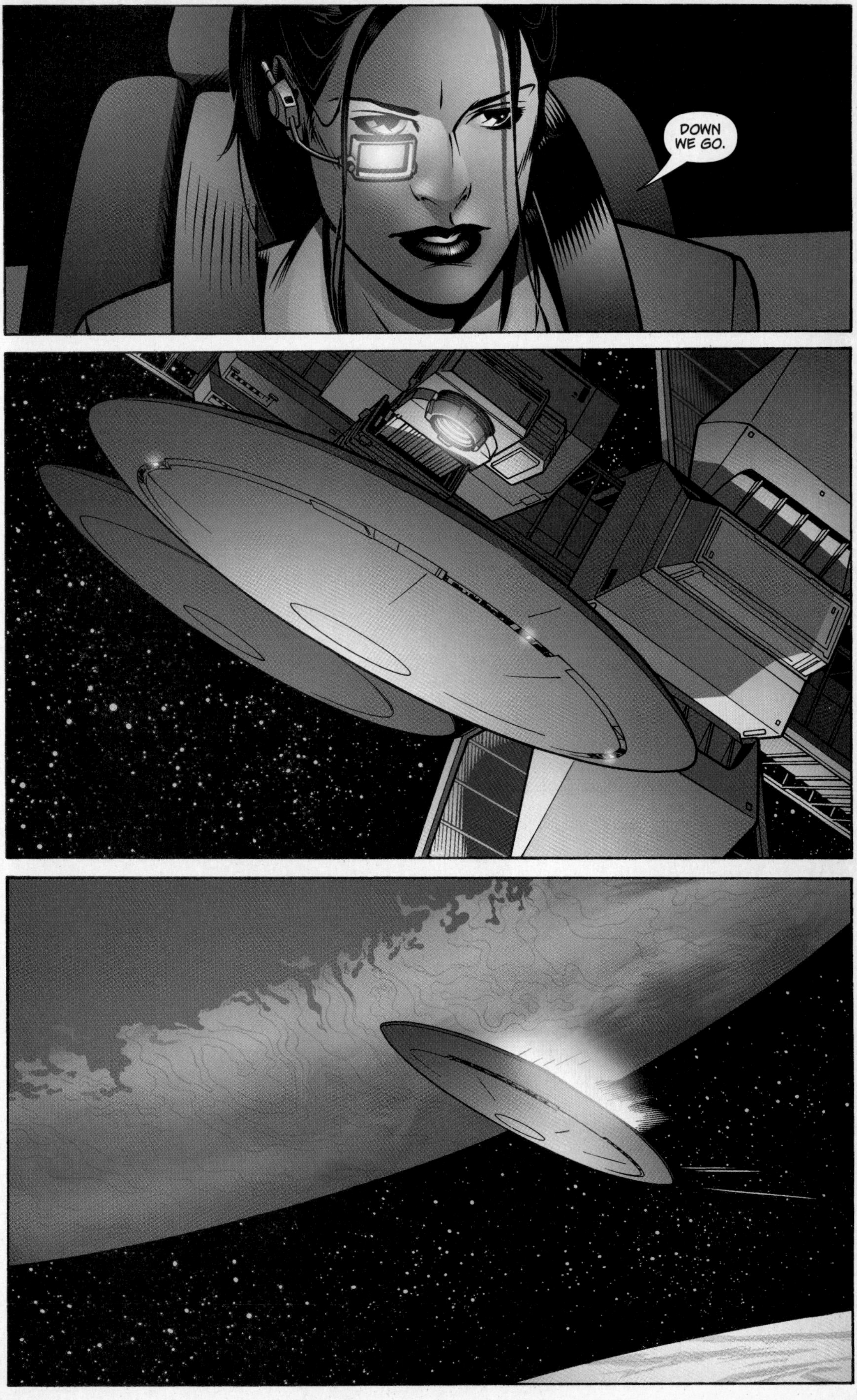
DOWN WE GO.

WHAT ARE THOSE LINES? NEVER SEEN ANYTHING LIKE THEM.

REGELATION MARKS.

THE OCEAN HAS JUPITER AND SEVENTEEN OTHER MOONS ACTING ON IT, SO ITS INTERNAL TIDES ARE WEIRD AND STRONG.

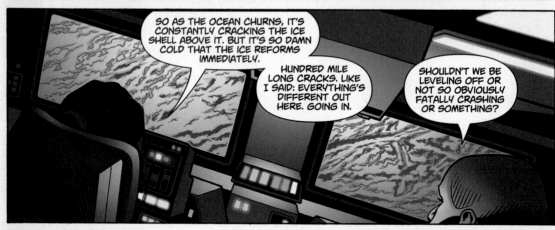

SO AS THE OCEAN CHURNS, IT'S CONSTANTLY CRACKING THE ICE SHELL ABOVE IT. BUT IT'S SO DAMN COLD THAT THE ICE REFORMS IMMEDIATELY.

HUNDRED MILE LONG CRACKS. LIKE I SAID: EVERYTHING'S DIFFERENT OUT HERE. GOING IN.

SHOULDN'T WE BE LEVELING OFF OR NOT SO OBVIOUSLY FATALLY CRASHING OR SOMETHING?

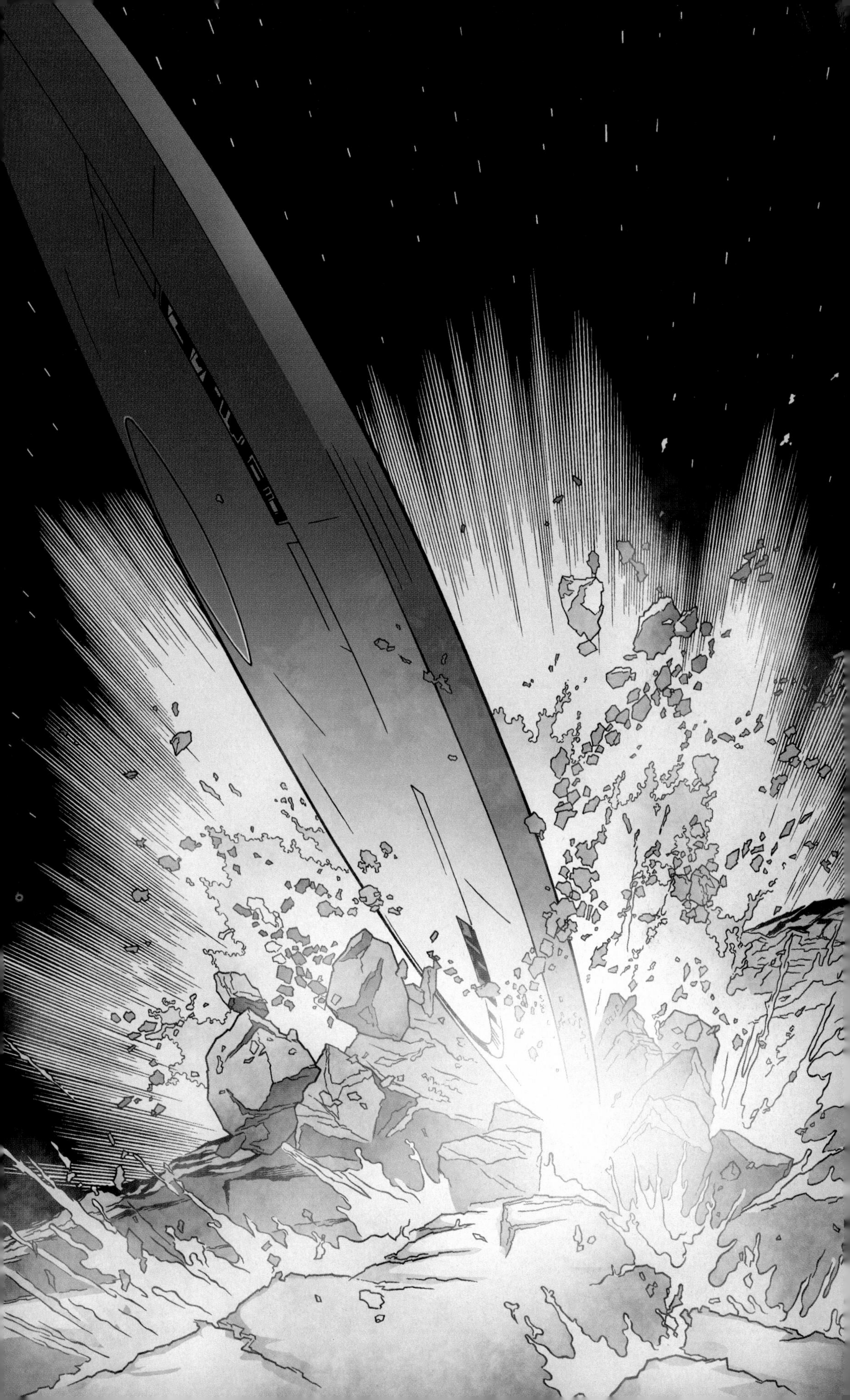

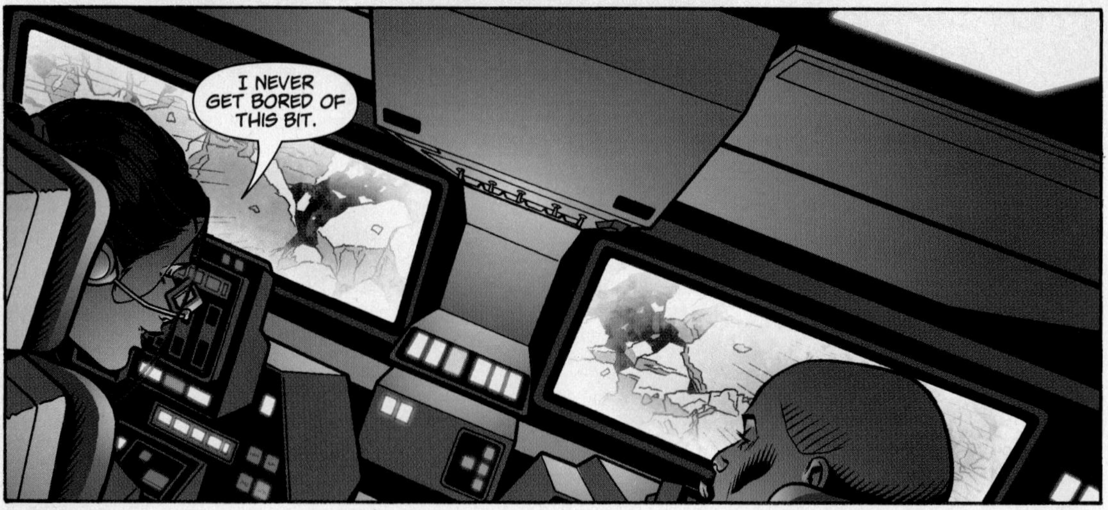
I NEVER GET BORED OF THIS BIT.

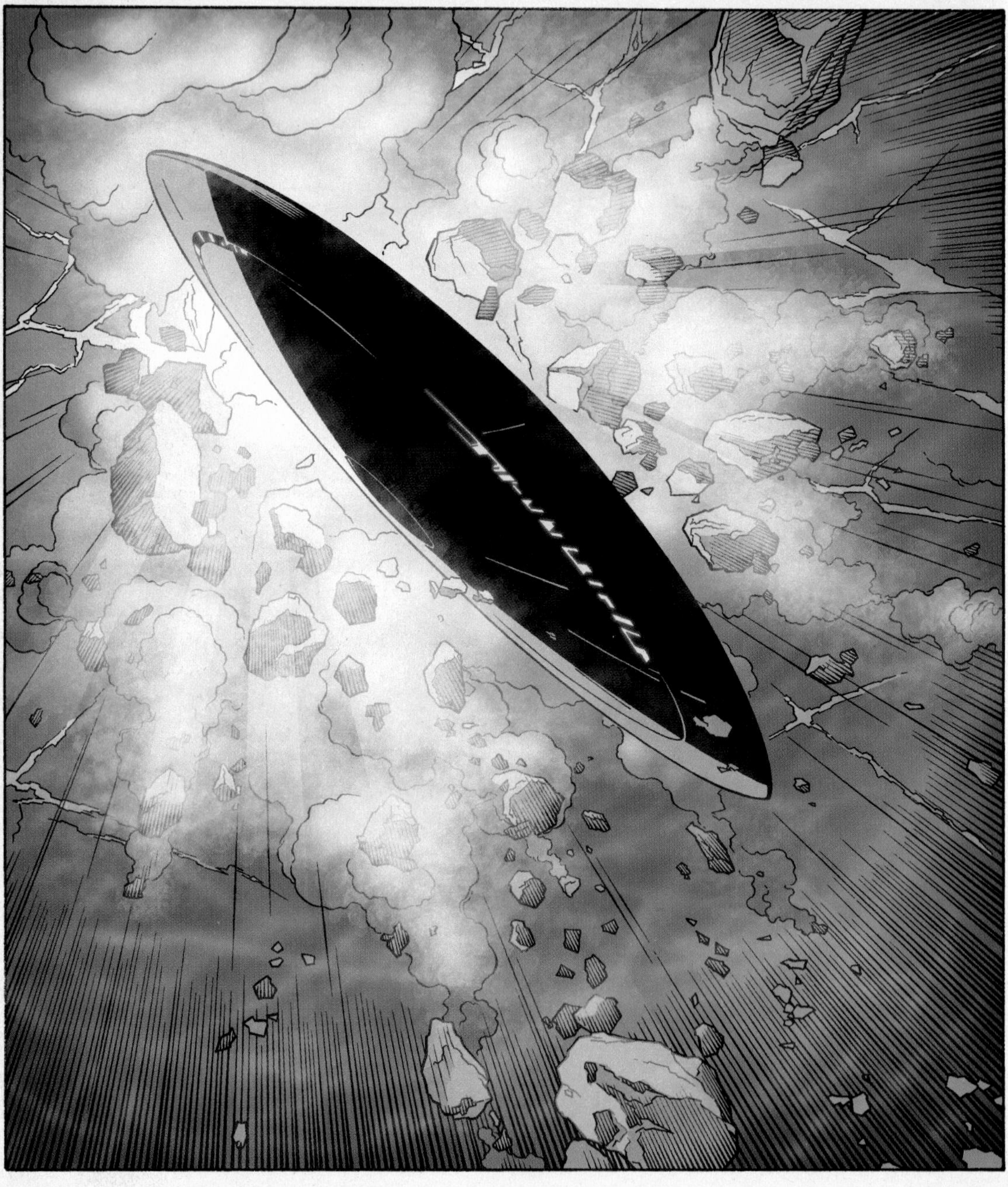

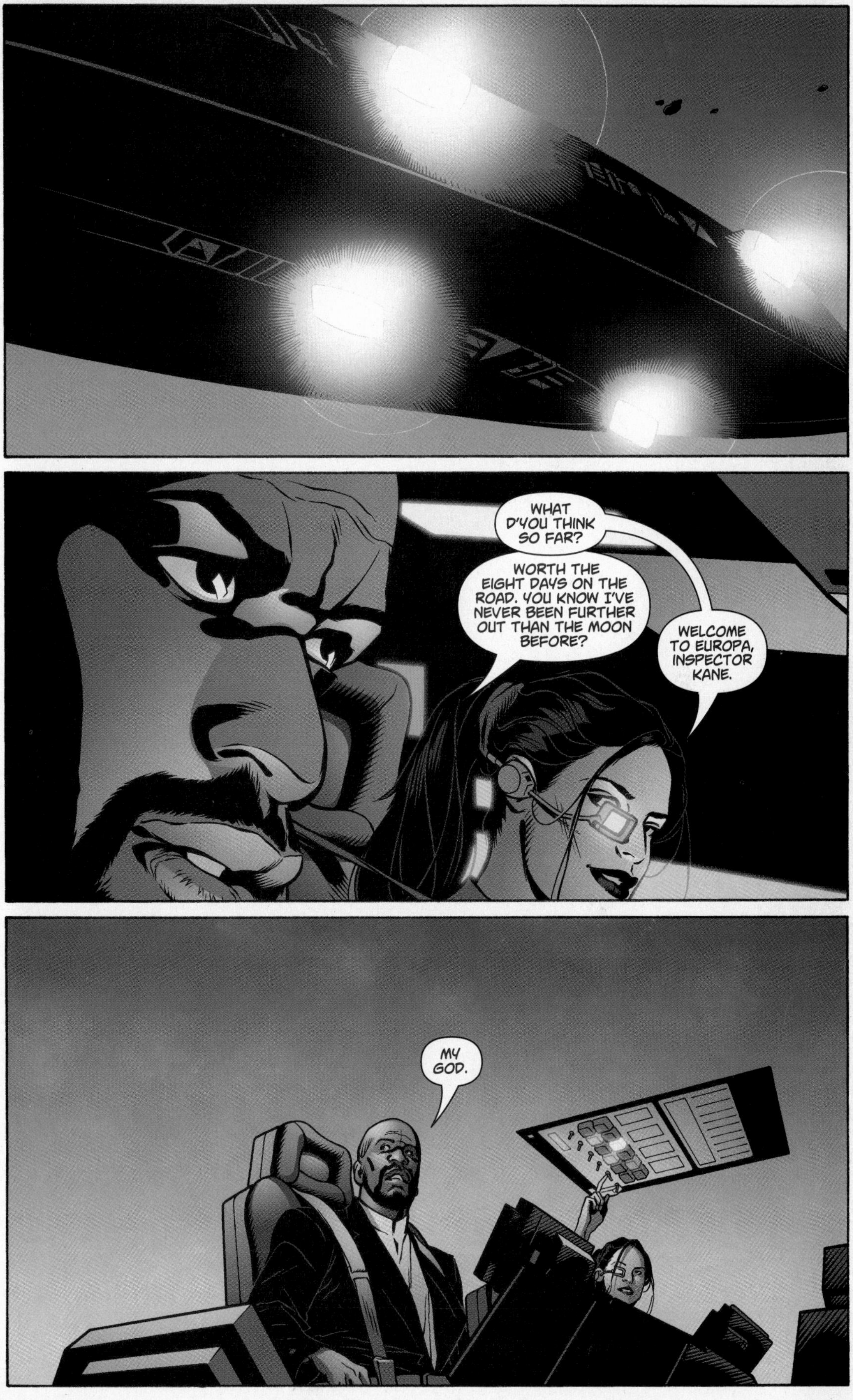
WHAT D'YOU THINK SO FAR?
WORTH THE EIGHT DAYS ON THE ROAD. YOU KNOW I'VE NEVER BEEN FURTHER OUT THAN THE MOON BEFORE?
WELCOME TO EUROPA, INSPECTOR KANE.
MY GOD.

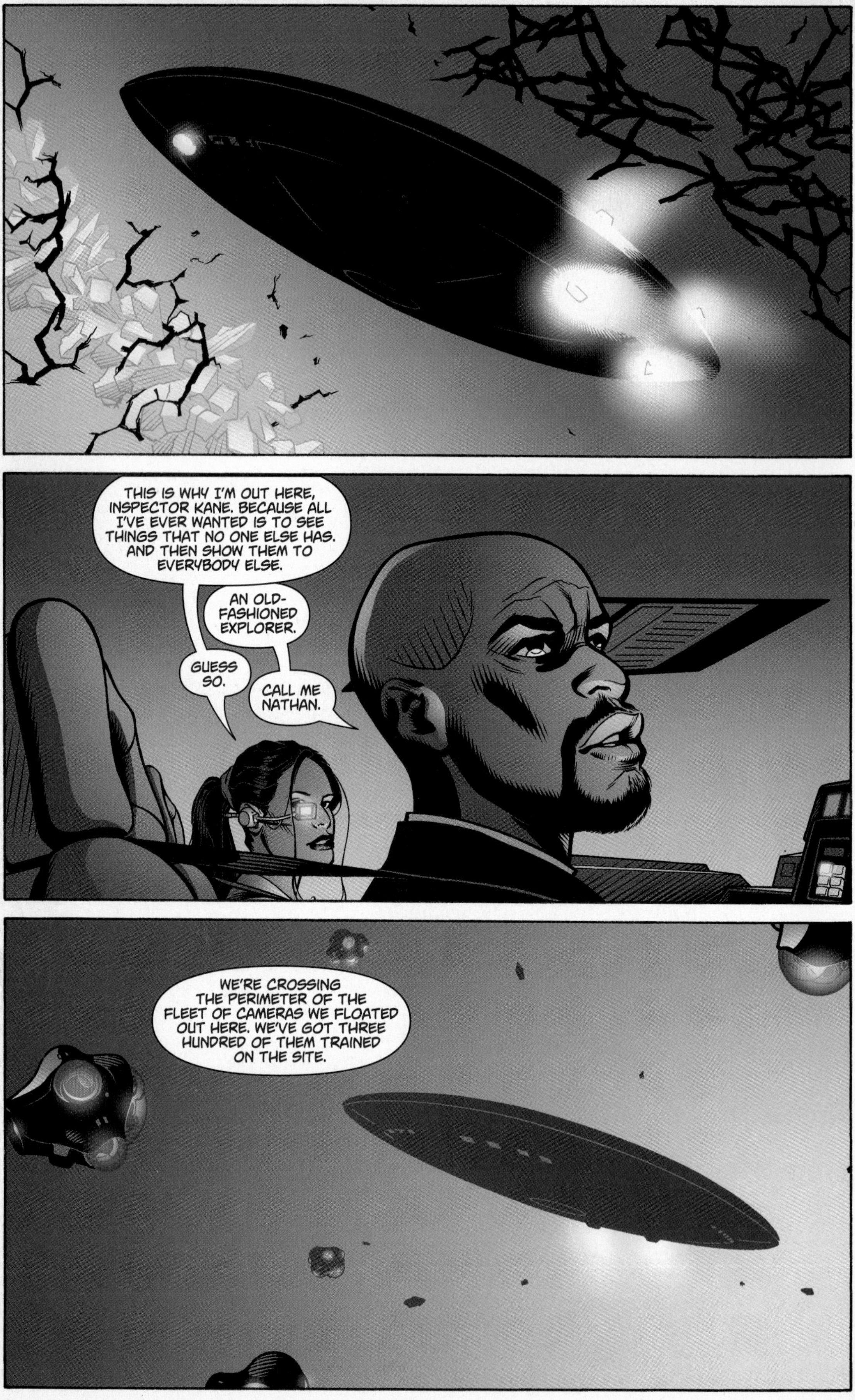
THIS IS WHY I'M OUT HERE, INSPECTOR KANE. BECAUSE ALL I'VE EVER WANTED IS TO SEE THINGS THAT NO ONE ELSE HAS. AND THEN SHOW THEM TO EVERYBODY ELSE.
AN OLD-FASHIONED EXPLORER.
GUESS SO.
CALL ME NATHAN.
WE'RE CROSSING THE PERIMETER OF THE FLEET OF CAMERAS WE FLOATED OUT HERE. WE'VE GOT THREE HUNDRED OF THEM TRAINED ON THE SITE.

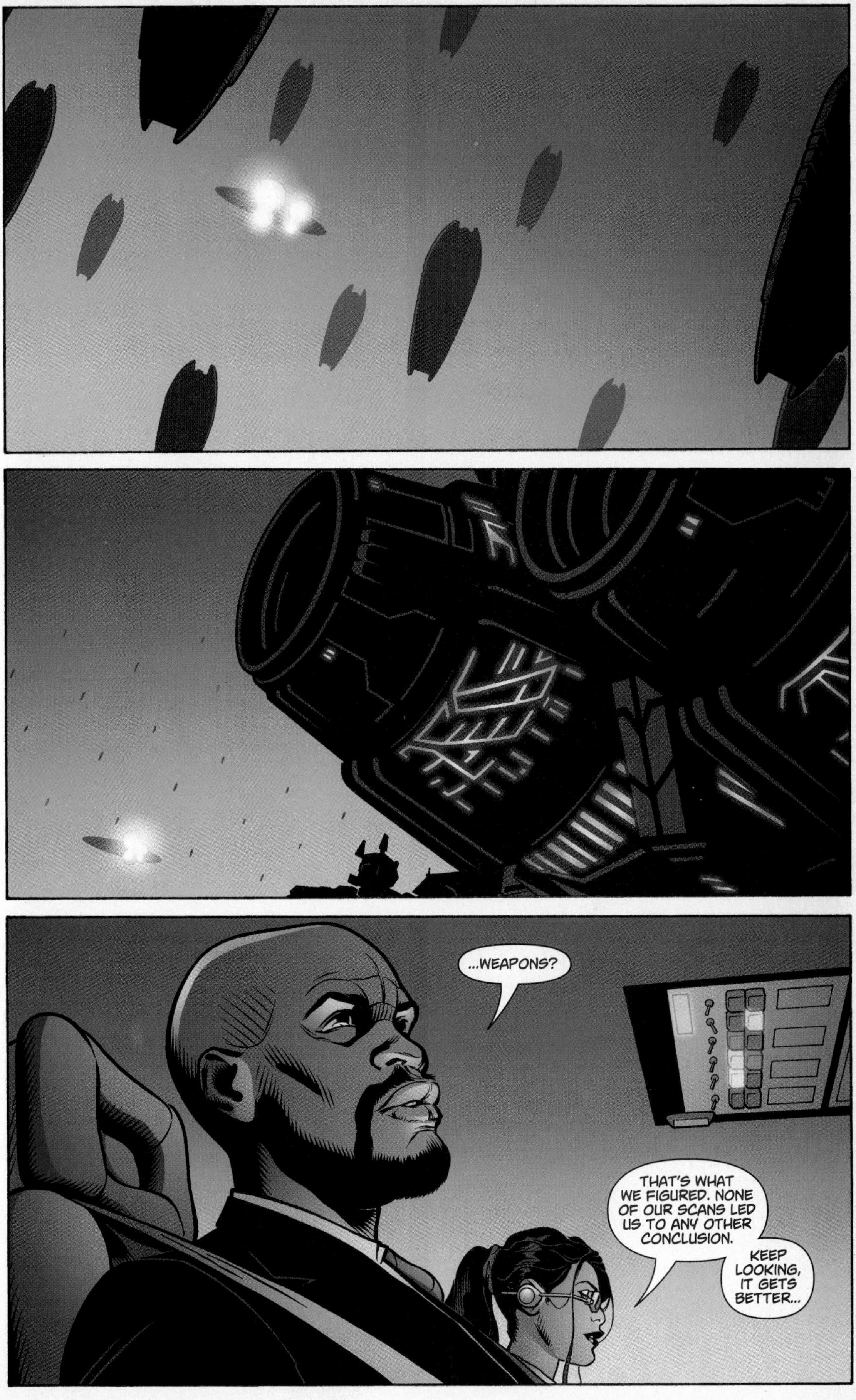
...WEAPONS?
THAT'S WHAT WE FIGURED. NONE OF OUR SCANS LED US TO ANY OTHER CONCLUSION.
KEEP LOOKING, IT GETS BETTER...

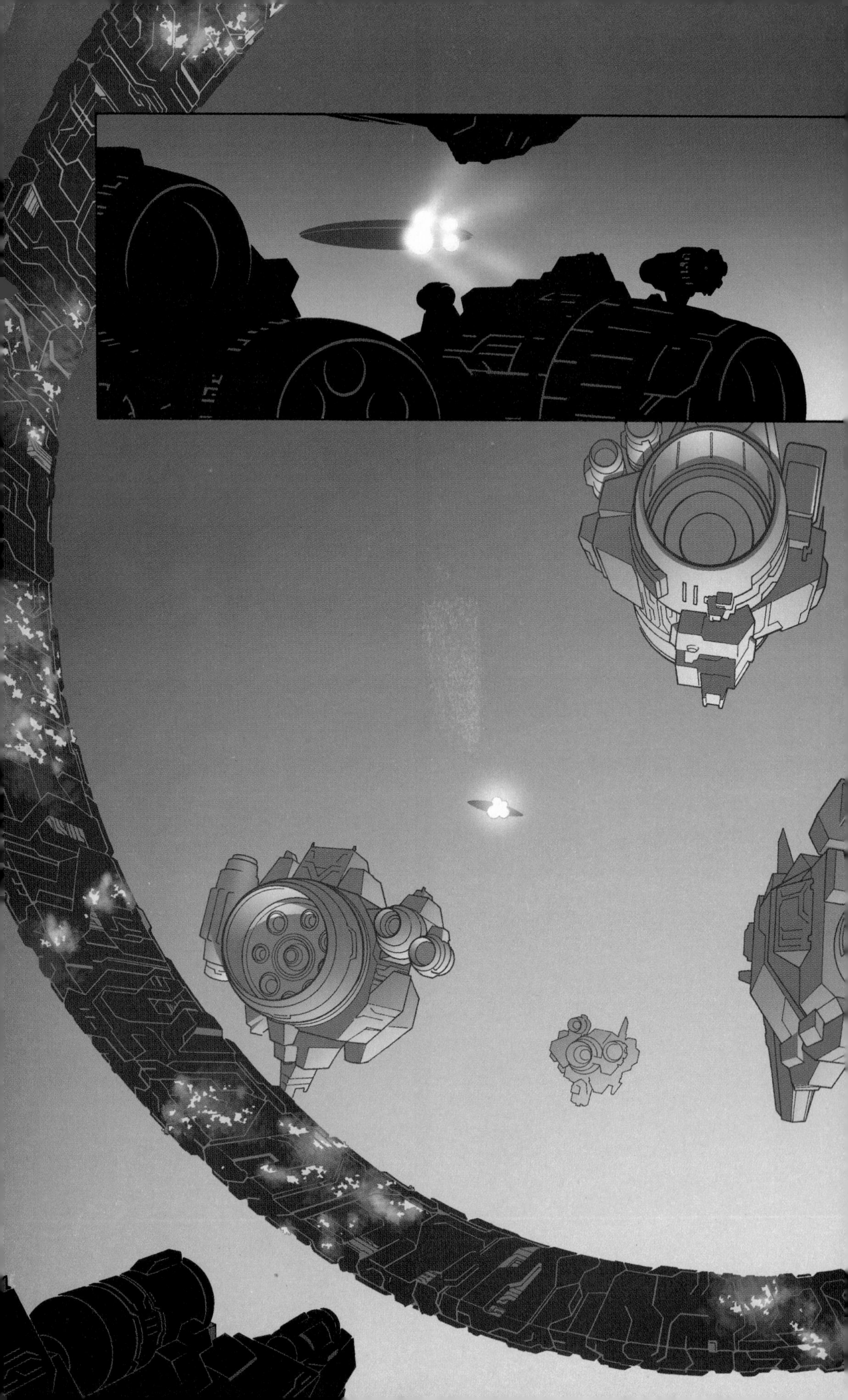

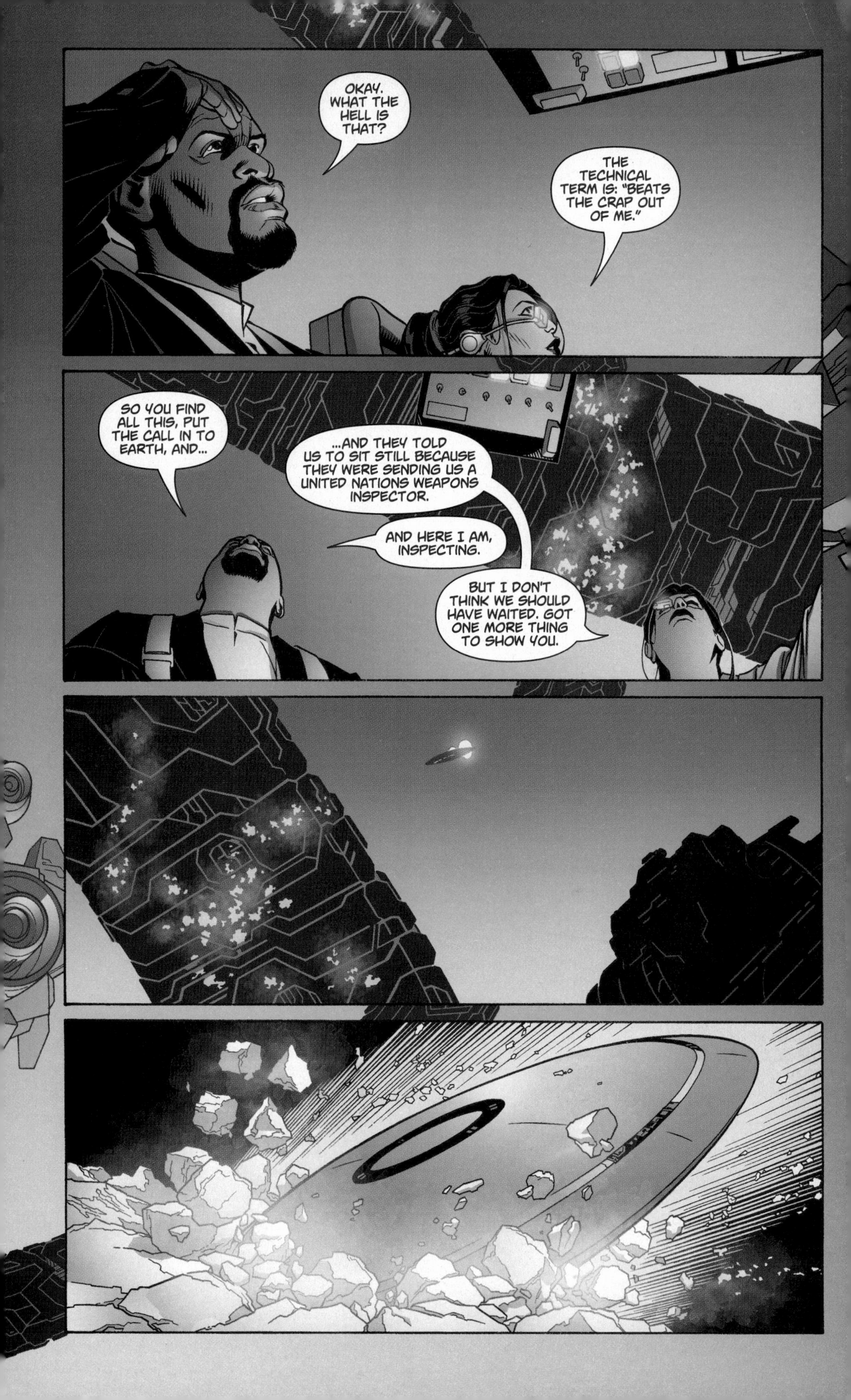
OKAY. WHAT THE HELL IS THAT?
THE TECHNICAL TERM IS: "BEATS THE CRAP OUT OF ME."
SO YOU FIND ALL THIS, PUT THE CALL IN TO EARTH, AND...
...AND THEY TOLD US TO SIT STILL BECAUSE THEY WERE SENDING US A UNITED NATIONS WEAPONS INSPECTOR.
AND HERE I AM, INSPECTING.
BUT I DON'T THINK WE SHOULD HAVE WAITED. GOT ONE MORE THING TO SHOW YOU.

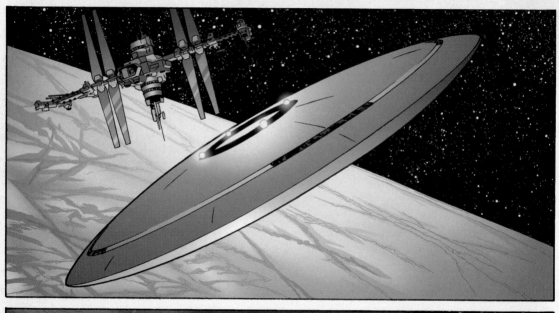

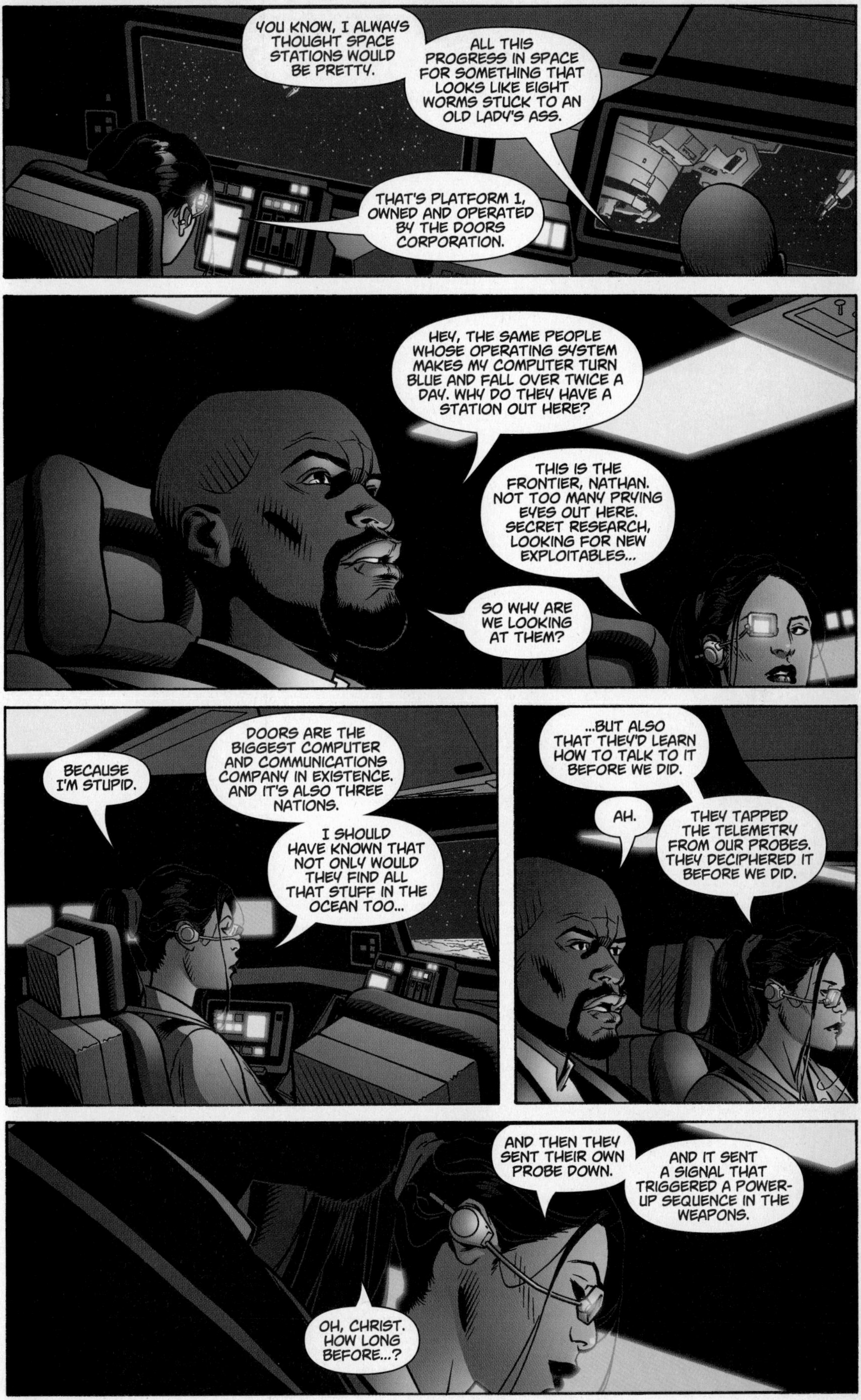
YOU KNOW, I ALWAYS THOUGHT SPACE STATIONS WOULD BE PRETTY.
ALL THIS PROGRESS IN SPACE FOR SOMETHING THAT LOOKS LIKE EIGHT WORMS STUCK TO AN OLD LADY'S ASS.
THAT'S PLATFORM 1, OWNED AND OPERATED BY THE DOORS CORPORATION.
HEY, THE SAME PEOPLE WHOSE OPERATING SYSTEM MAKES MY COMPUTER TURN BLUE AND FALL OVER TWICE A DAY. WHY DO THEY HAVE A STATION OUT HERE?
THIS IS THE FRONTIER, NATHAN. NOT TOO MANY PRYING EYES OUT HERE. SECRET RESEARCH, LOOKING FOR NEW EXPLOITABLES...
SO WHY ARE WE LOOKING AT THEM?
BECAUSE I'M STUPID.
DOORS ARE THE BIGGEST COMPUTER AND COMMUNICATIONS COMPANY IN EXISTENCE. AND IT'S ALSO THREE NATIONS.
I SHOULD HAVE KNOWN THAT NOT ONLY WOULD THEY FIND ALL THAT STUFF IN THE OCEAN TOO...
...BUT ALSO THAT THEY'D LEARN HOW TO TALK TO IT BEFORE WE DID.
AH.
THEY TAPPED THE TELEMETRY FROM OUR PROBES. THEY DECIPHERED IT BEFORE WE DID.
AND THEN THEY SENT THEIR OWN PROBE DOWN.
AND IT SENT A SIGNAL THAT TRIGGERED A POWER-UP SEQUENCE IN THE WEAPONS.
OH, CHRIST. HOW LONG BEFORE...?

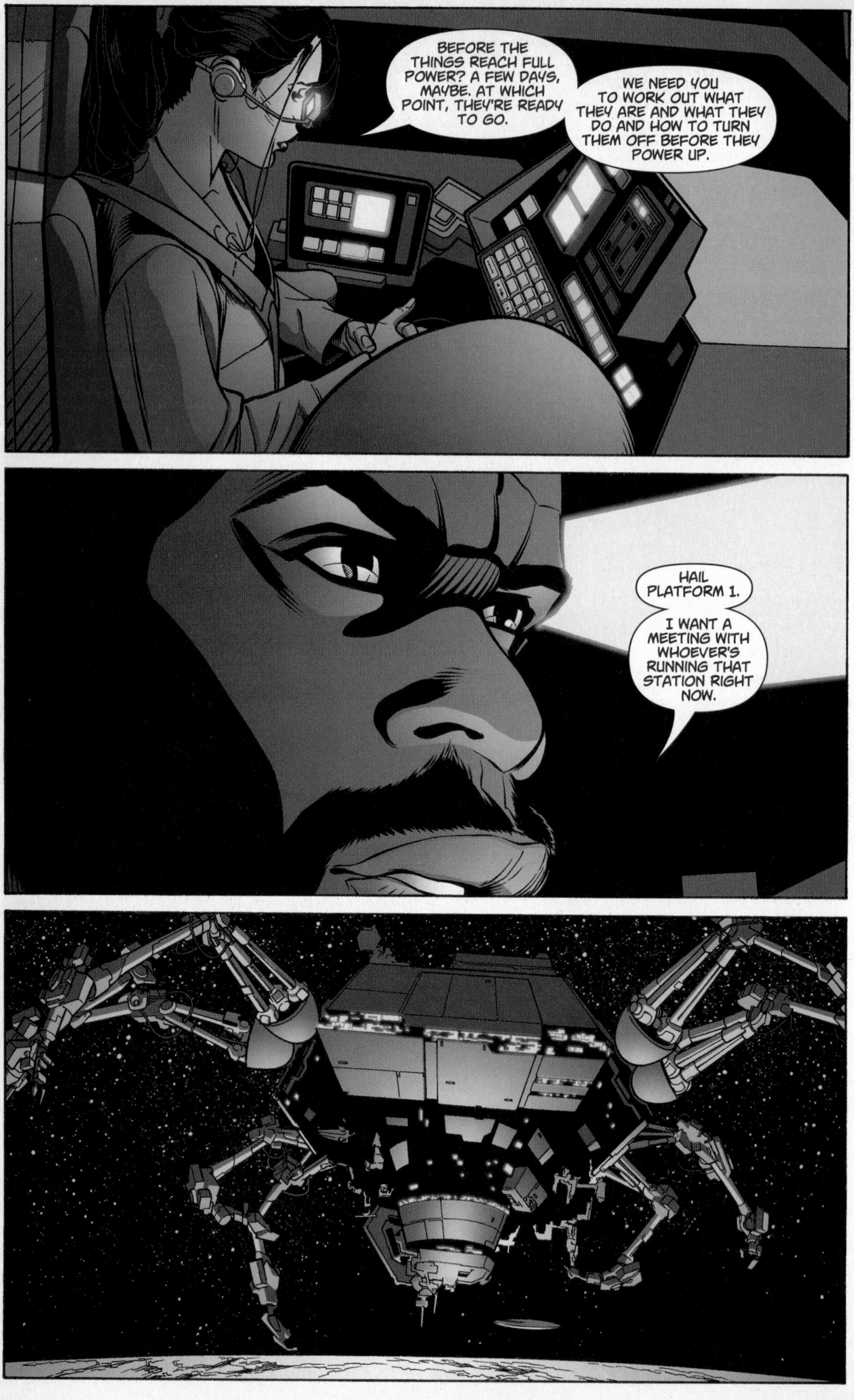
BEFORE THE THINGS REACH FULL POWER? A FEW DAYS, MAYBE. AT WHICH POINT, THEY'RE READY TO GO.
WE NEED YOU TO WORK OUT WHAT THEY ARE AND WHAT THEY DO AND HOW TO TURN THEM OFF BEFORE THEY POWER UP.
HAIL PLATFORM 1.
I WANT A MEETING WITH WHOEVER'S RUNNING THAT STATION RIGHT NOW.

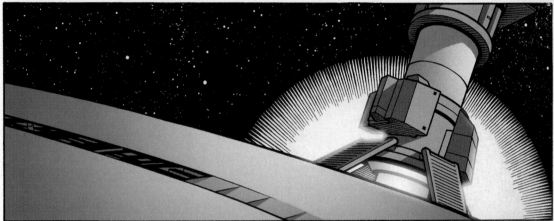

NATHAN KANE, UNITED NATIONS WEAPONS INSPECTORATE. THIS IS FADIA AZIZ, COMMANDING COLD HARBOR.

WE'VE ARRANGED TO SEE THE STATION MANAGER.

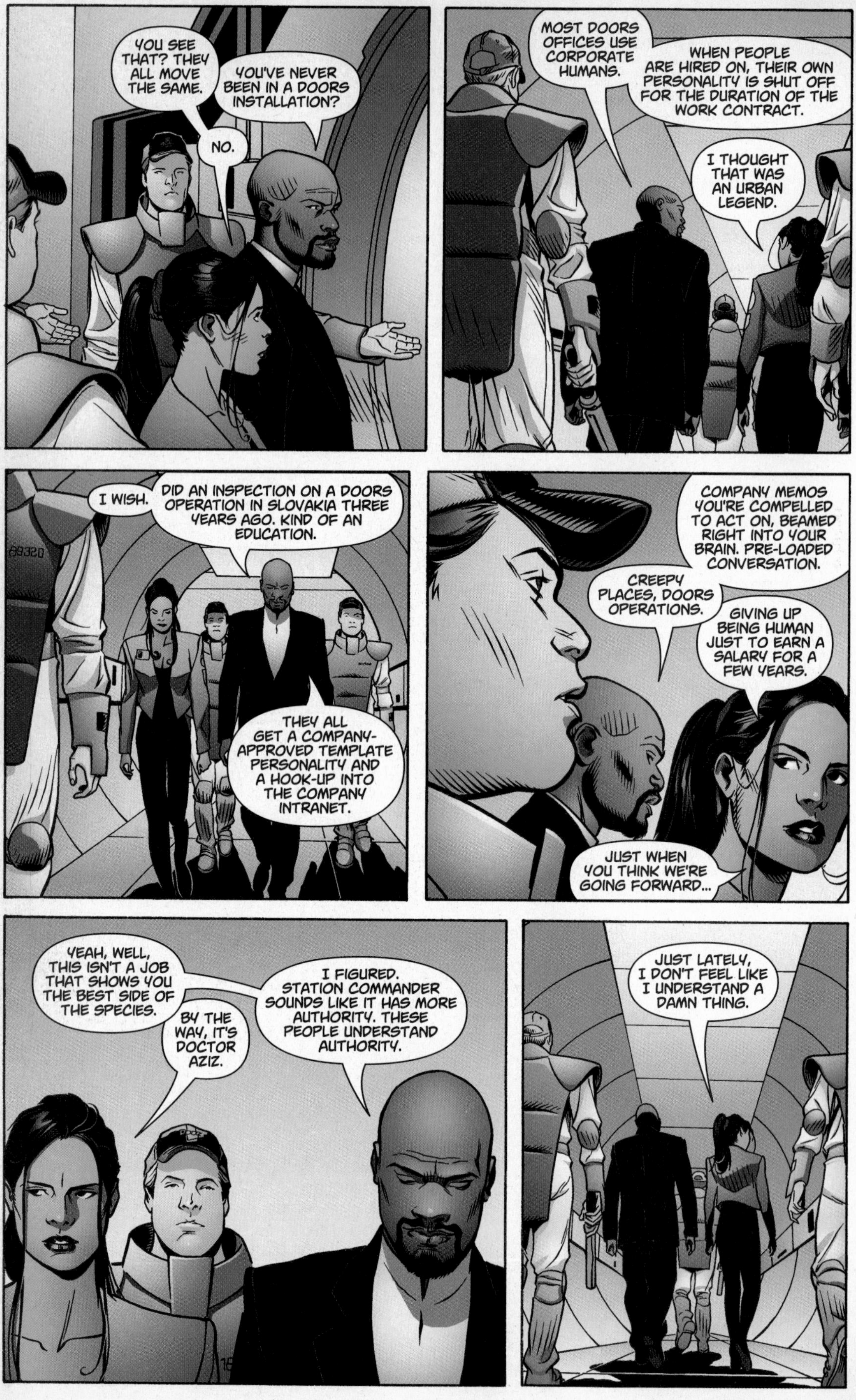

YOU SEE THAT? THEY ALL MOVE THE SAME.
YOU'VE NEVER BEEN IN A DOORS INSTALLATION?
NO.
MOST DOORS OFFICES USE CORPORATE HUMANS.
WHEN PEOPLE ARE HIRED ON, THEIR OWN PERSONALITY IS SHUT OFF FOR THE DURATION OF THE WORK CONTRACT.
I THOUGHT THAT WAS AN URBAN LEGEND.
I WISH.
DID AN INSPECTION ON A DOORS OPERATION IN SLOVAKIA THREE YEARS AGO. KIND OF AN EDUCATION.
THEY ALL GET A COMPANY-APPROVED TEMPLATE PERSONALITY AND A HOOK-UP INTO THE COMPANY INTRANET.
COMPANY MEMOS YOU'RE COMPELLED TO ACT ON, BEAMED RIGHT INTO YOUR BRAIN. PRE-LOADED CONVERSATION.
CREEPY PLACES, DOORS OPERATIONS.
GIVING UP BEING HUMAN JUST TO EARN A SALARY FOR A FEW YEARS.
JUST WHEN YOU THINK WE'RE GOING FORWARD...
YEAH, WELL, THIS ISN'T A JOB THAT SHOWS YOU THE BEST SIDE OF THE SPECIES.
BY THE WAY, IT'S DOCTOR AZIZ.
I FIGURED. STATION COMMANDER SOUNDS LIKE IT HAS MORE AUTHORITY. THESE PEOPLE UNDERSTAND AUTHORITY.
JUST LATELY, I DON'T FEEL LIKE I UNDERSTAND A DAMN THING.

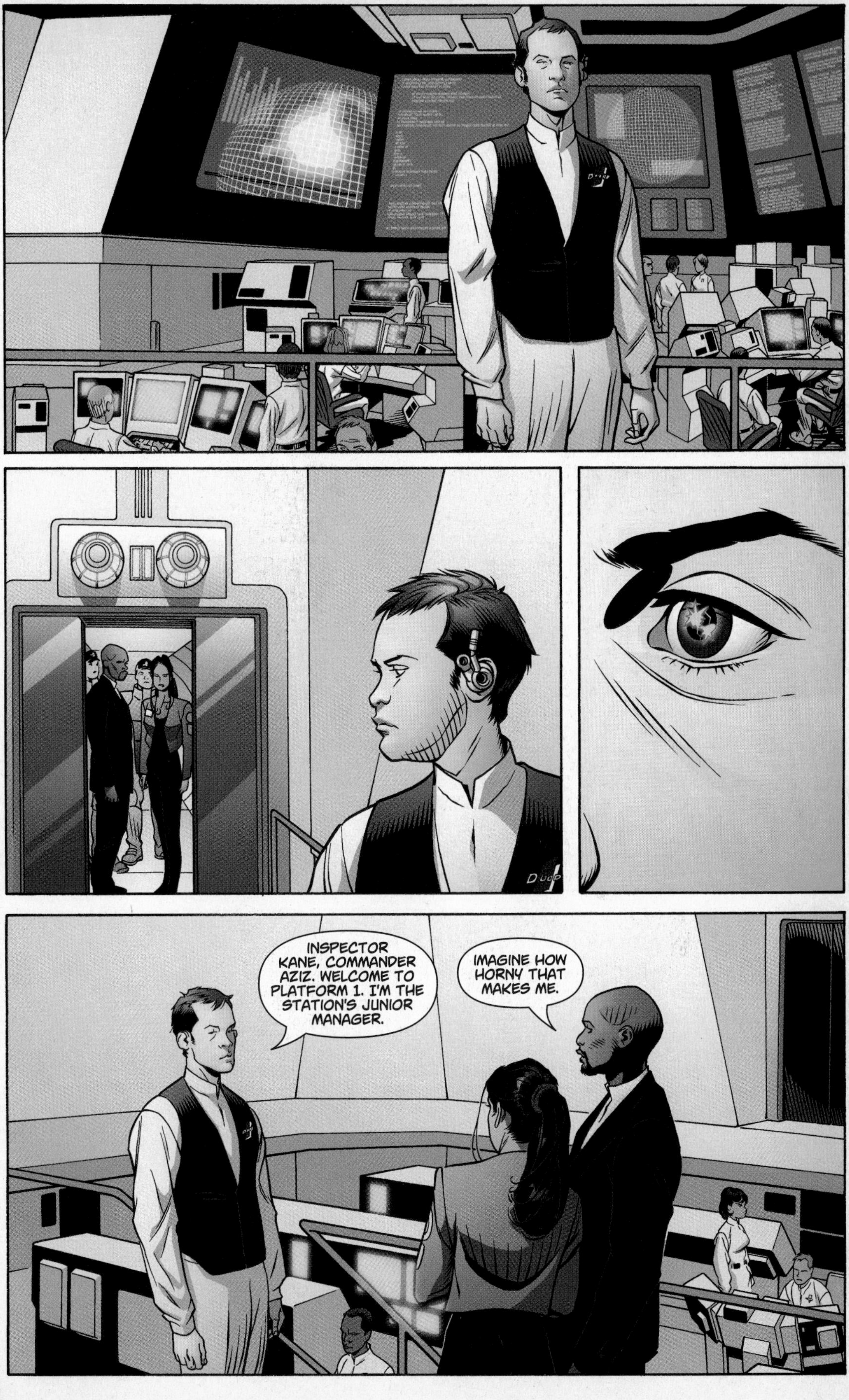
INSPECTOR KANE, COMMANDER AZIZ. WELCOME TO PLATFORM 1. I'M THE STATION'S JUNIOR MANAGER.
IMAGINE HOW HORNY THAT MAKES ME.

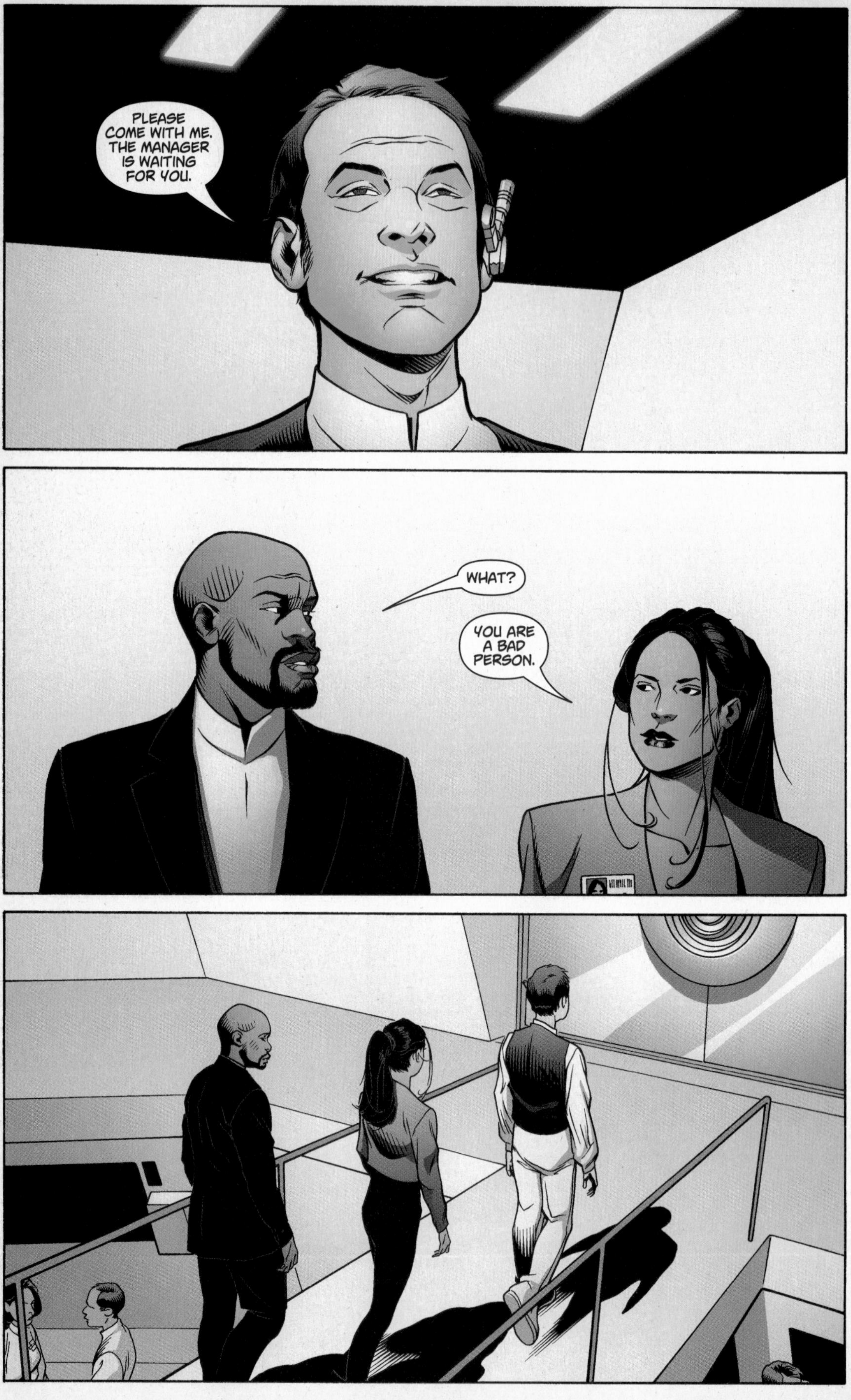
PLEASE COME WITH ME. THE MANAGER IS WAITING FOR YOU.
WHAT?
YOU ARE A BAD PERSON.

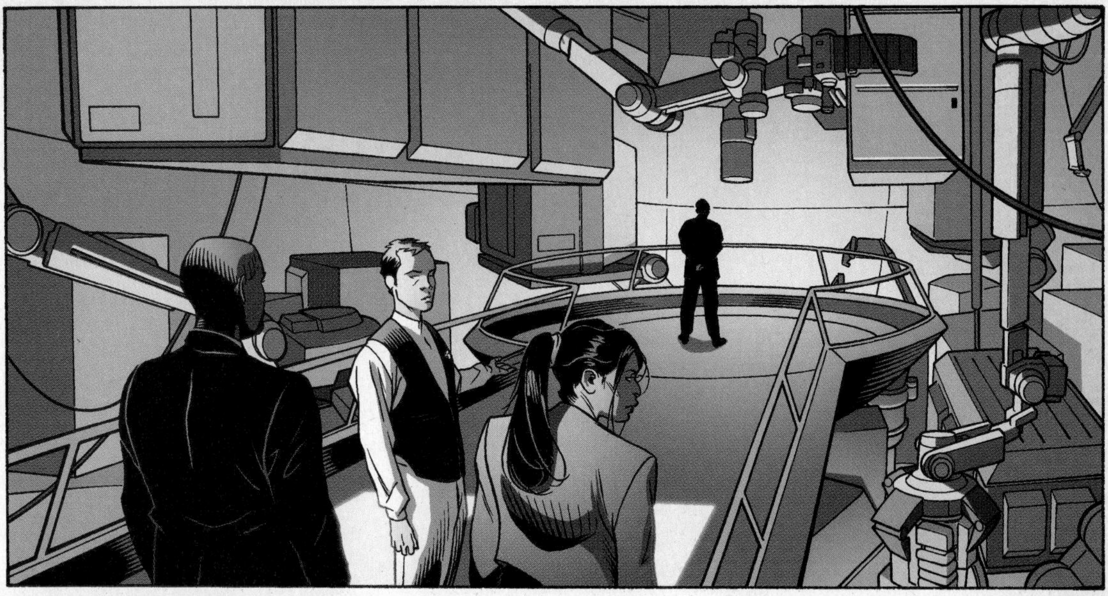

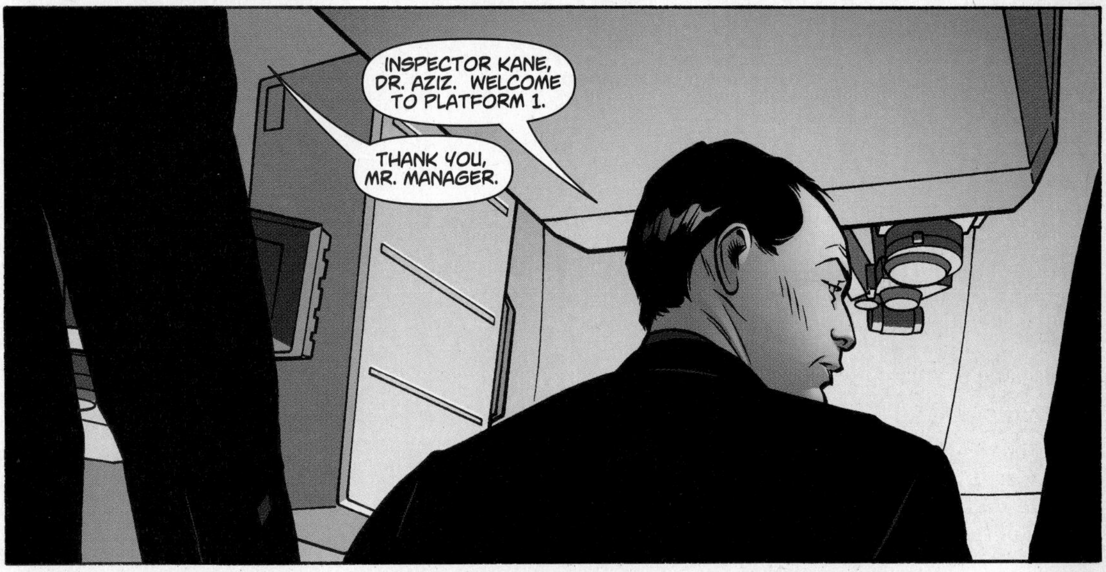
INSPECTOR KANE, DR. AZIZ. WELCOME TO PLATFORM 1.
THANK YOU, MR. MANAGER.

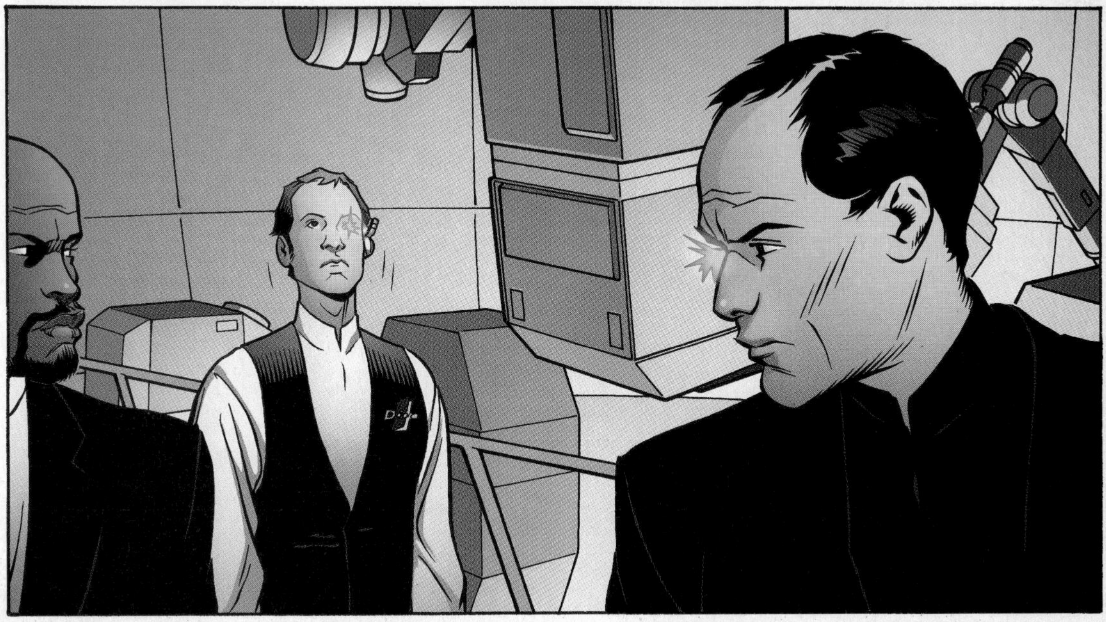

STRANGE DAYS INDEED, NO?

WHAT'S GOING ON DOWN THERE?

WELL, I THOUGHT I'D PUT TOGETHER A WAY TO HELP YOU RETRIEVE THE WEAPONRY AND CRYOGENIC STASIS UNITS FROM EUROPA'S OCEAN.

I'M WELL AWARE THAT AN EXFOR STATION REALLY DOESN'T HAVE THE HEAVY LIFTING EQUIPMENT NECESSARY FOR THE TASK.

WE, HOWEVER, DO.

AND IT'S REALLY JUST YOU AND US OUT HERE, AFTER ALL.

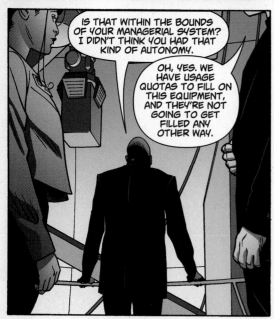

IS THAT WITHIN THE BOUNDS OF YOUR MANAGERIAL SYSTEM? I DIDN'T THINK YOU HAD THAT KIND OF AUTONOMY.

OH, YES. WE HAVE USAGE QUOTAS TO FILL ON THIS EQUIPMENT, AND THEY'RE NOT GOING TO GET FILLED ANY OTHER WAY.

IT REALLY IS MY PLEASURE TO BE ABLE TO PUT THIS CRAP TOWARDS A GOOD CAUSE.

NOT TO MENTION TALKING TO PEOPLE WHOSE RESPONSES AREN'T LARGELY PRE-WRITTEN.

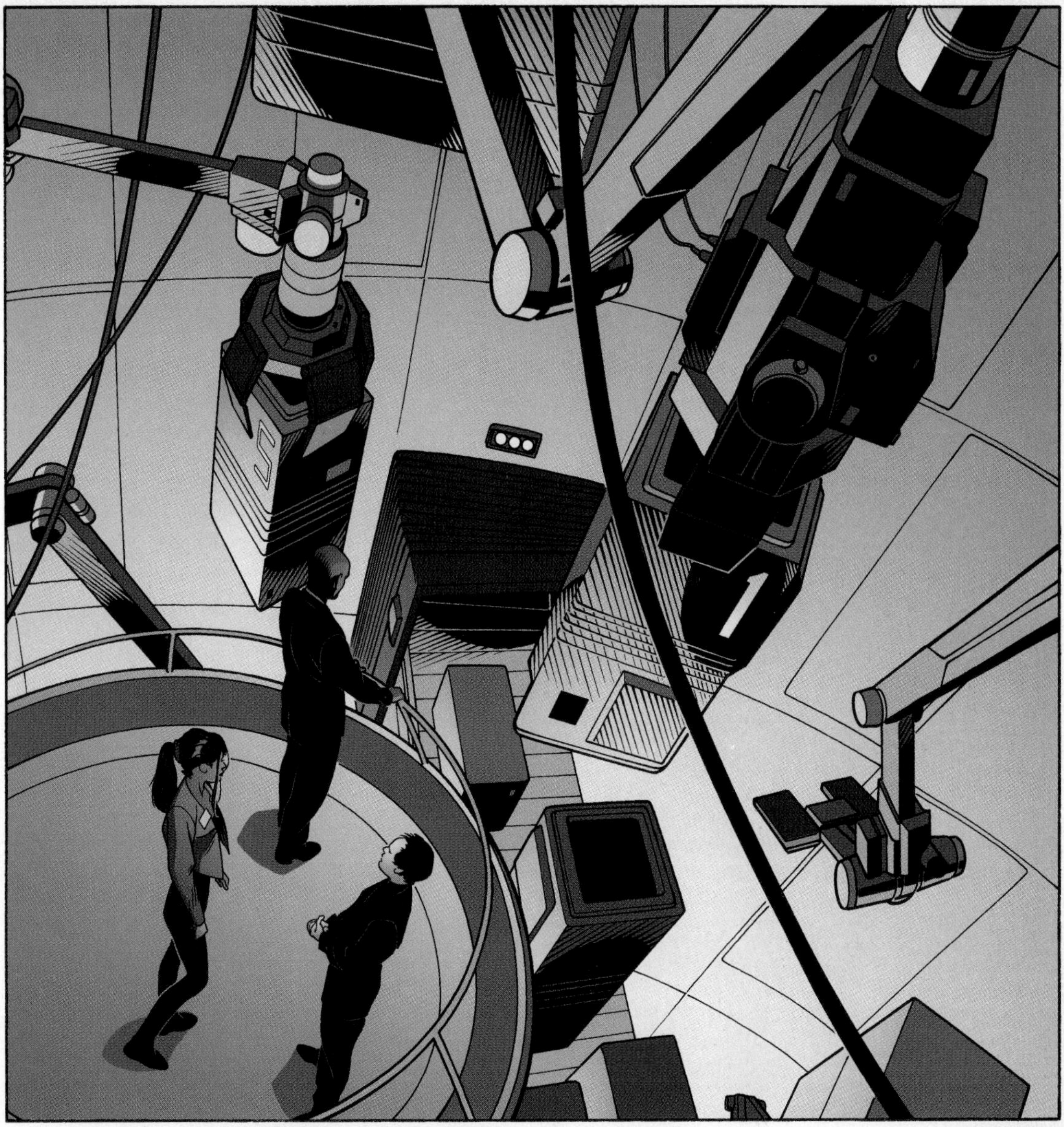

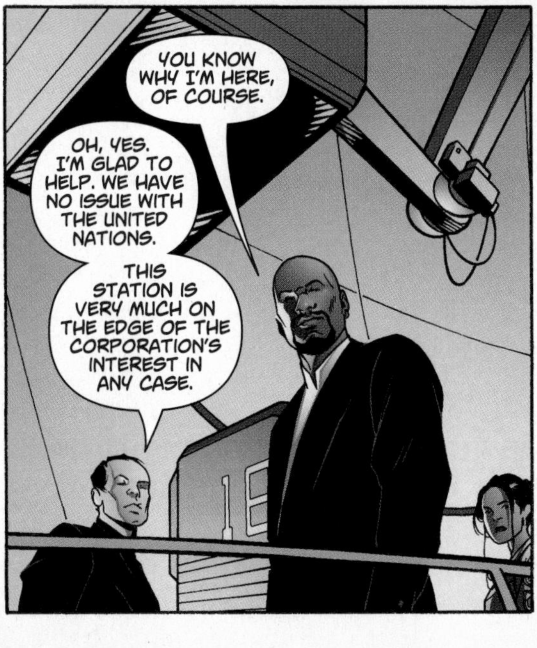
YOU KNOW WHY I'M HERE, OF COURSE.
OH, YES. I'M GLAD TO HELP. WE HAVE NO ISSUE WITH THE UNITED NATIONS.
THIS STATION IS VERY MUCH ON THE EDGE OF THE CORPORATION'S INTEREST IN ANY CASE.

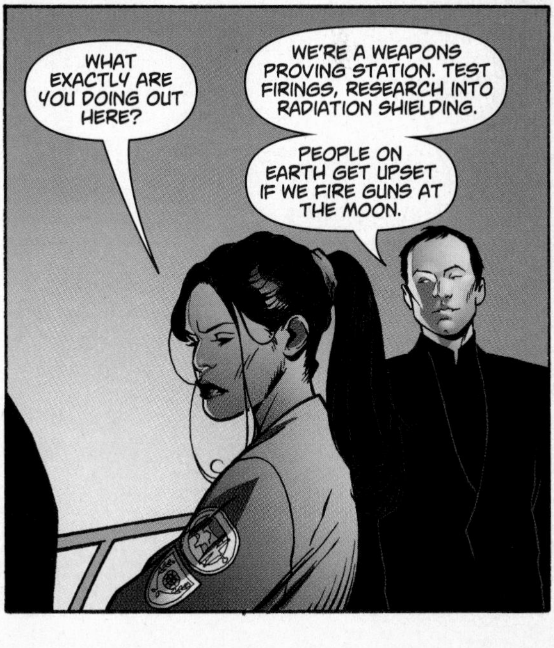
WHAT EXACTLY ARE YOU DOING OUT HERE?
WE'RE A WEAPONS PROVING STATION. TEST FIRINGS, RESEARCH INTO RADIATION SHIELDING.
PEOPLE ON EARTH GET UPSET IF WE FIRE GUNS AT THE MOON.

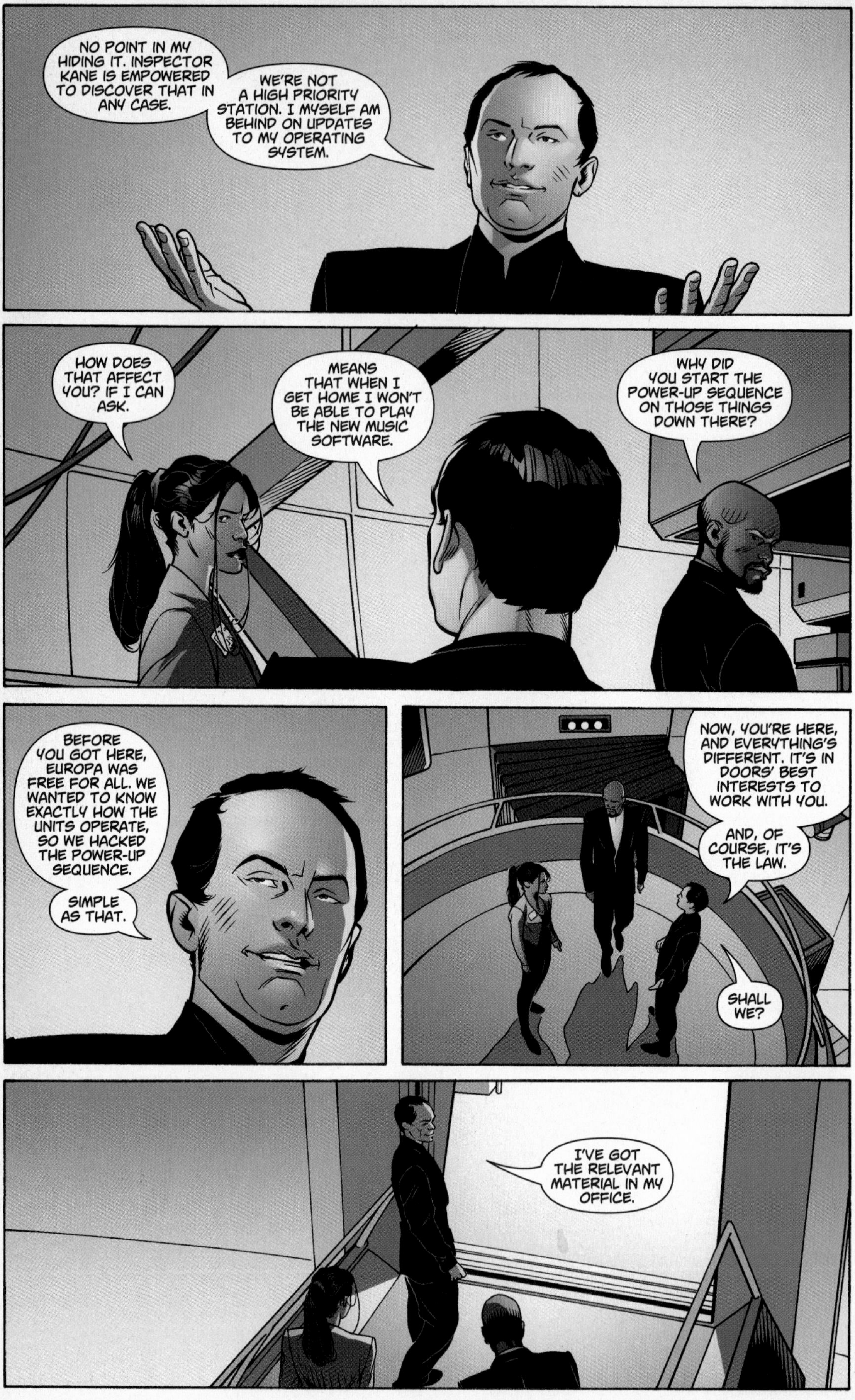
NO POINT IN MY HIDING IT. INSPECTOR KANE IS EMPOWERED TO DISCOVER THAT IN ANY CASE.
WE'RE NOT A HIGH PRIORITY STATION. I MYSELF AM BEHIND ON UPDATES TO MY OPERATING SYSTEM.
HOW DOES THAT AFFECT YOU? IF I CAN ASK.
MEANS THAT WHEN I GET HOME I WON'T BE ABLE TO PLAY THE NEW MUSIC SOFTWARE.
WHY DID YOU START THE POWER-UP SEQUENCE ON THOSE THINGS DOWN THERE?
BEFORE YOU GOT HERE, EUROPA WAS FREE FOR ALL. WE WANTED TO KNOW EXACTLY HOW THE UNITS OPERATE, SO WE HACKED THE POWER-UP SEQUENCE.
SIMPLE AS THAT.
NOW, YOU'RE HERE, AND EVERYTHING'S DIFFERENT. IT'S IN DOORS' BEST INTERESTS TO WORK WITH YOU.
AND, OF COURSE, IT'S THE LAW.
SHALL WE?
I'VE GOT THE RELEVANT MATERIAL IN MY OFFICE.

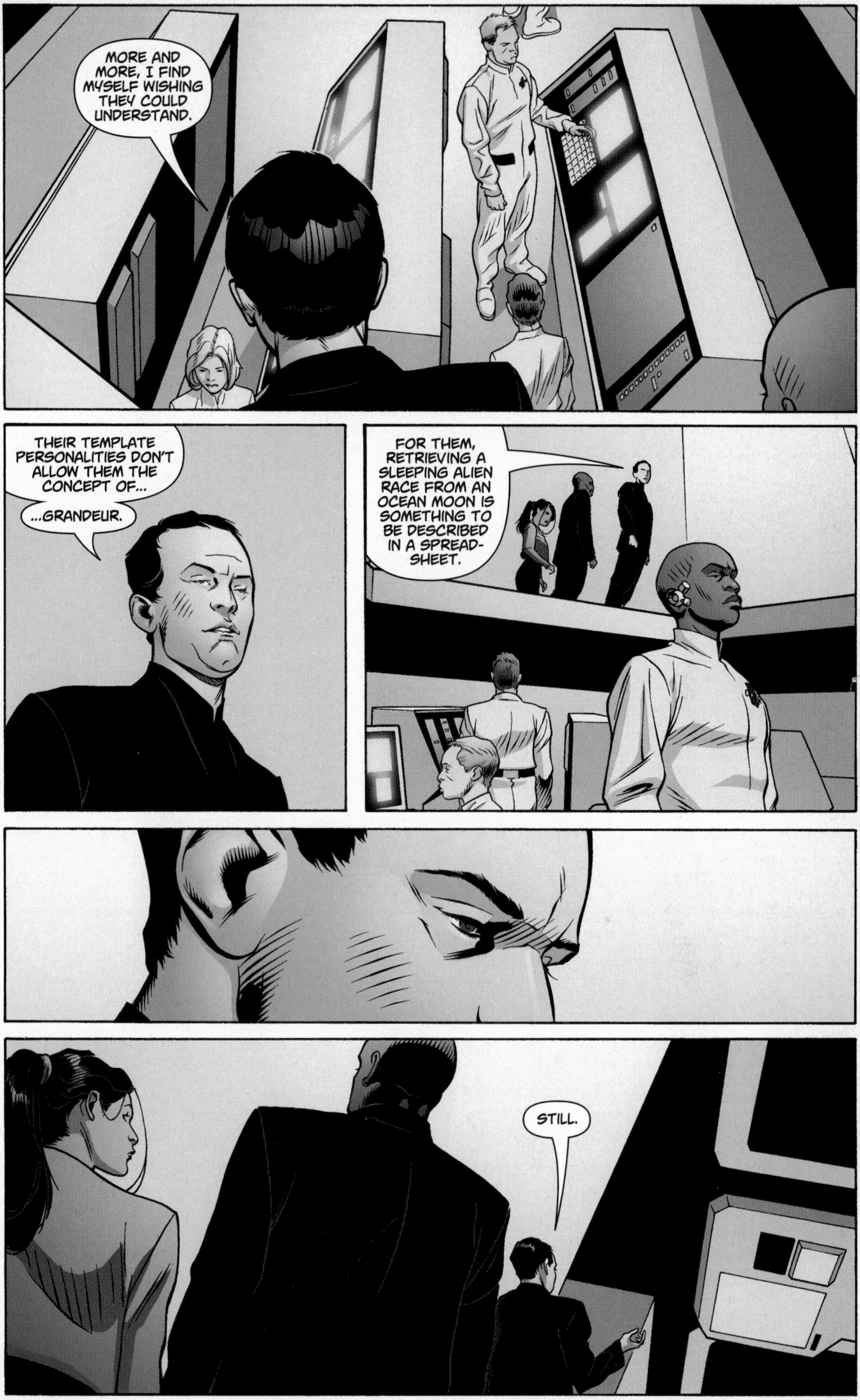
MORE AND MORE, I FIND MYSELF WISHING THEY COULD UNDERSTAND.
THEIR TEMPLATE PERSONALITIES DON'T ALLOW THEM THE CONCEPT OF...
...GRANDEUR.
FOR THEM, RETRIEVING A SLEEPING ALIEN RACE FROM AN OCEAN MOON IS SOMETHING TO BE DESCRIBED IN A SPREAD-SHEET.
STILL.

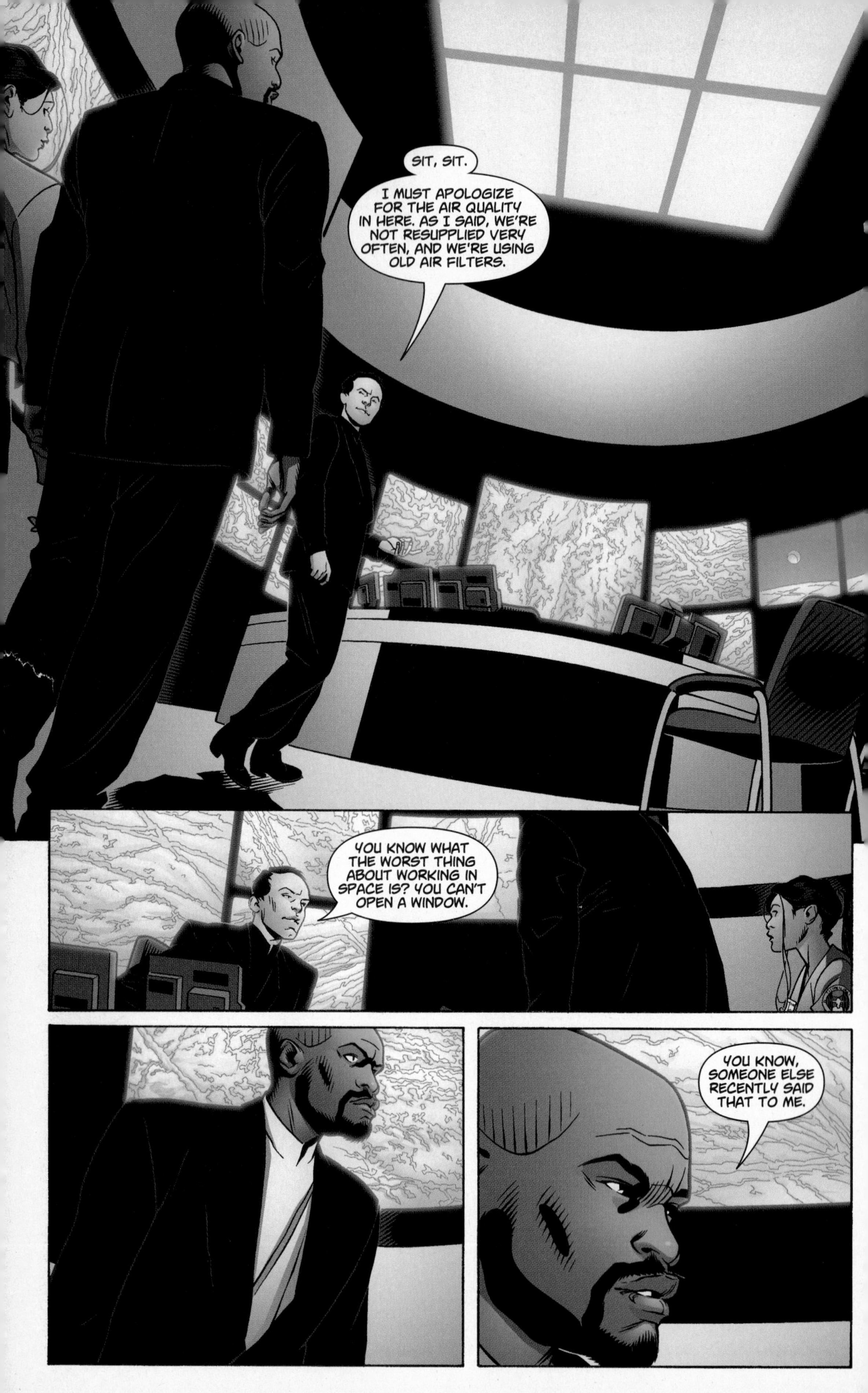
SIT, SIT.
I MUST APOLOGIZE FOR THE AIR QUALITY IN HERE. AS I SAID, WE'RE NOT RESUPPLIED VERY OFTEN, AND WE'RE USING OLD AIR FILTERS.
YOU KNOW WHAT THE WORST THING ABOUT WORKING IN SPACE IS? YOU CAN'T OPEN A WINDOW.
YOU KNOW, SOMEONE ELSE RECENTLY SAID THAT TO ME.

JUST BEFORE I WAS ATTACKED, ON DEIMOS.

MAKES ME WONDER, YOU KNOW?

MAKES ME CONSIDER EXACTLY WHO WOULD NOT WANT ME OUT HERE.

MAYBE PEOPLE WHO SHARE A PERSONALITY THAT COMES PRELOADED WITH LINES AND PHRASES.

YOU KNOW, DON'T YOU? AND WE WOULD HAVE LET YOU EXTRACT THEM FROM THE OCEAN.

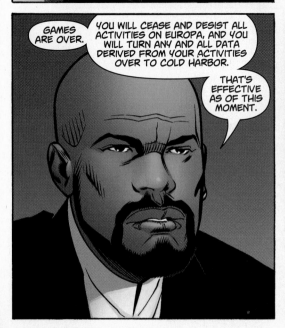

GAMES ARE OVER.

YOU WILL CEASE AND DESIST ALL ACTIVITIES ON EUROPA, AND YOU WILL TURN ANY AND ALL DATA DERIVED FROM YOUR ACTIVITIES OVER TO COLD HARBOR.

THAT'S EFFECTIVE AS OF THIS MOMENT.

YOU'RE WORKING FROM A FEW MISCONCEPTIONS HERE, INSPECTOR.

THE FIRST, OF COURSE, IS THAT I GIVE A $#!+ ABOUT ANYTHING YOU SAY.

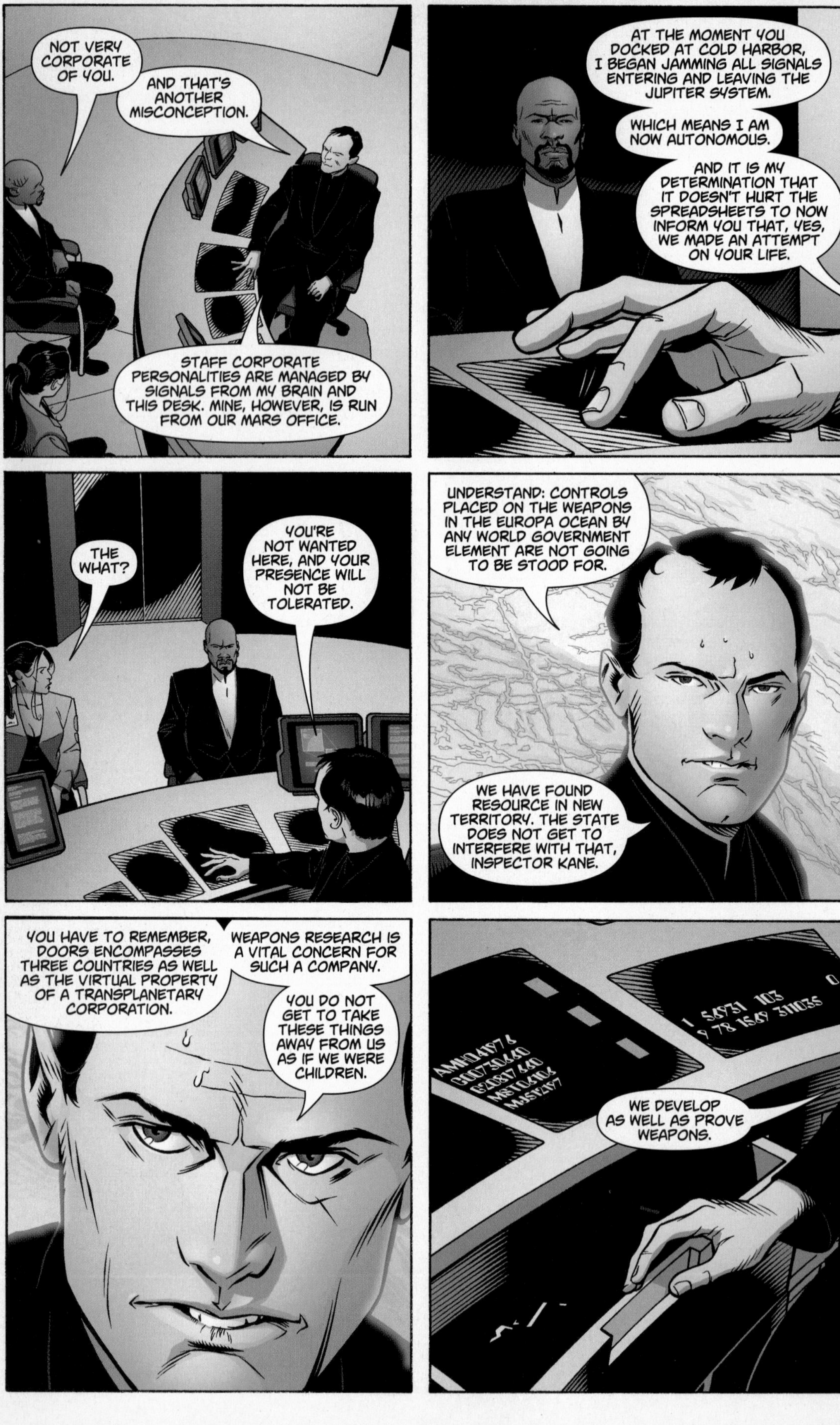
NOT VERY CORPORATE OF YOU.
AND THAT'S ANOTHER MISCONCEPTION.
STAFF CORPORATE PERSONALITIES ARE MANAGED BY SIGNALS FROM MY BRAIN AND THIS DESK. MINE, HOWEVER, IS RUN FROM OUR MARS OFFICE.
AT THE MOMENT YOU DOCKED AT COLD HARBOR, I BEGAN JAMMING ALL SIGNALS ENTERING AND LEAVING THE JUPITER SYSTEM.
WHICH MEANS I AM NOW AUTONOMOUS.
AND IT IS MY DETERMINATION THAT IT DOESN'T HURT THE SPREADSHEETS TO NOW INFORM YOU THAT, YES, WE MADE AN ATTEMPT ON YOUR LIFE.
THE WHAT?
YOU'RE NOT WANTED HERE, AND YOUR PRESENCE WILL NOT BE TOLERATED.
UNDERSTAND: CONTROLS PLACED ON THE WEAPONS IN THE EUROPA OCEAN BY ANY WORLD GOVERNMENT ELEMENT ARE NOT GOING TO BE STOOD FOR.
WE HAVE FOUND RESOURCE IN NEW TERRITORY. THE STATE DOES NOT GET TO INTERFERE WITH THAT, INSPECTOR KANE.
YOU HAVE TO REMEMBER, DOORS ENCOMPASSES THREE COUNTRIES AS WELL AS THE VIRTUAL PROPERTY OF A TRANSPLANETARY CORPORATION.
WEAPONS RESEARCH IS A VITAL CONCERN FOR SUCH A COMPANY.
YOU DO NOT GET TO TAKE THESE THINGS AWAY FROM US AS IF WE WERE CHILDREN.
WE DEVELOP AS WELL AS PROVE WEAPONS.

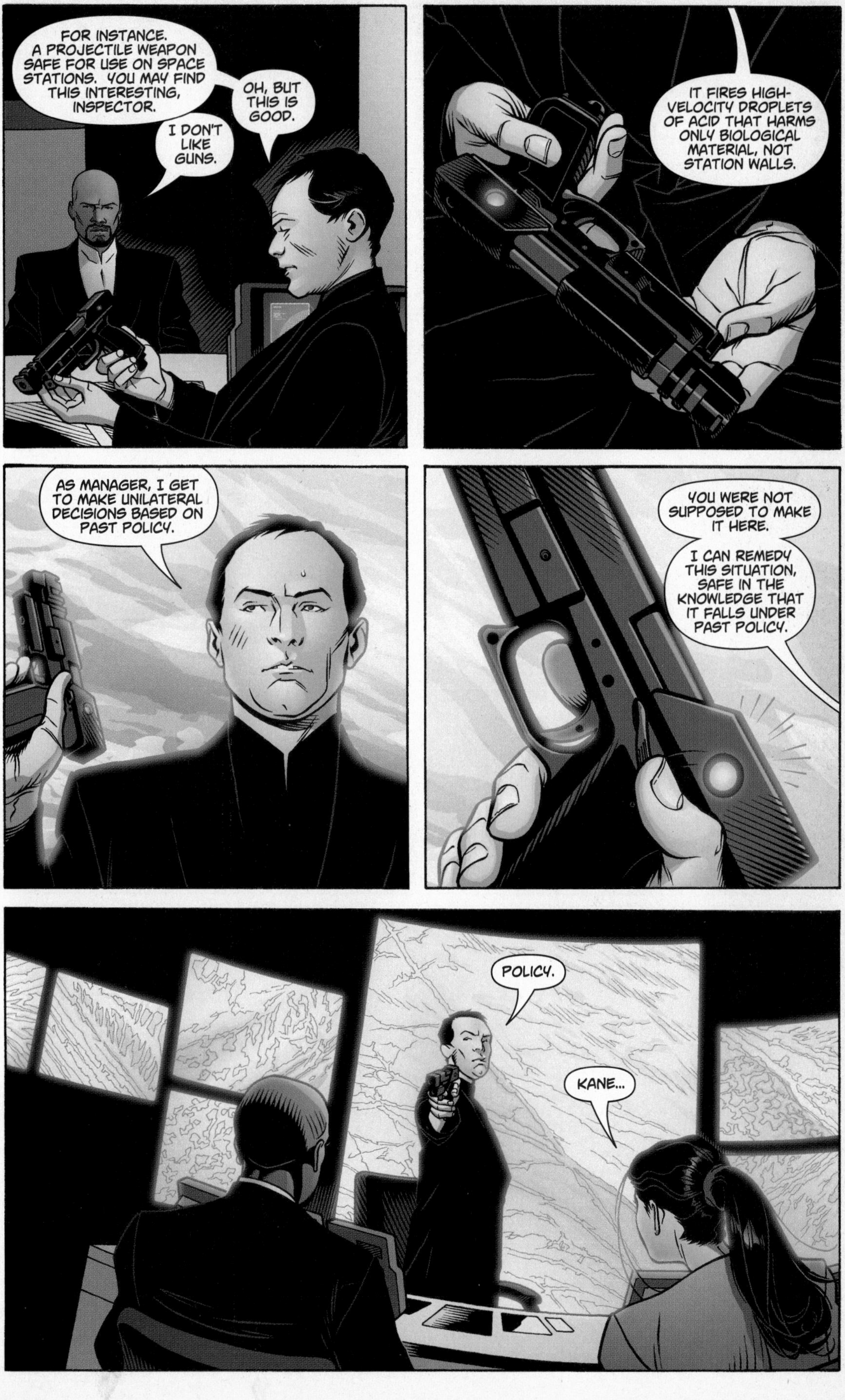
FOR INSTANCE. A PROJECTILE WEAPON SAFE FOR USE ON SPACE STATIONS. YOU MAY FIND THIS INTERESTING, INSPECTOR.
OH, BUT THIS IS GOOD.
I DON'T LIKE GUNS.
IT FIRES HIGH-VELOCITY DROPLETS OF ACID THAT HARMS ONLY BIOLOGICAL MATERIAL, NOT STATION WALLS.
AS MANAGER, I GET TO MAKE UNILATERAL DECISIONS BASED ON PAST POLICY.
YOU WERE NOT SUPPOSED TO MAKE IT HERE.
I CAN REMEDY THIS SITUATION, SAFE IN THE KNOWLEDGE THAT IT FALLS UNDER PAST POLICY.
POLICY.
KANE...

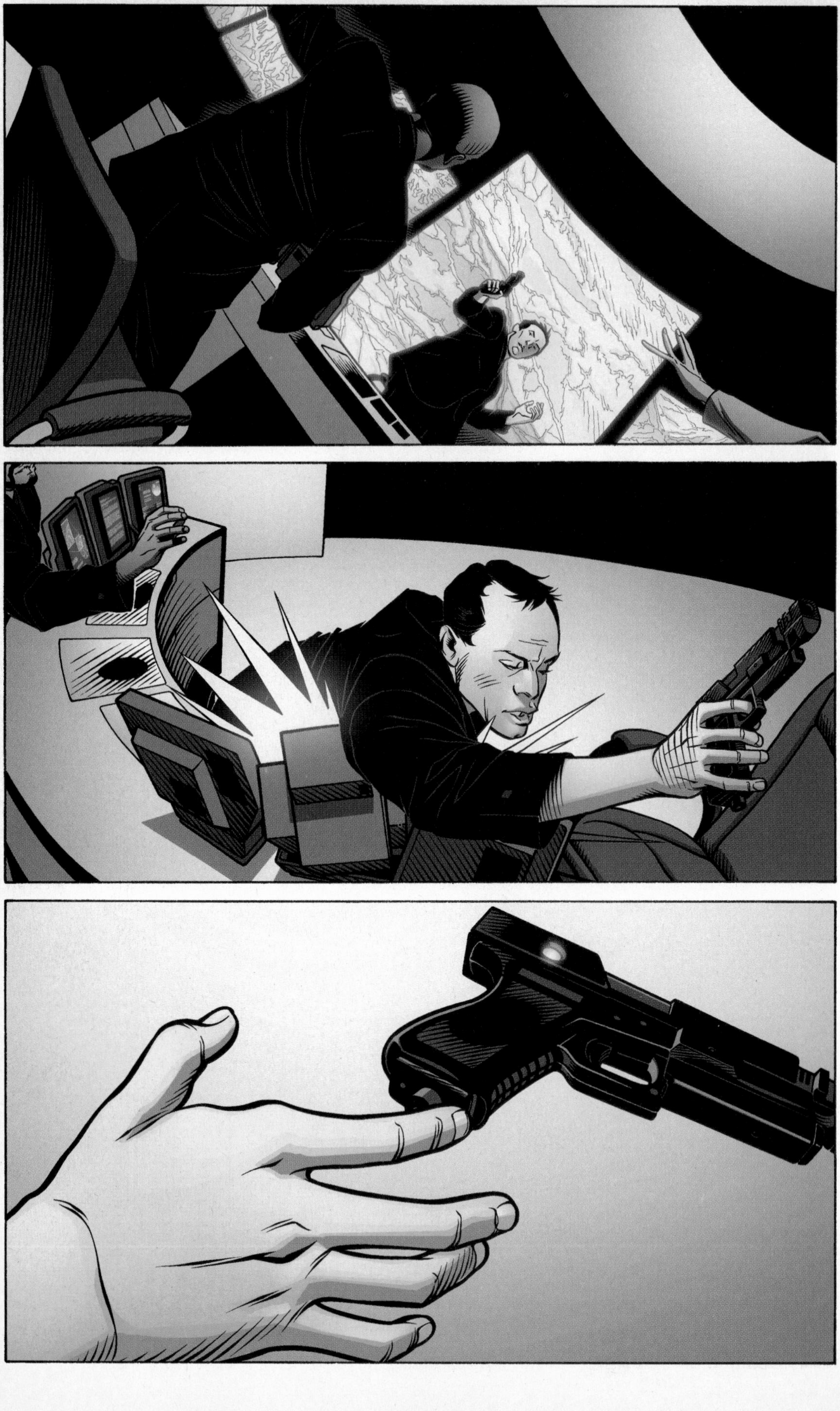

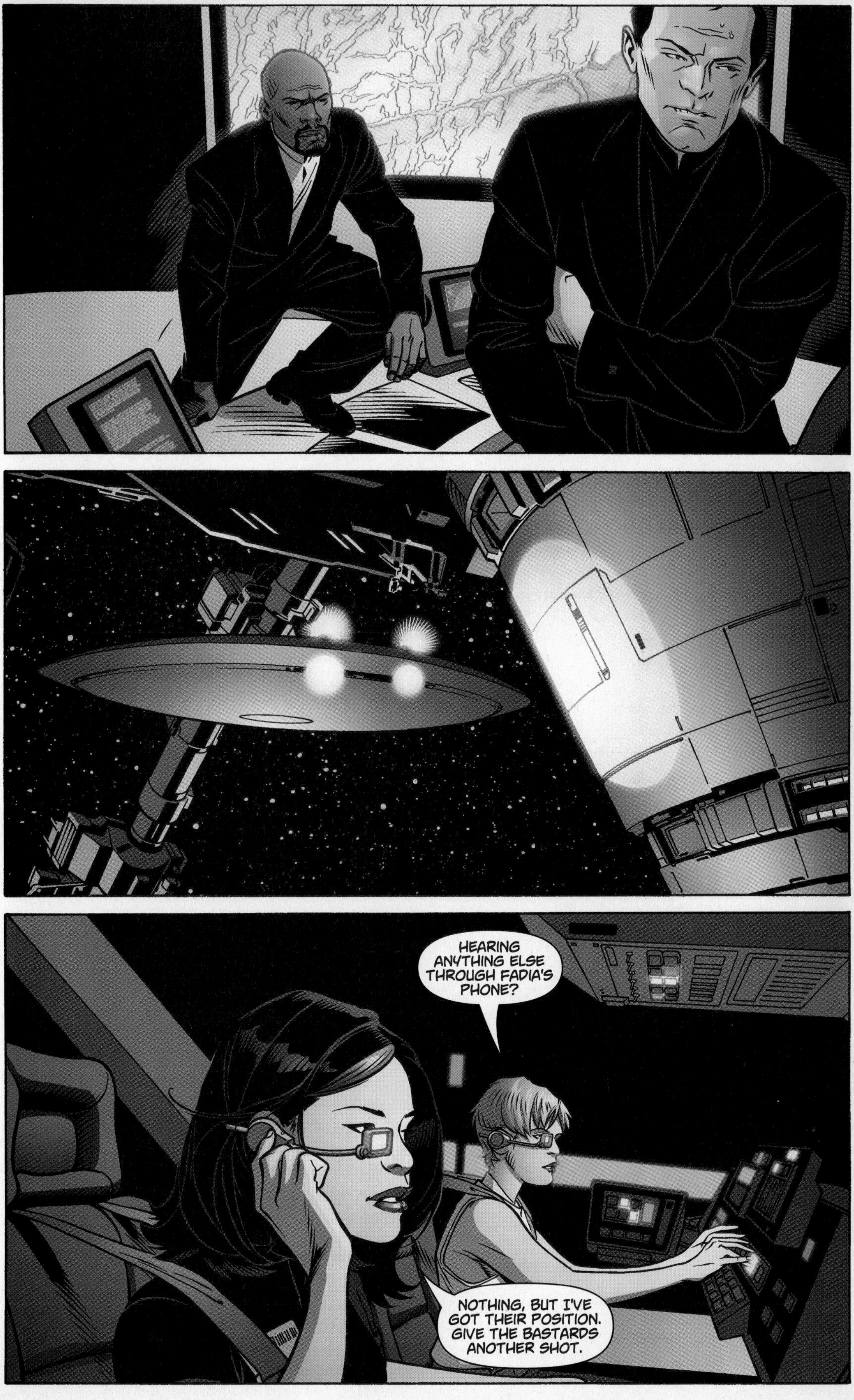
HEARING ANYTHING ELSE THROUGH FADIA'S PHONE?
NOTHING, BUT I'VE GOT THEIR POSITION. GIVE THE BASTARDS ANOTHER SHOT.

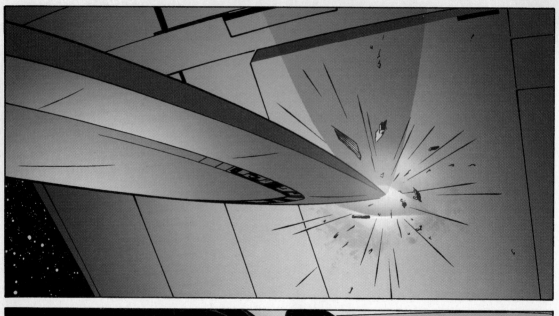

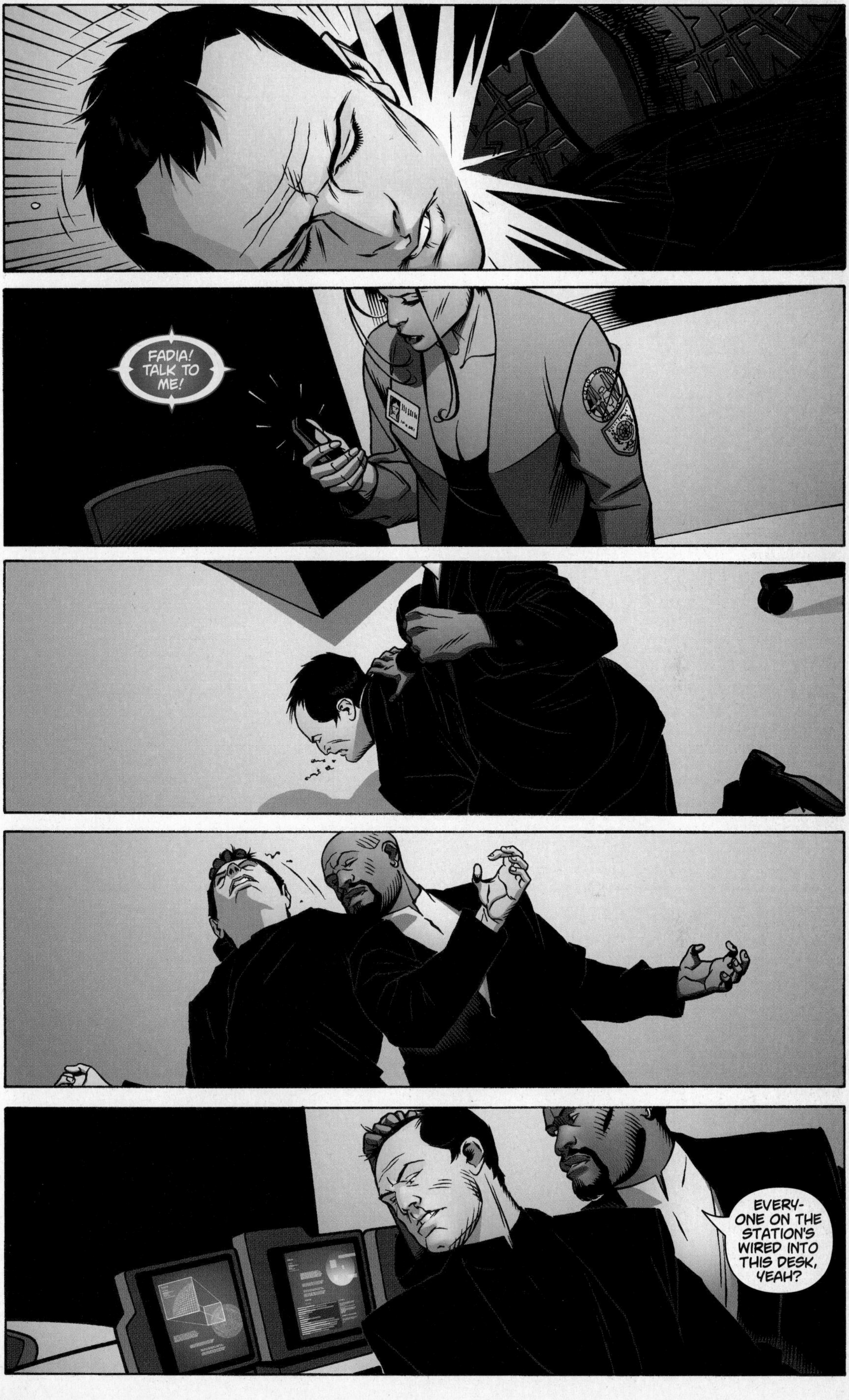
FADIA! TALK TO ME!
EVERY-ONE ON THE STATION'S WIRED INTO THIS DESK, YEAH?

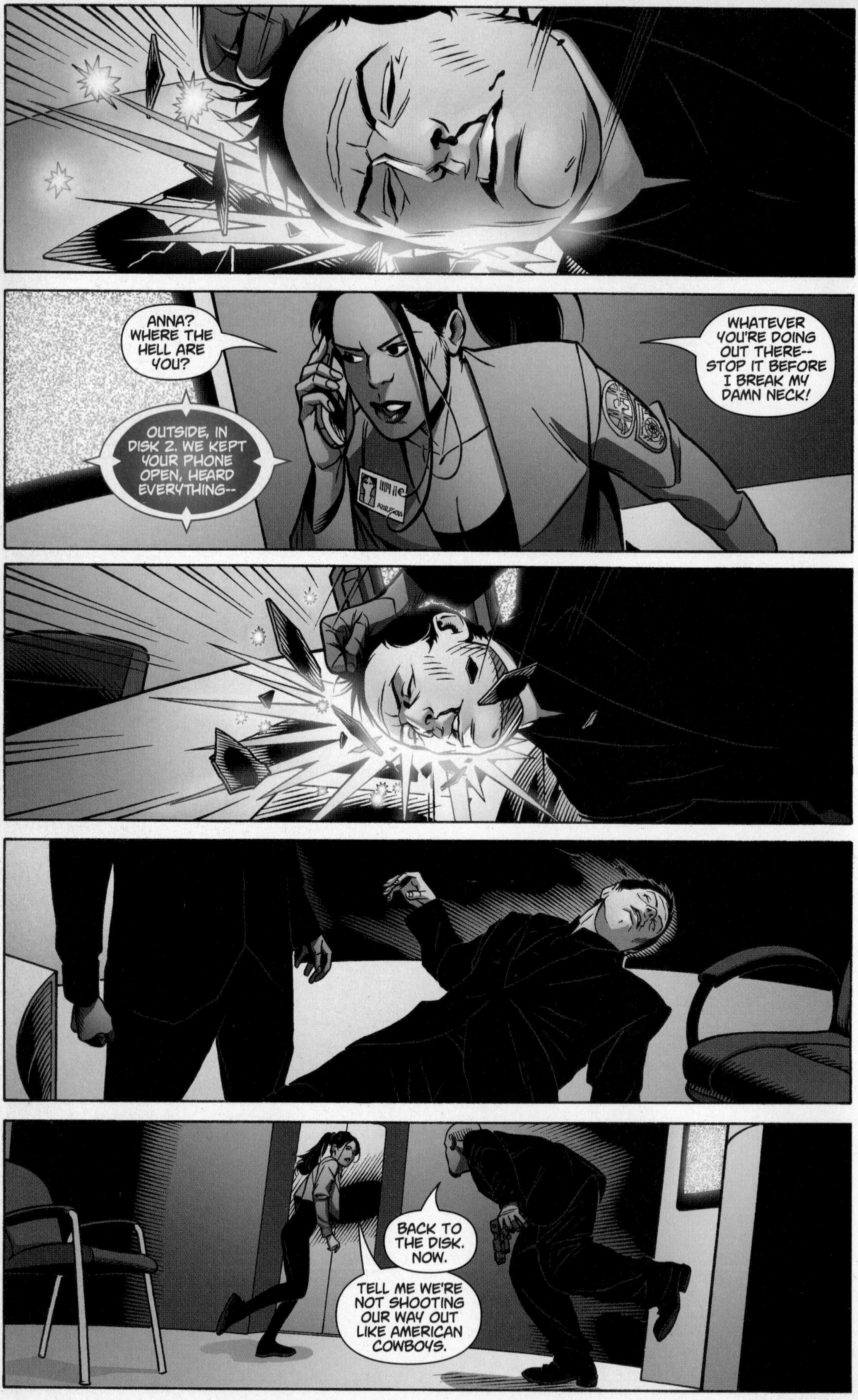
ANNA? WHERE THE HELL ARE YOU?
OUTSIDE, IN DISK 2. WE KEPT YOUR PHONE OPEN, HEARD EVERYTHING--
WHATEVER YOU'RE DOING OUT THERE-- STOP IT BEFORE I BREAK MY DAMN NECK!
BACK TO THE DISK. NOW.
TELL ME WE'RE NOT SHOOTING OUR WAY OUT LIKE AMERICAN COWBOYS.

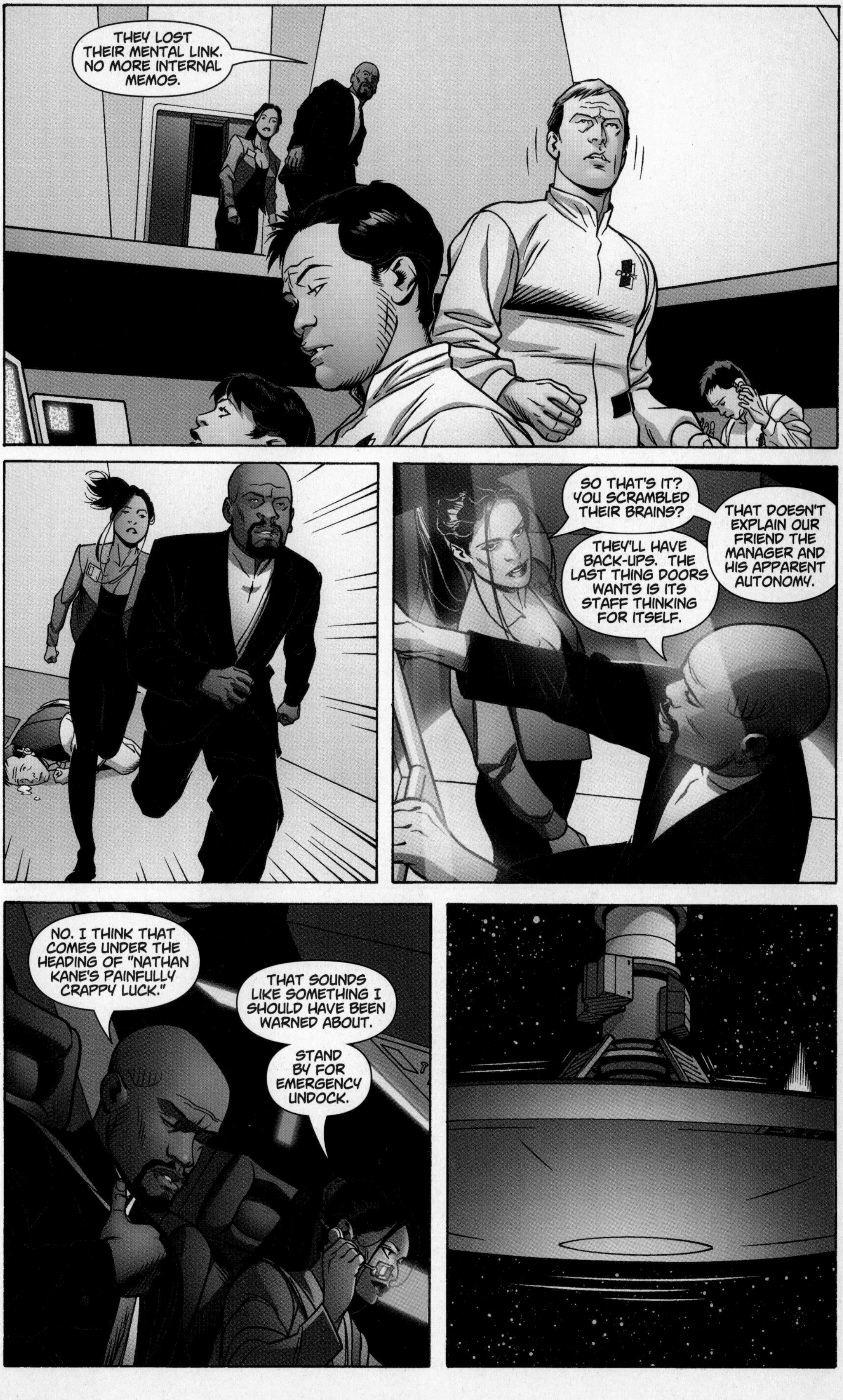
THEY LOST THEIR MENTAL LINK. NO MORE INTERNAL MEMOS.
SO THAT'S IT? YOU SCRAMBLED THEIR BRAINS?
THEY'LL HAVE BACK-UPS. THE LAST THING DOORS WANTS IS ITS STAFF THINKING FOR ITSELF.
THAT DOESN'T EXPLAIN OUR FRIEND THE MANAGER AND HIS APPARENT AUTONOMY.
NO. I THINK THAT COMES UNDER THE HEADING OF "NATHAN KANE'S PAINFULLY CRAPPY LUCK."
THAT SOUNDS LIKE SOMETHING I SHOULD HAVE BEEN WARNED ABOUT.
STAND BY FOR EMERGENCY UNDOCK.

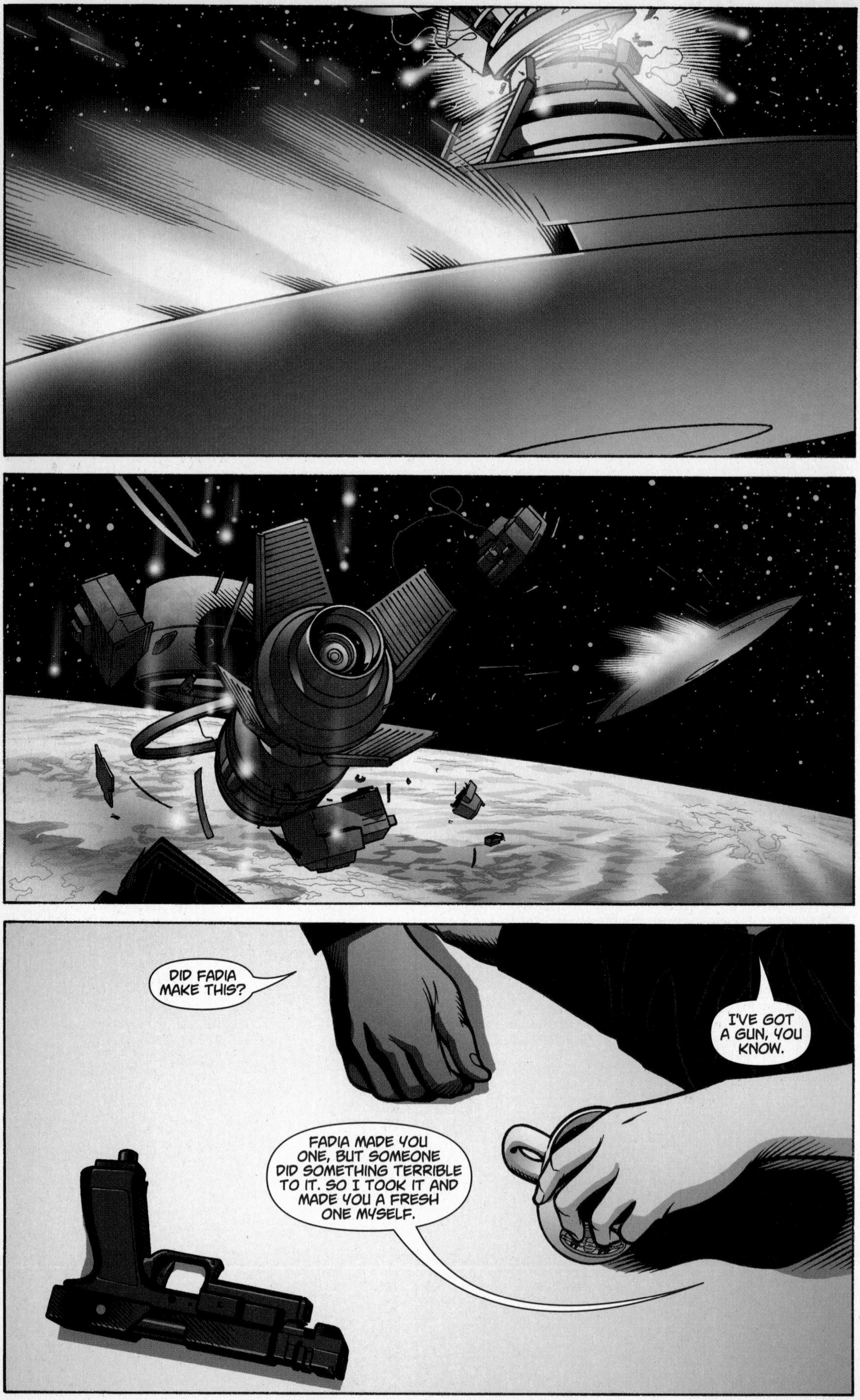
DID FADIA MAKE THIS?
I'VE GOT A GUN, YOU KNOW.
FADIA MADE YOU ONE, BUT SOMEONE DID SOMETHING TERRIBLE TO IT. SO I TOOK IT AND MADE YOU A FRESH ONE MYSELF.

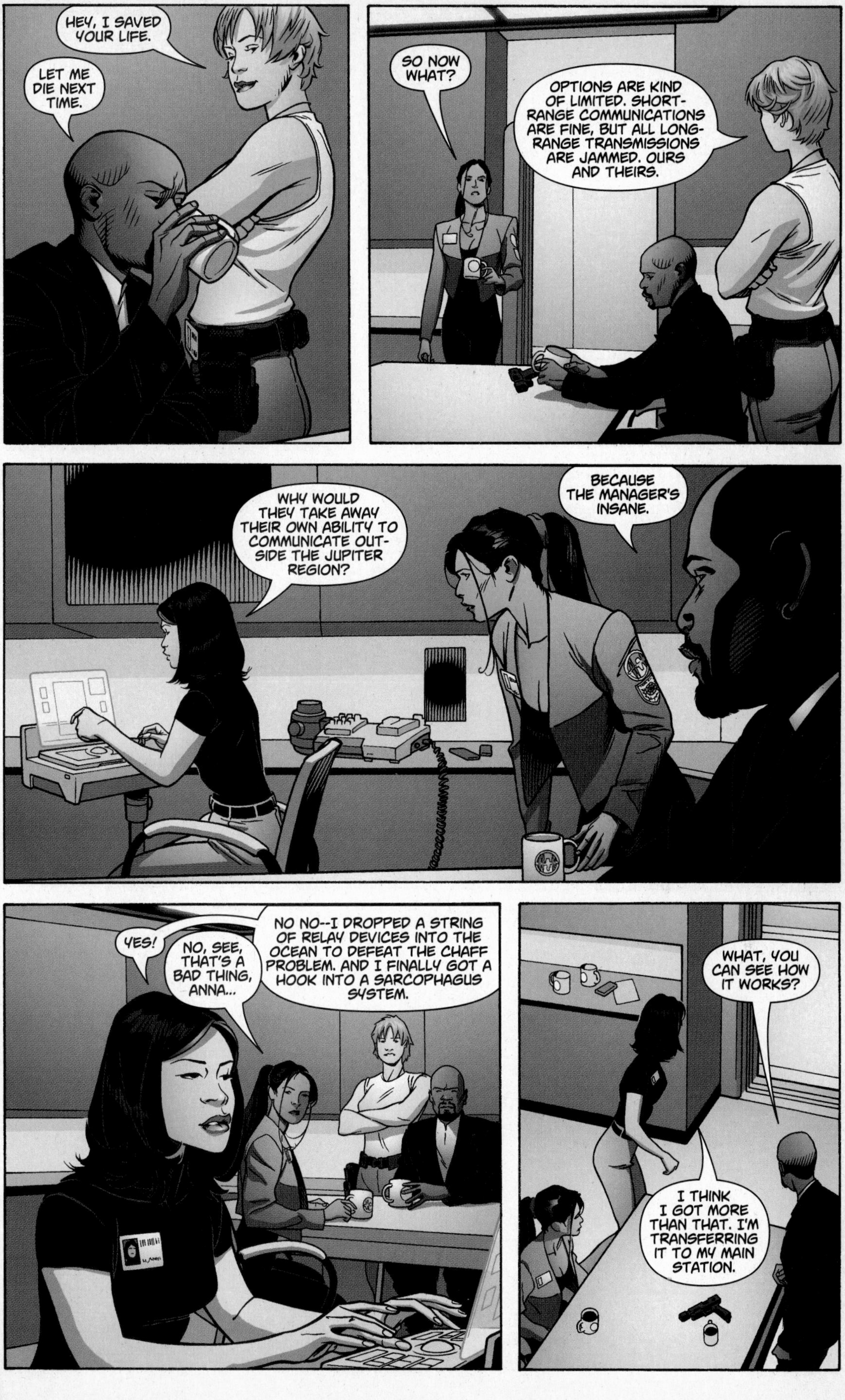
HEY, I SAVED YOUR LIFE.
LET ME DIE NEXT TIME.
SO NOW WHAT?
OPTIONS ARE KIND OF LIMITED. SHORT-RANGE COMMUNICATIONS ARE FINE, BUT ALL LONG-RANGE TRANSMISSIONS ARE JAMMED. OURS AND THEIRS.
WHY WOULD THEY TAKE AWAY THEIR OWN ABILITY TO COMMUNICATE OUT-SIDE THE JUPITER REGION?
BECAUSE THE MANAGER'S INSANE.
YES!
NO, SEE, THAT'S A BAD THING, ANNA...
NO NO--I DROPPED A STRING OF RELAY DEVICES INTO THE OCEAN TO DEFEAT THE CHAFF PROBLEM. AND I FINALLY GOT A HOOK INTO A SARCOPHAGUS SYSTEM.
WHAT, YOU CAN SEE HOW IT WORKS?
I THINK I GOT MORE THAN THAT. I'M TRANSFERRING IT TO MY MAIN STATION.

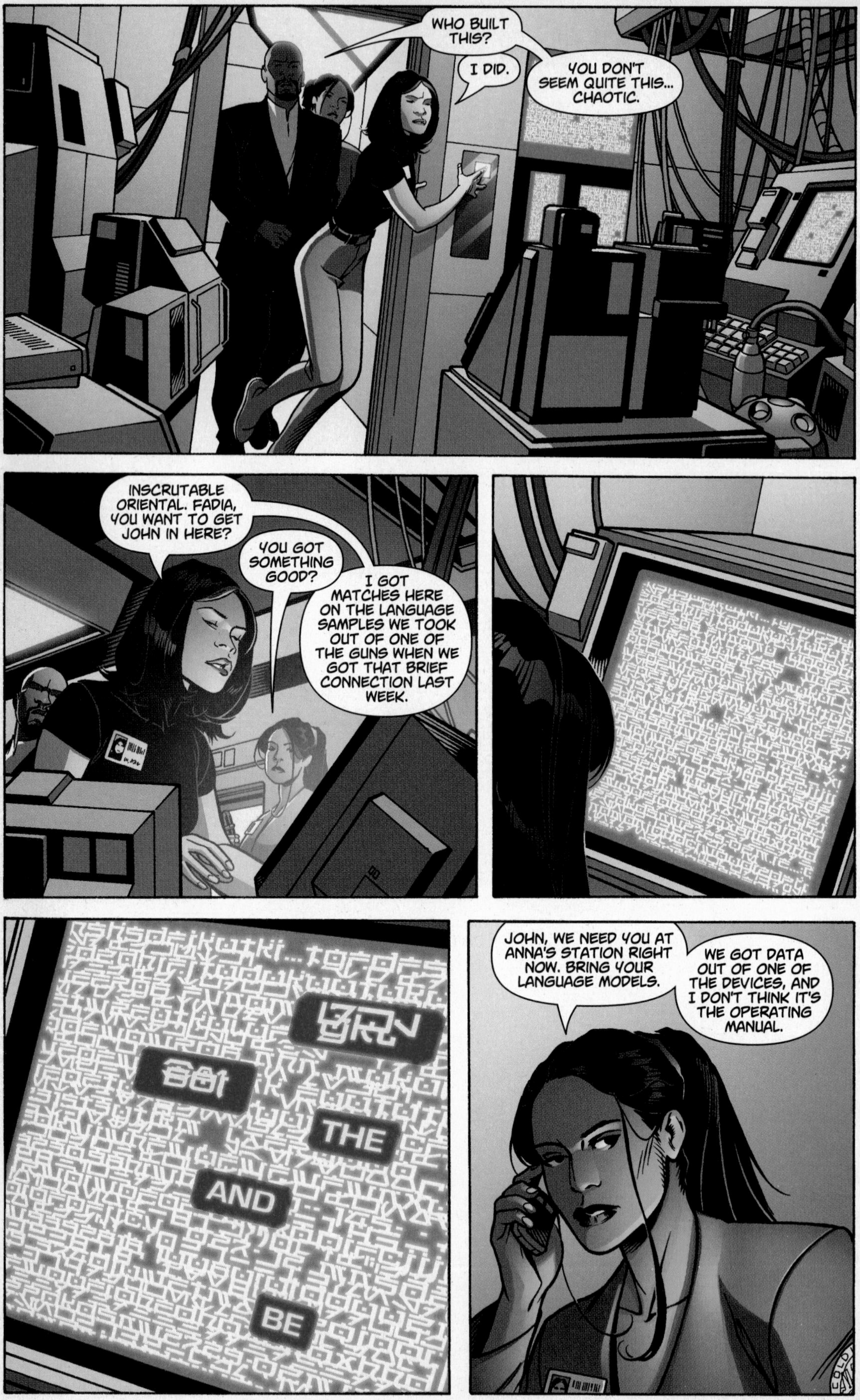
WHO BUILT THIS?
I DID.
YOU DON'T SEEM QUITE THIS... CHAOTIC.
INSCRUTABLE ORIENTAL. FADIA, YOU WANT TO GET JOHN IN HERE?
YOU GOT SOMETHING GOOD?
I GOT MATCHES HERE ON THE LANGUAGE SAMPLES WE TOOK OUT OF ONE OF THE GUNS WHEN WE GOT THAT BRIEF CONNECTION LAST WEEK.
THE
AND
BE
JOHN, WE NEED YOU AT ANNA'S STATION RIGHT NOW. BRING YOUR LANGUAGE MODELS.
WE GOT DATA OUT OF ONE OF THE DEVICES, AND I DON'T THINK IT'S THE OPERATING MANUAL.

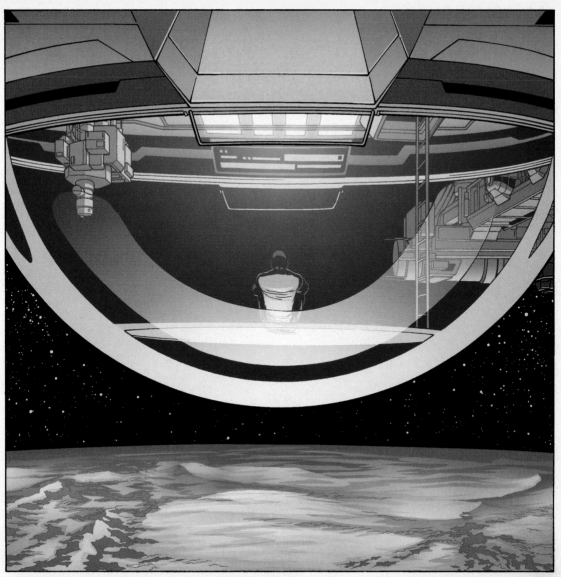

IT'S LATE.

I CAN NEVER TELL. MY BODYCLOCK NEVER ADJUSTS TO SPACE STATION TIME.

I CAN GET YOU SOME MEDS FOR THAT.

NAH. BEING UNSLEPT AND CRANKY KIND OF SUITS ME TO THE JOB AT HAND.

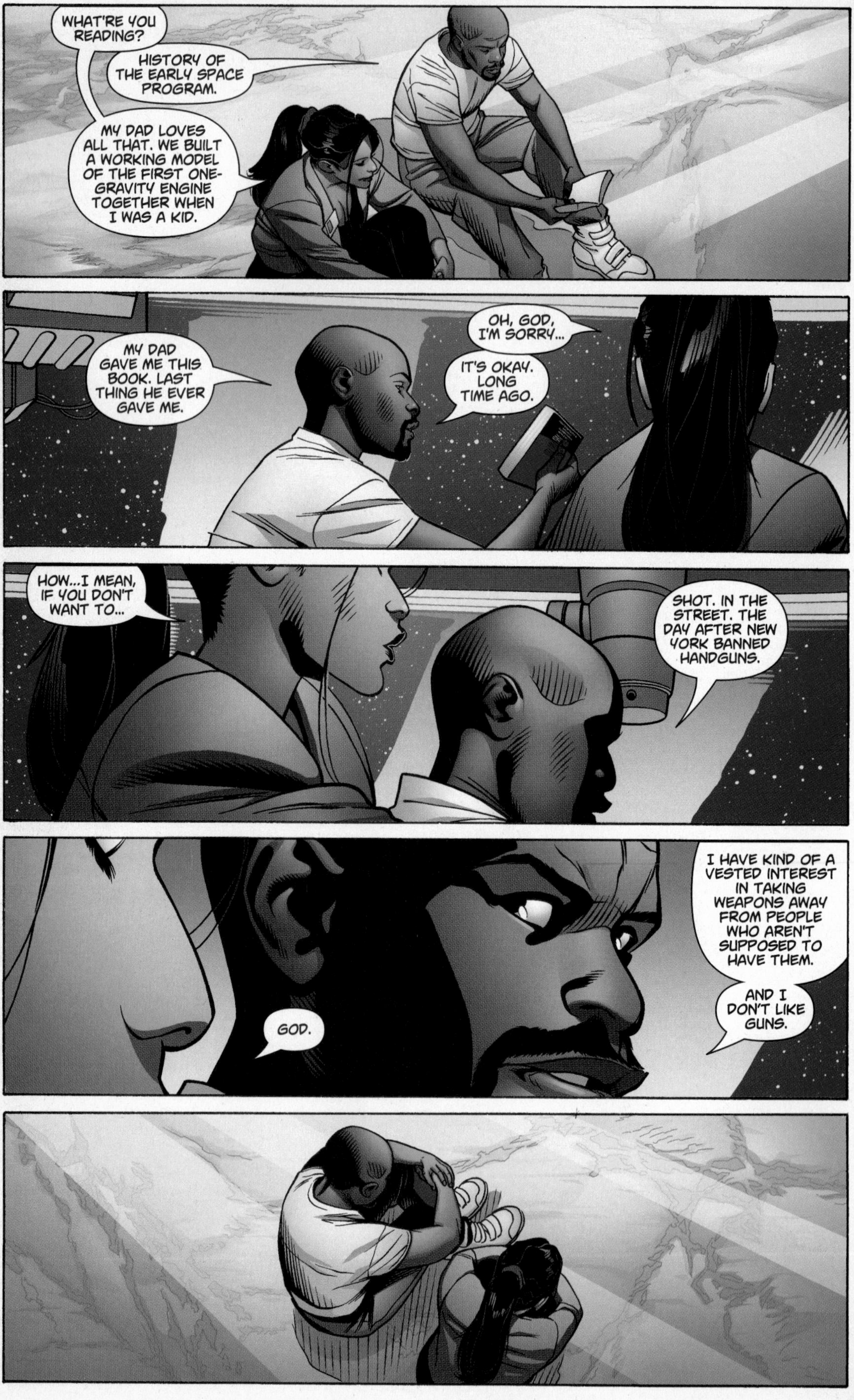
WHAT'RE YOU READING?
HISTORY OF THE EARLY SPACE PROGRAM.
MY DAD LOVES ALL THAT. WE BUILT A WORKING MODEL OF THE FIRST ONE-GRAVITY ENGINE TOGETHER WHEN I WAS A KID.
MY DAD GAVE ME THIS BOOK. LAST THING HE EVER GAVE ME.
OH, GOD, I'M SORRY...
IT'S OKAY. LONG TIME AGO.
HOW...I MEAN, IF YOU DON'T WANT TO...
SHOT. IN THE STREET. THE DAY AFTER NEW YORK BANNED HANDGUNS.
I HAVE KIND OF A VESTED INTEREST IN TAKING WEAPONS AWAY FROM PEOPLE WHO AREN'T SUPPOSED TO HAVE THEM.
AND I DON'T LIKE GUNS.
GOD.

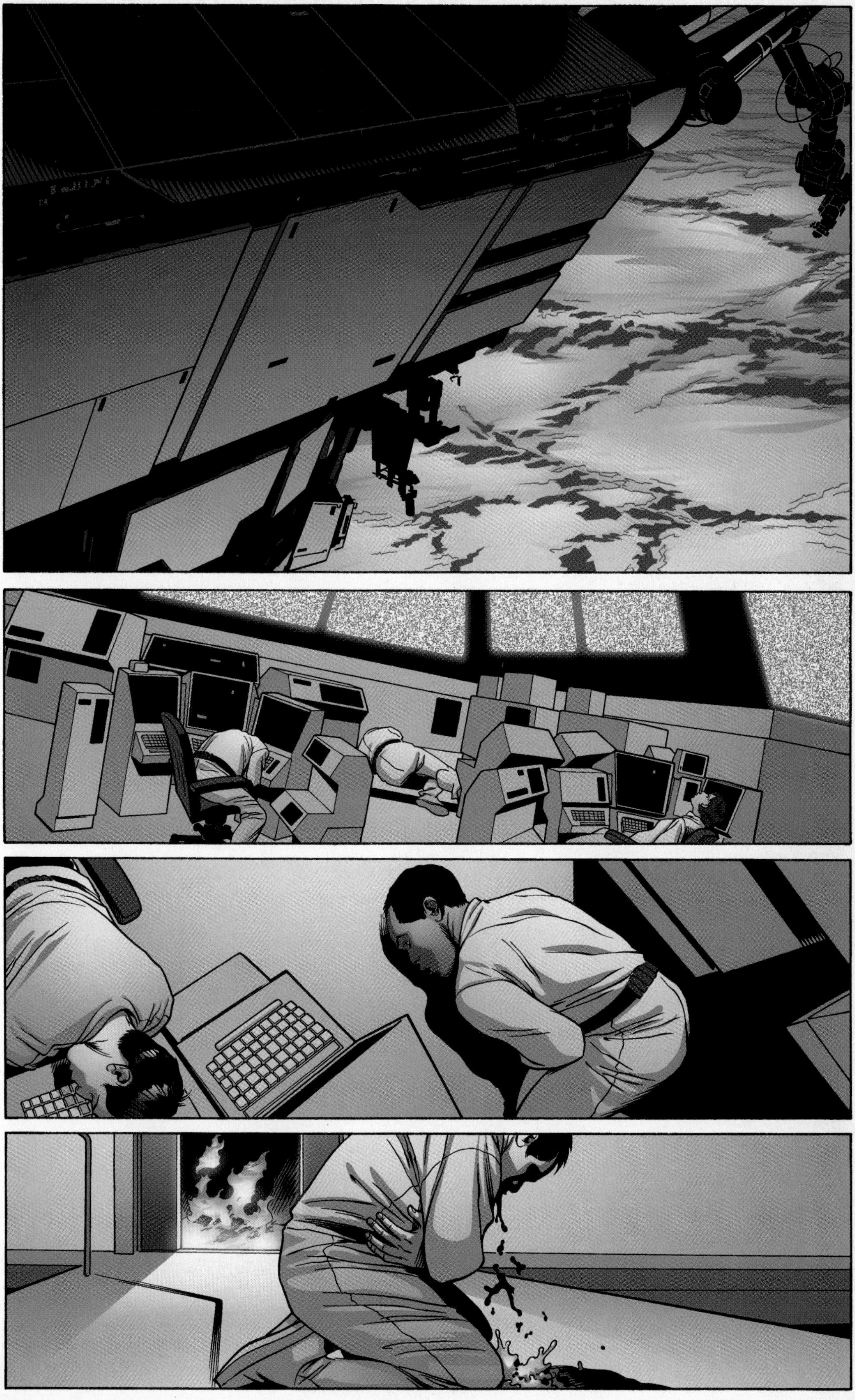

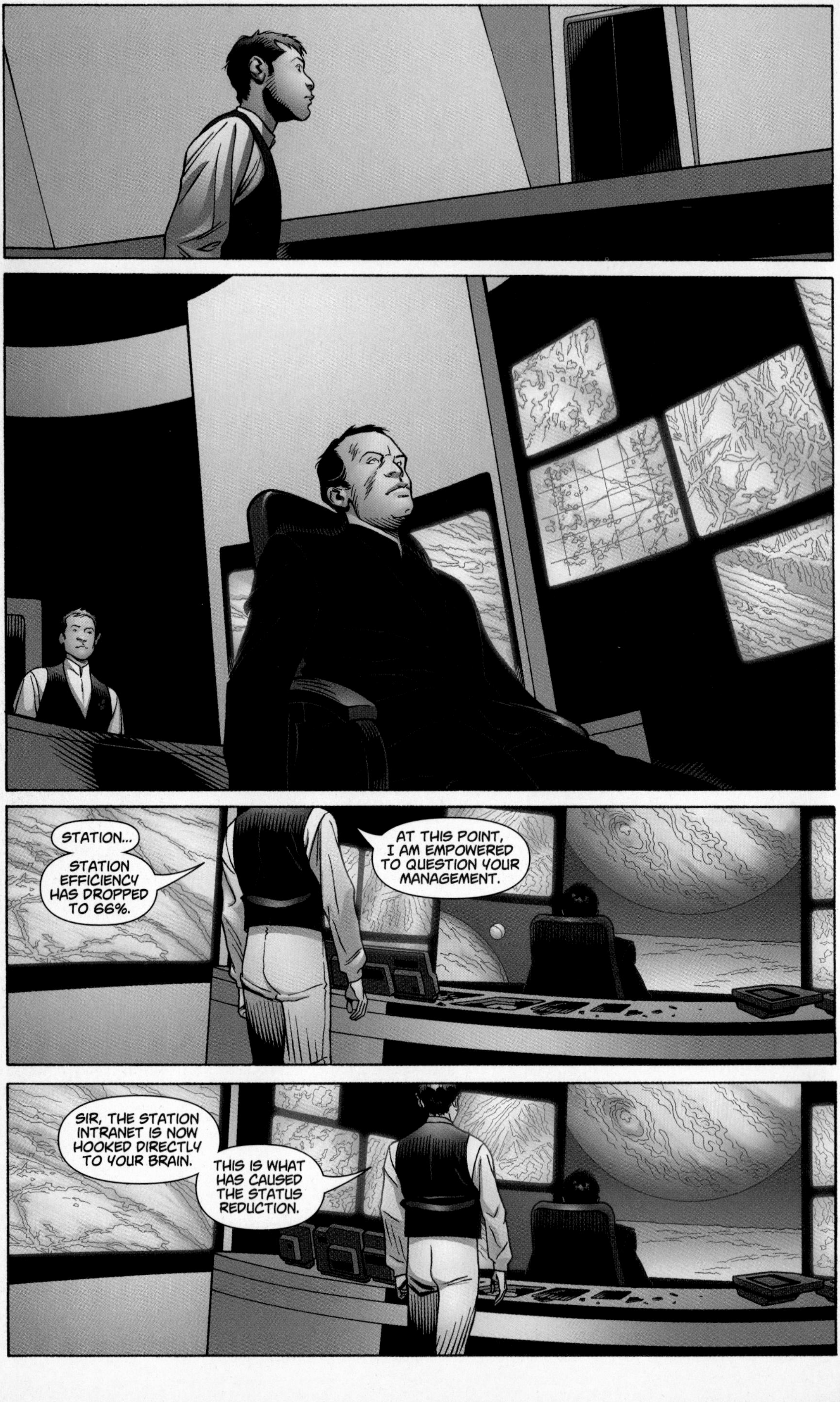
STATION...
STATION EFFICIENCY HAS DROPPED TO 66%.
AT THIS POINT, I AM EMPOWERED TO QUESTION YOUR MANAGEMENT.
SIR, THE STATION INTRANET IS NOW HOOKED DIRECTLY TO YOUR BRAIN.
THIS IS WHAT HAS CAUSED THE STATUS REDUCTION.

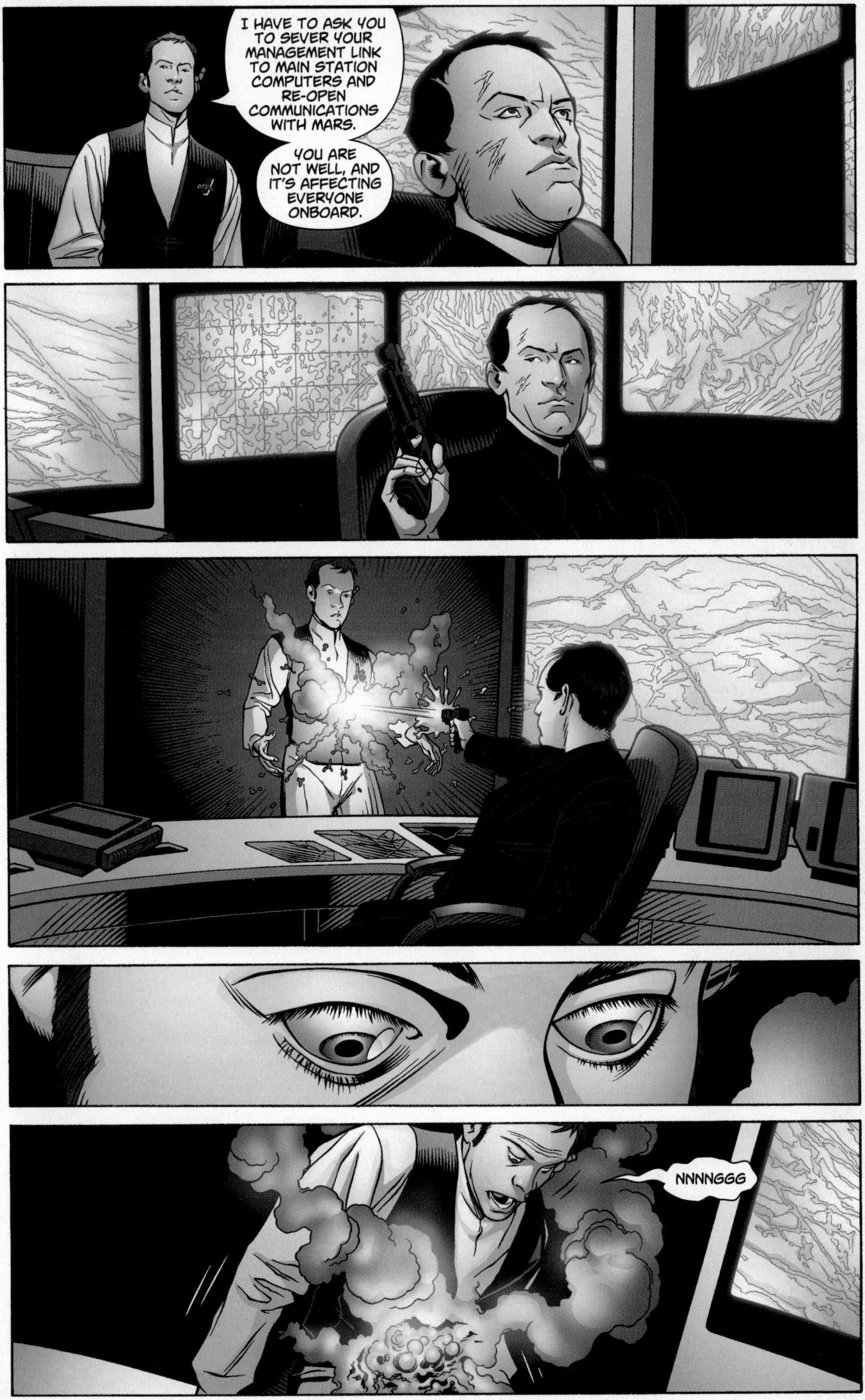
I HAVE TO ASK YOU TO SEVER YOUR MANAGEMENT LINK TO MAIN STATION COMPUTERS AND RE-OPEN COMMUNICATIONS WITH MARS.
YOU ARE NOT WELL, AND IT'S AFFECTING EVERYONE ONBOARD.
NNNNGGG

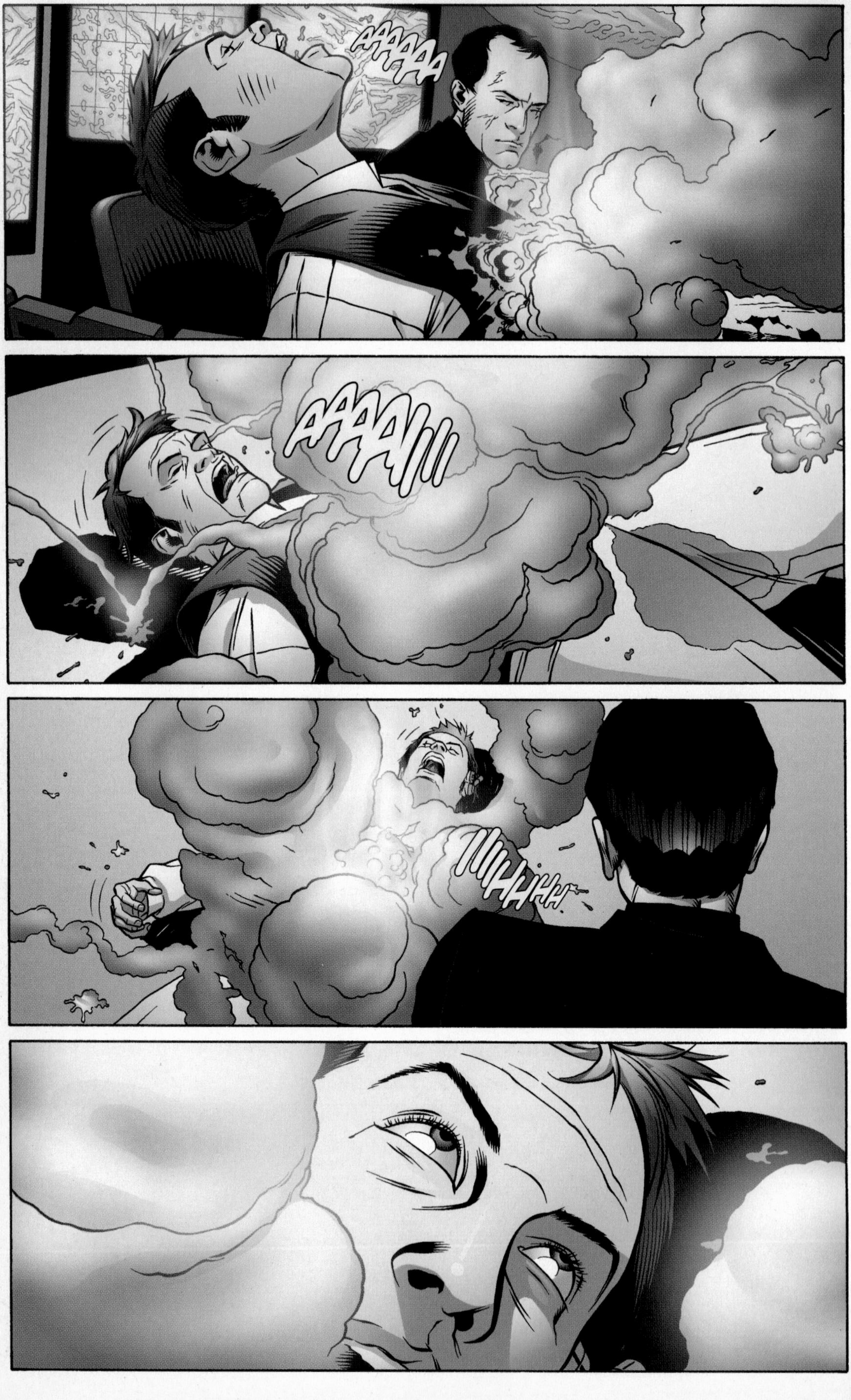
AAAAAA
AAAAIII
IIIHHHHH

YOU'RE THE NEW JUNIOR MANAGER. PREPARE FOR UPGRADE.

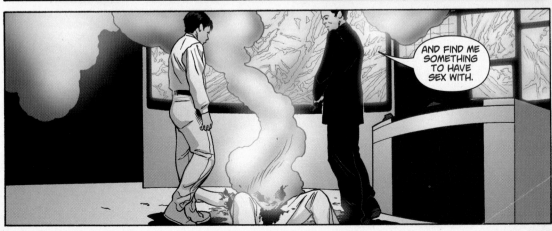

AND FIND ME SOMETHING TO HAVE SEX WITH.

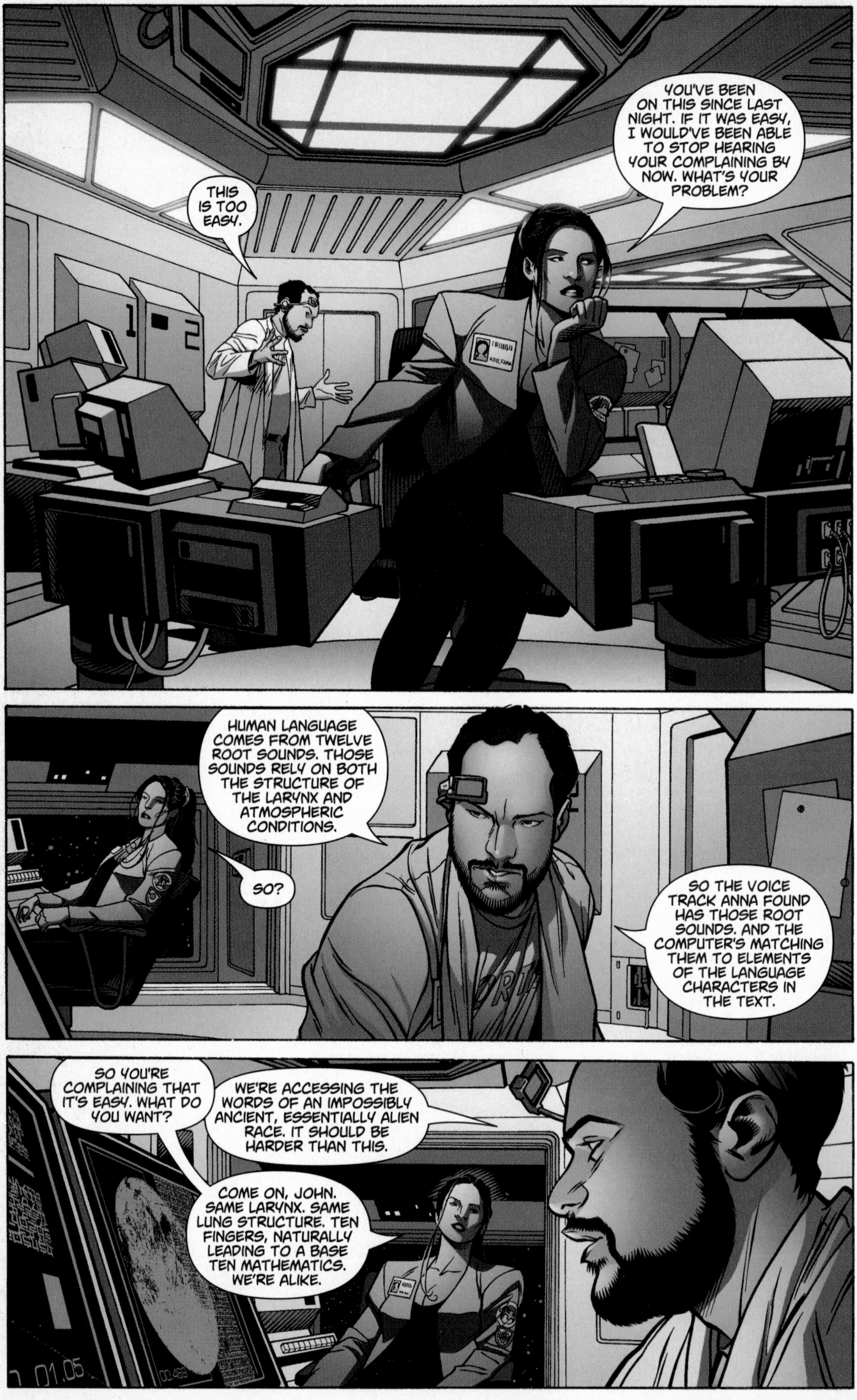
THIS IS TOO EASY.
YOU'VE BEEN ON THIS SINCE LAST NIGHT. IF IT WAS EASY, I WOULD'VE BEEN ABLE TO STOP HEARING YOUR COMPLAINING BY NOW. WHAT'S YOUR PROBLEM?
HUMAN LANGUAGE COMES FROM TWELVE ROOT SOUNDS. THOSE SOUNDS RELY ON BOTH THE STRUCTURE OF THE LARYNX AND ATMOSPHERIC CONDITIONS.
SO?
SO THE VOICE TRACK ANNA FOUND HAS THOSE ROOT SOUNDS. AND THE COMPUTER'S MATCHING THEM TO ELEMENTS OF THE LANGUAGE CHARACTERS IN THE TEXT.
SO YOU'RE COMPLAINING THAT IT'S EASY. WHAT DO YOU WANT?
WE'RE ACCESSING THE WORDS OF AN IMPOSSIBLY ANCIENT, ESSENTIALLY ALIEN RACE. IT SHOULD BE HARDER THAN THIS.
COME ON, JOHN. SAME LARYNX. SAME LUNG STRUCTURE. TEN FINGERS, NATURALLY LEADING TO A BASE TEN MATHEMATICS. WE'RE ALIKE.

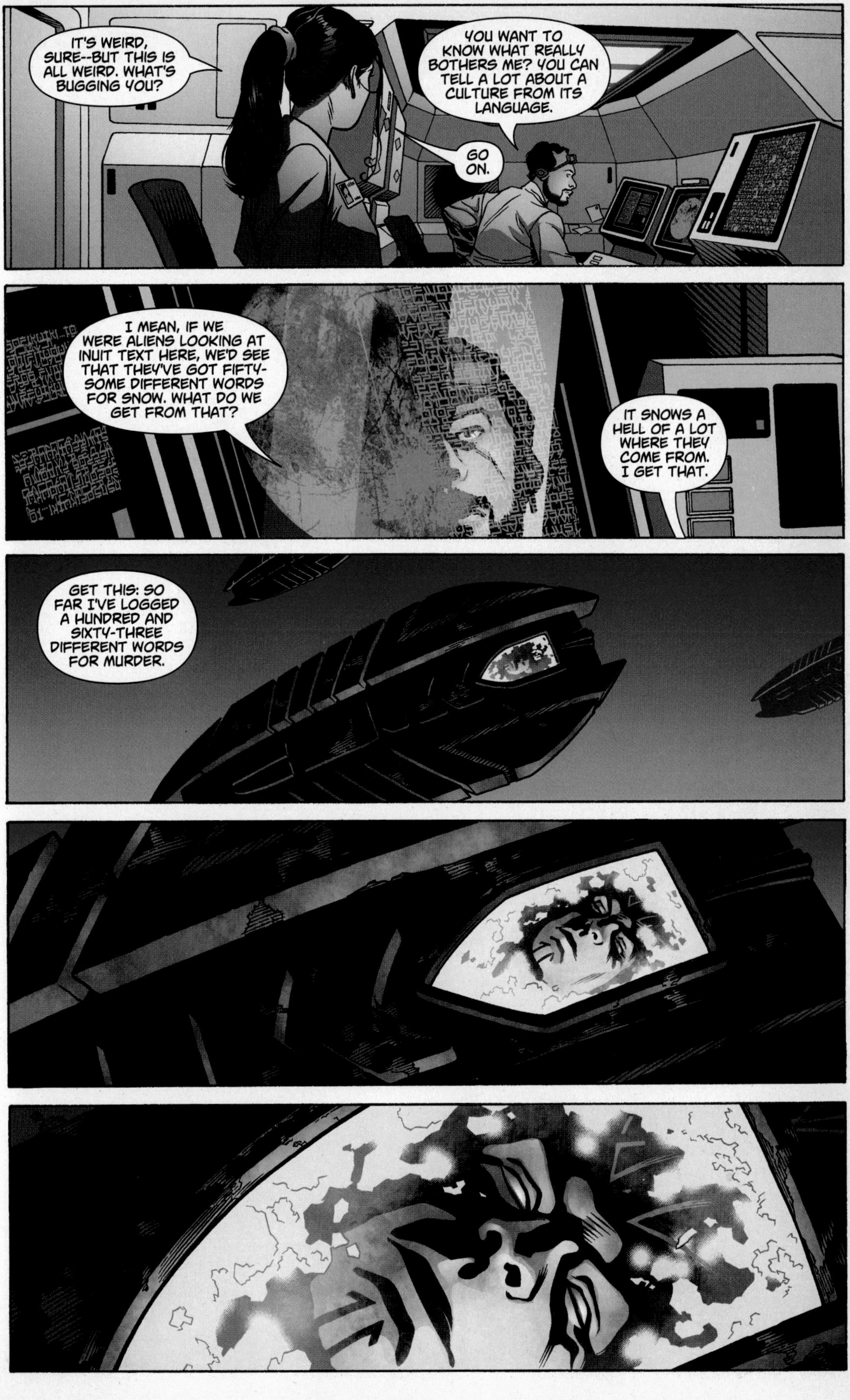
IT'S WEIRD, SURE--BUT THIS IS ALL WEIRD. WHAT'S BUGGING YOU?
YOU WANT TO KNOW WHAT REALLY BOTHERS ME? YOU CAN TELL A LOT ABOUT A CULTURE FROM ITS LANGUAGE.
GO ON.
I MEAN, IF WE WERE ALIENS LOOKING AT INUIT TEXT HERE, WE'D SEE THAT THEY'VE GOT FIFTY-SOME DIFFERENT WORDS FOR SNOW. WHAT DO WE GET FROM THAT?
IT SNOWS A HELL OF A LOT WHERE THEY COME FROM. I GET THAT.
GET THIS: SO FAR I'VE LOGGED A HUNDRED AND SIXTY-THREE DIFFERENT WORDS FOR MURDER.

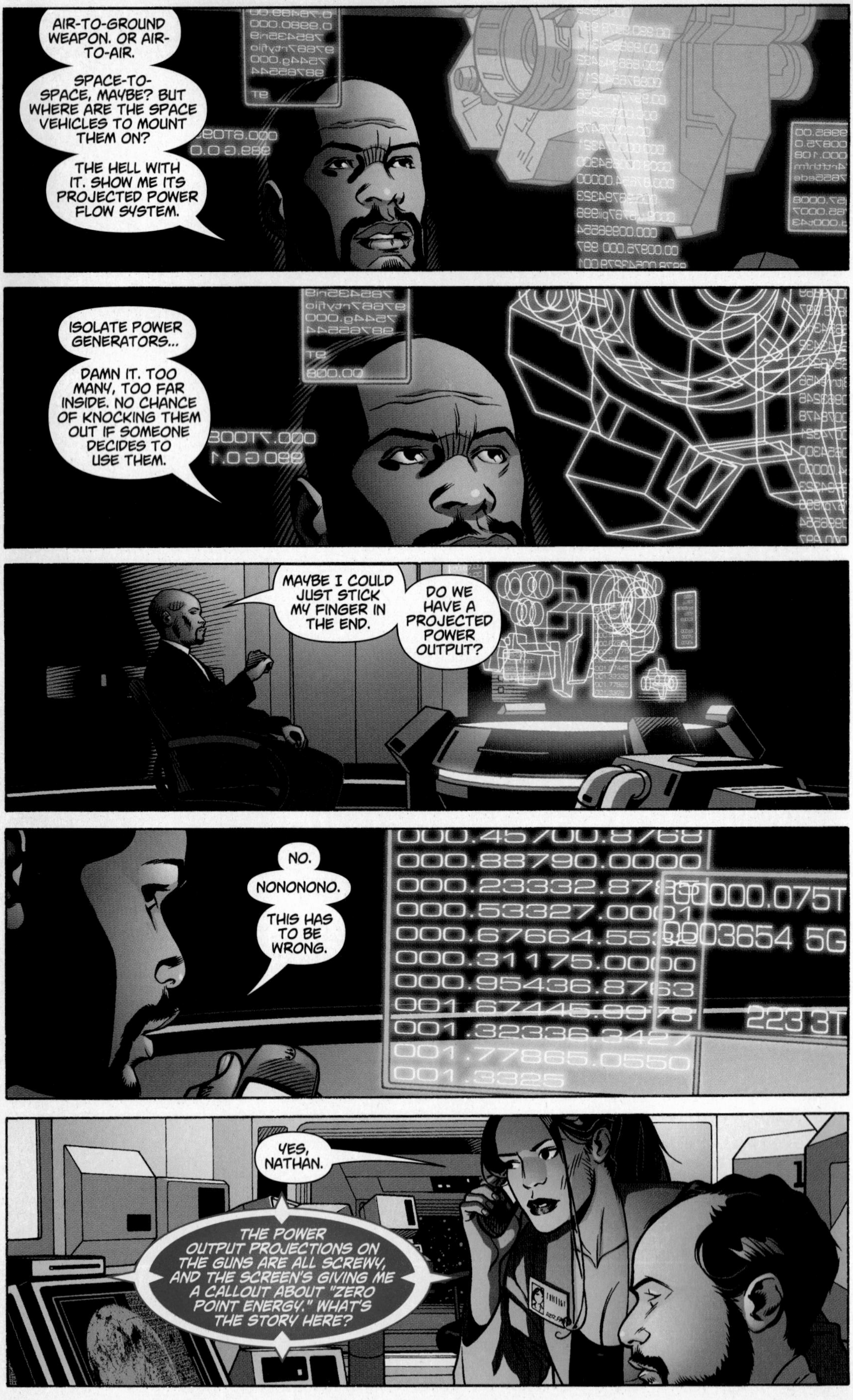
AIR-TO-GROUND WEAPON. OR AIR-TO-AIR.
SPACE-TO-SPACE, MAYBE? BUT WHERE ARE THE SPACE VEHICLES TO MOUNT THEM ON?
THE HELL WITH IT. SHOW ME ITS PROJECTED POWER FLOW SYSTEM.
ISOLATE POWER GENERATORS...
DAMN IT. TOO MANY, TOO FAR INSIDE. NO CHANCE OF KNOCKING THEM OUT IF SOMEONE DECIDES TO USE THEM.
MAYBE I COULD JUST STICK MY FINGER IN THE END.
DO WE HAVE A PROJECTED POWER OUTPUT?
NO.
NONONONO.
THIS HAS TO BE WRONG.
YES, NATHAN.
THE POWER OUTPUT PROJECTIONS ON THE GUNS ARE ALL SCREWY, AND THE SCREEN'S GIVING ME A CALLOUT ABOUT "ZERO POINT ENERGY." WHAT'S THE STORY HERE?

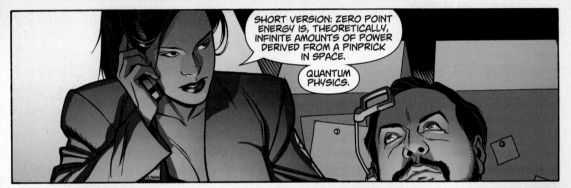

SHORT VERSION: ZERO POINT ENERGY IS, THEORETICALLY, INFINITE AMOUNTS OF POWER DERIVED FROM A PINPRICK IN SPACE.

QUANTUM PHYSICS.

THEN HERE'S THE NEWS.

ONE OF THESE GUNS THROWS OUT ENOUGH POWER TO SET A PLANET ON FIRE.

DOOR LOCK.

HELLO?

BUSY. WHO IS IT?

IT WAS UNLOCKED.

NO IT DAMN WELL WASN'T.

YOUR DOORLOCK'S BROKEN. I'M THE MECHANIC. I'M HERE TO FIX IT. WANT A BEER?

WHAT'S THIS?

MY LUGGAGE.

YOU TRAVEL LIGHT.

OOH, GUNS.

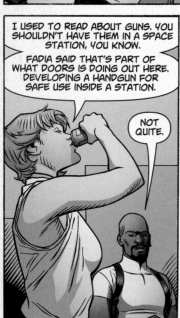

I USED TO READ ABOUT GUNS. YOU SHOULDN'T HAVE THEM IN A SPACE STATION, YOU KNOW.

FADIA SAID THAT'S PART OF WHAT DOORS IS DOING OUT HERE. DEVELOPING A HANDGUN FOR SAFE USE INSIDE A STATION.

NOT QUITE.

THESE ARE DESIGNED FOR USE IN SPACE. THEY HAVE NO RECOIL. GAS-FIRED.

SO IF YOU'RE IN A ZERO-GRAVITY SITUATION, FIRING THEM WON'T SEND YOU FLYING BACK-WARD AT SEVEN HUNDRED MILES AN HOUR.

I CAN SEE WHERE THAT WOULD BE USEFUL.

FIRST TIME I WAS ON THE MOON, I HAD TO USE A PISTOL ON THE SURFACE.

THE RECOIL SENT ME SHOOTING OFF AT ESCAPE VELOCITY.

MOONBASE ALPHA HAD TO SCRAMBLE A SHUTTLE TO CATCH ME.

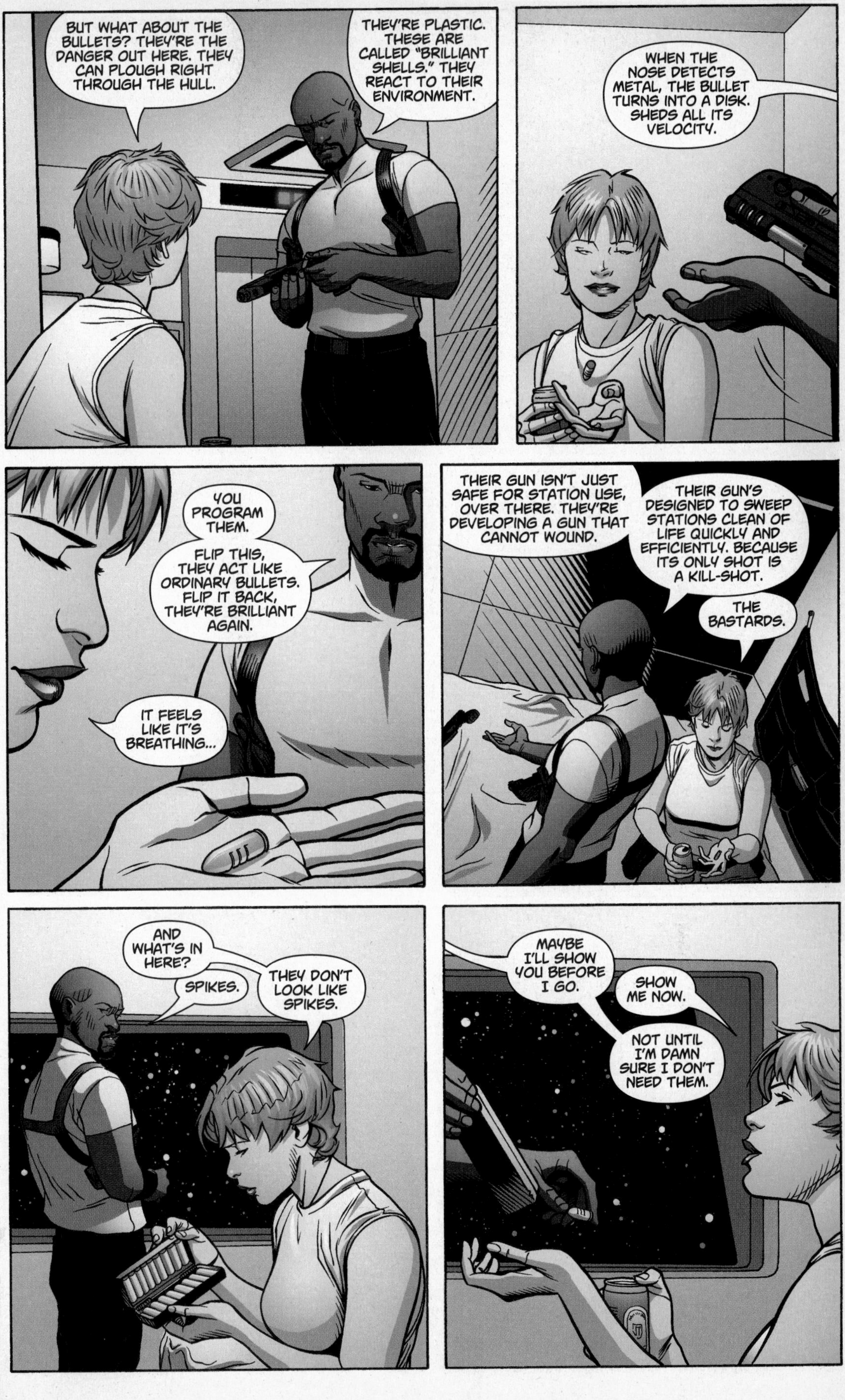
BUT WHAT ABOUT THE BULLETS? THEY'RE THE DANGER OUT HERE. THEY CAN PLOUGH RIGHT THROUGH THE HULL.
THEY'RE PLASTIC. THESE ARE CALLED "BRILLIANT SHELLS." THEY REACT TO THEIR ENVIRONMENT.
WHEN THE NOSE DETECTS METAL, THE BULLET TURNS INTO A DISK. SHEDS ALL ITS VELOCITY.
YOU PROGRAM THEM.
FLIP THIS, THEY ACT LIKE ORDINARY BULLETS. FLIP IT BACK, THEY'RE BRILLIANT AGAIN.
IT FEELS LIKE IT'S BREATHING...
THEIR GUN ISN'T JUST SAFE FOR STATION USE, OVER THERE. THEY'RE DEVELOPING A GUN THAT CANNOT WOUND.
THEIR GUN'S DESIGNED TO SWEEP STATIONS CLEAN OF LIFE QUICKLY AND EFFICIENTLY. BECAUSE ITS ONLY SHOT IS A KILL-SHOT.
THE BASTARDS.
AND WHAT'S IN HERE?
SPIKES.
THEY DON'T LOOK LIKE SPIKES.
MAYBE I'LL SHOW YOU BEFORE I GO.
SHOW ME NOW.
NOT UNTIL I'M DAMN SURE I DON'T NEED THEM.

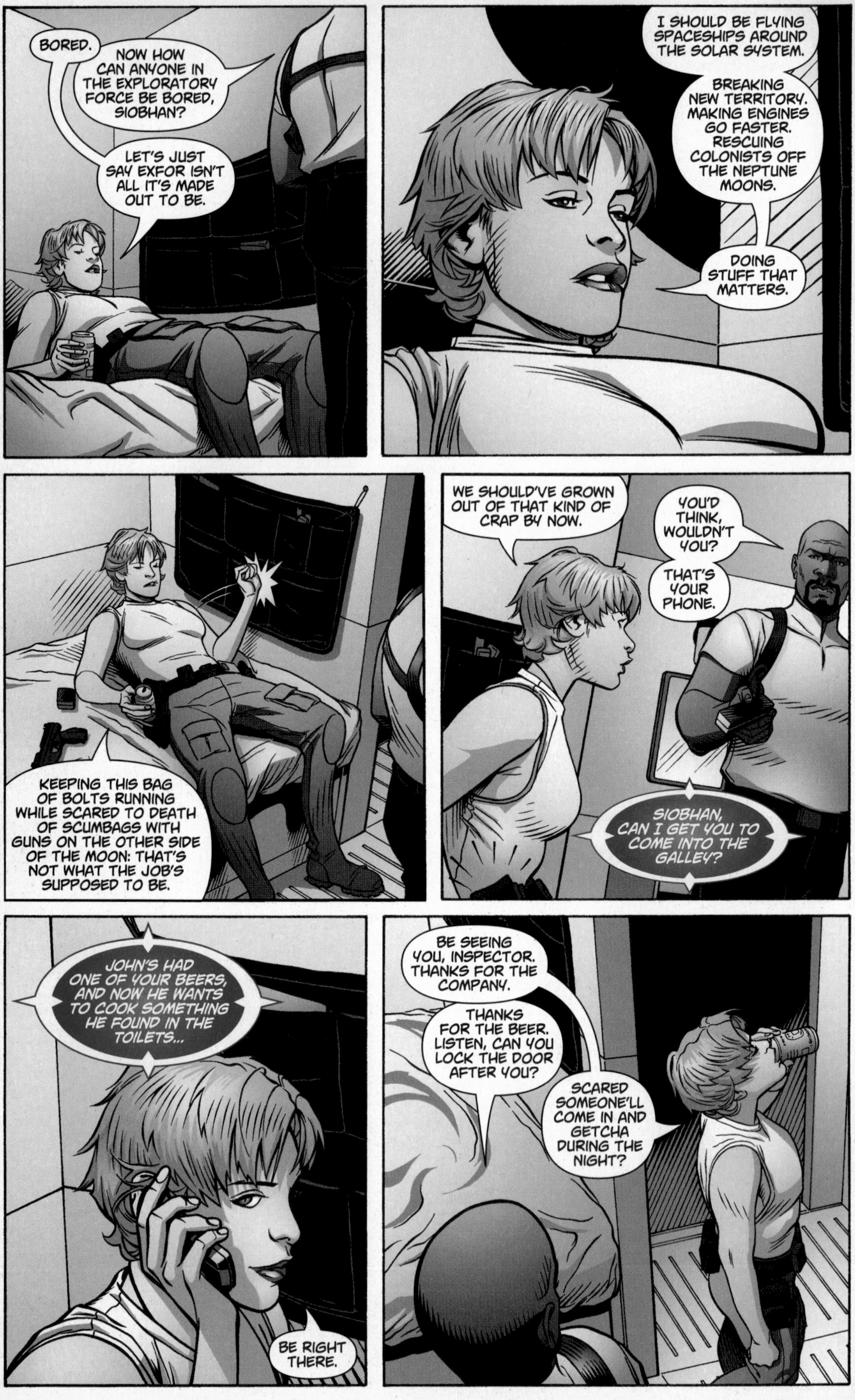
BORED.
NOW HOW CAN ANYONE IN THE EXPLORATORY FORCE BE BORED, SIOBHAN?
LET'S JUST SAY EXFOR ISN'T ALL IT'S MADE OUT TO BE.
I SHOULD BE FLYING SPACESHIPS AROUND THE SOLAR SYSTEM.
BREAKING NEW TERRITORY. MAKING ENGINES GO FASTER. RESCUING COLONISTS OFF THE NEPTUNE MOONS.
DOING STUFF THAT MATTERS.
KEEPING THIS BAG OF BOLTS RUNNING WHILE SCARED TO DEATH OF SCUMBAGS WITH GUNS ON THE OTHER SIDE OF THE MOON: THAT'S NOT WHAT THE JOB'S SUPPOSED TO BE.
WE SHOULD'VE GROWN OUT OF THAT KIND OF CRAP BY NOW.
YOU'D THINK, WOULDN'T YOU?
THAT'S YOUR PHONE.
SIOBHAN, CAN I GET YOU TO COME INTO THE GALLEY?
JOHN'S HAD ONE OF YOUR BEERS, AND NOW HE WANTS TO COOK SOMETHING HE FOUND IN THE TOILETS...
BE RIGHT THERE.
BE SEEING YOU, INSPECTOR. THANKS FOR THE COMPANY.
THANKS FOR THE BEER. LISTEN, CAN YOU LOCK THE DOOR AFTER YOU?
SCARED SOMEONE'LL COME IN AND GETCHA DURING THE NIGHT?

CALL ME A HEALTHY PARANOID.

PARANOIDS ARE JUST PEOPLE WITH ALL THE FACTS. G'NIGHT.

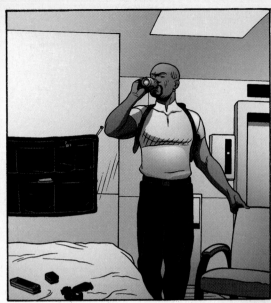

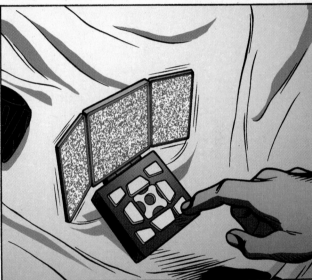

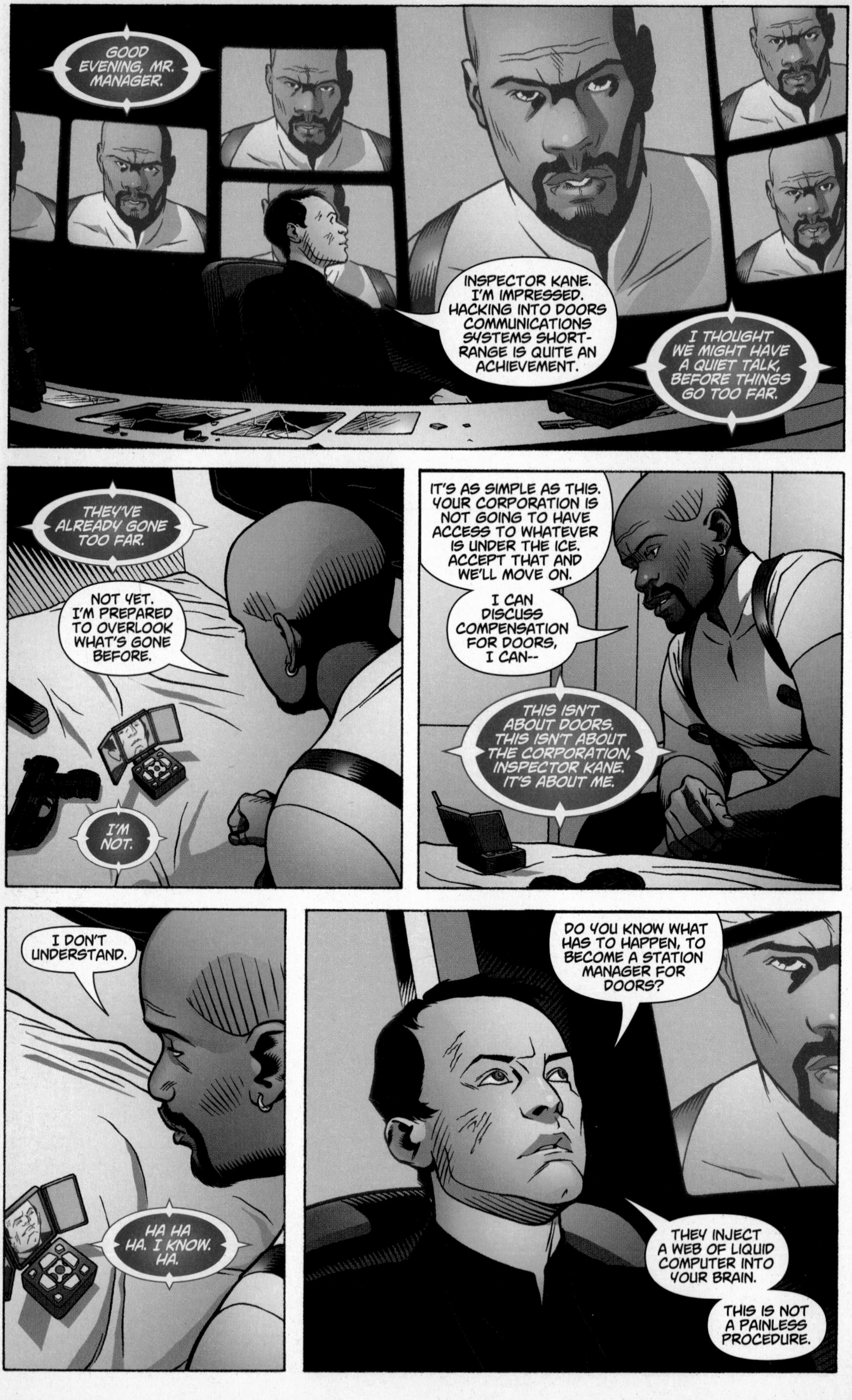

GOOD EVENING, MR. MANAGER.
INSPECTOR KANE. I'M IMPRESSED. HACKING INTO DOORS COMMUNICATIONS SYSTEMS SHORT-RANGE IS QUITE AN ACHIEVEMENT.
I THOUGHT WE MIGHT HAVE A QUIET TALK, BEFORE THINGS GO TOO FAR.
THEY'VE ALREADY GONE TOO FAR.
NOT YET. I'M PREPARED TO OVERLOOK WHAT'S GONE BEFORE.
I'M NOT.
IT'S AS SIMPLE AS THIS. YOUR CORPORATION IS NOT GOING TO HAVE ACCESS TO WHATEVER IS UNDER THE ICE. ACCEPT THAT AND WE'LL MOVE ON.
I CAN DISCUSS COMPENSATION FOR DOORS, I CAN--
THIS ISN'T ABOUT DOORS. THIS ISN'T ABOUT THE CORPORATION, INSPECTOR KANE. IT'S ABOUT ME.
I DON'T UNDERSTAND.
HA HA HA. I KNOW. HA.
DO YOU KNOW WHAT HAS TO HAPPEN, TO BECOME A STATION MANAGER FOR DOORS?
THEY INJECT A WEB OF LIQUID COMPUTER INTO YOUR BRAIN.
THIS IS NOT A PAINLESS PROCEDURE.

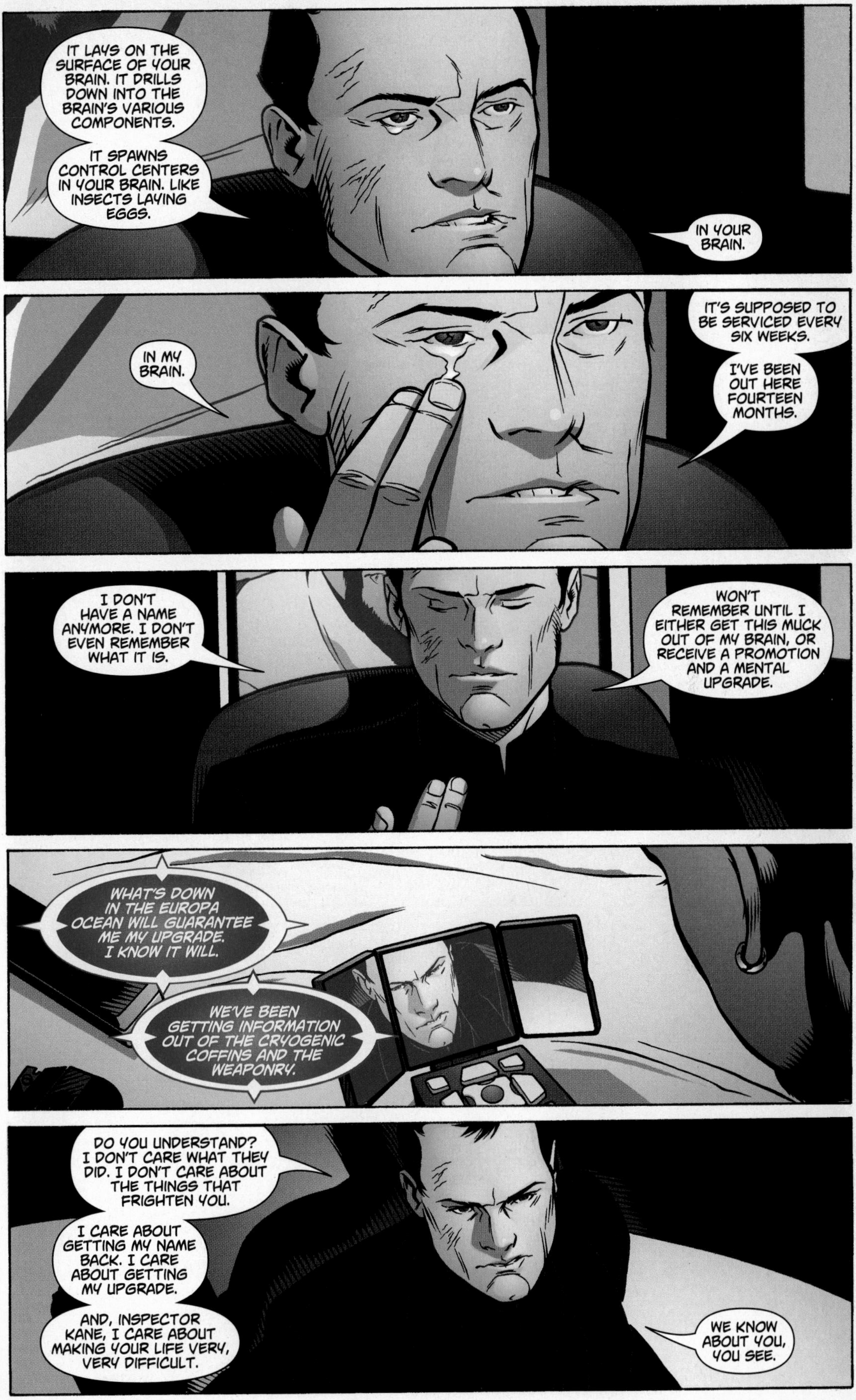
IT LAYS ON THE SURFACE OF YOUR BRAIN. IT DRILLS DOWN INTO THE BRAIN'S VARIOUS COMPONENTS.
IT SPAWNS CONTROL CENTERS IN YOUR BRAIN. LIKE INSECTS LAYING EGGS.
IN YOUR BRAIN.
IN MY BRAIN.
IT'S SUPPOSED TO BE SERVICED EVERY SIX WEEKS.
I'VE BEEN OUT HERE FOURTEEN MONTHS.
I DON'T HAVE A NAME ANYMORE. I DON'T EVEN REMEMBER WHAT IT IS.
WON'T REMEMBER UNTIL I EITHER GET THIS MUCK OUT OF MY BRAIN, OR RECEIVE A PROMOTION AND A MENTAL UPGRADE.
WHAT'S DOWN IN THE EUROPA OCEAN WILL GUARANTEE ME MY UPGRADE. I KNOW IT WILL.
WE'VE BEEN GETTING INFORMATION OUT OF THE CRYOGENIC COFFINS AND THE WEAPONRY.
DO YOU UNDERSTAND? I DON'T CARE WHAT THEY DID. I DON'T CARE ABOUT THE THINGS THAT FRIGHTEN YOU.
I CARE ABOUT GETTING MY NAME BACK. I CARE ABOUT GETTING MY UPGRADE.
AND, INSPECTOR KANE, I CARE ABOUT MAKING YOUR LIFE VERY, VERY DIFFICULT.
WE KNOW ABOUT YOU, YOU SEE.

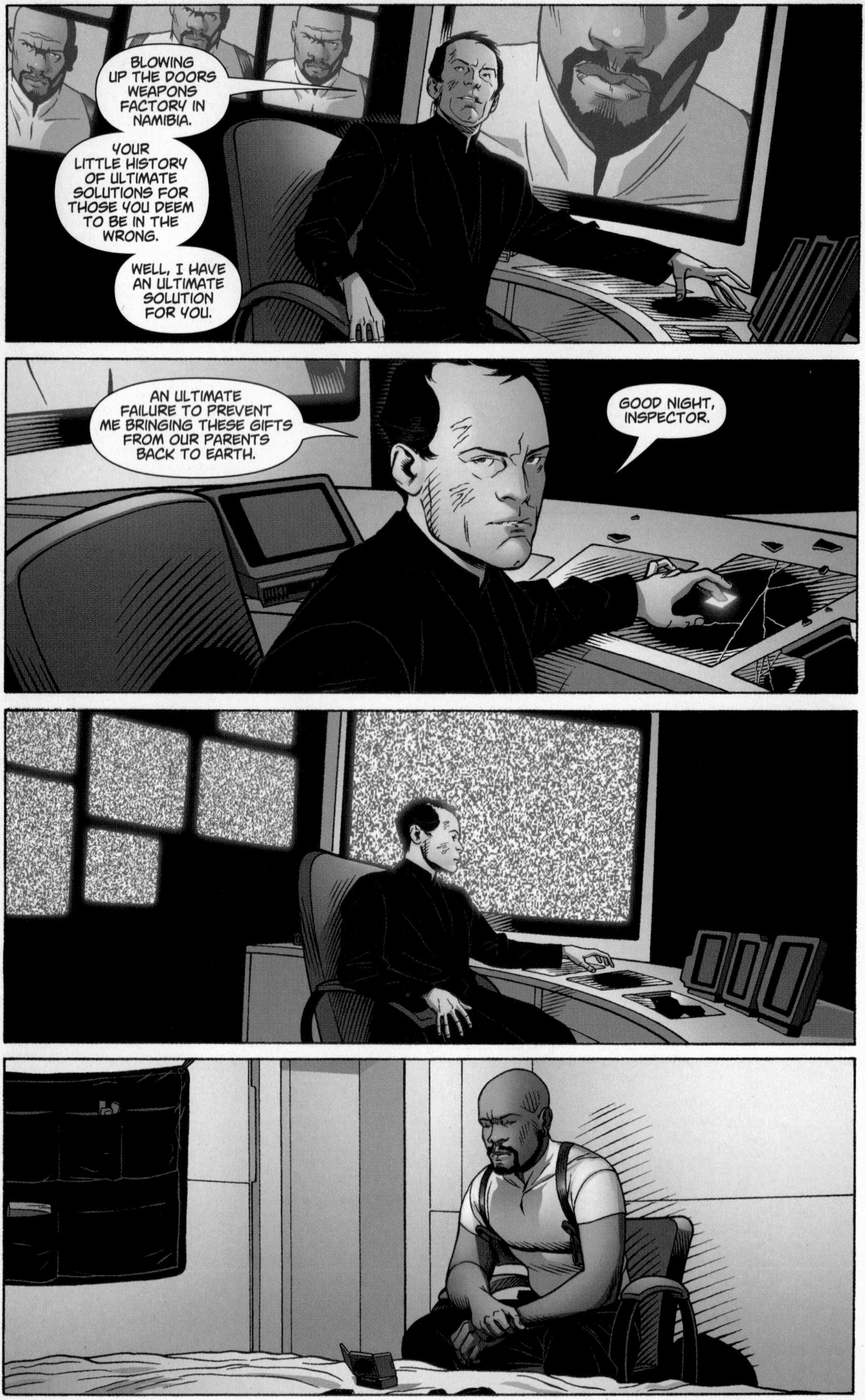
BLOWING UP THE DOORS WEAPONS FACTORY IN NAMIBIA.
YOUR LITTLE HISTORY OF ULTIMATE SOLUTIONS FOR THOSE YOU DEEM TO BE IN THE WRONG.
WELL, I HAVE AN ULTIMATE SOLUTION FOR YOU.
AN ULTIMATE FAILURE TO PREVENT ME BRINGING THESE GIFTS FROM OUR PARENTS BACK TO EARTH.
GOOD NIGHT, INSPECTOR.

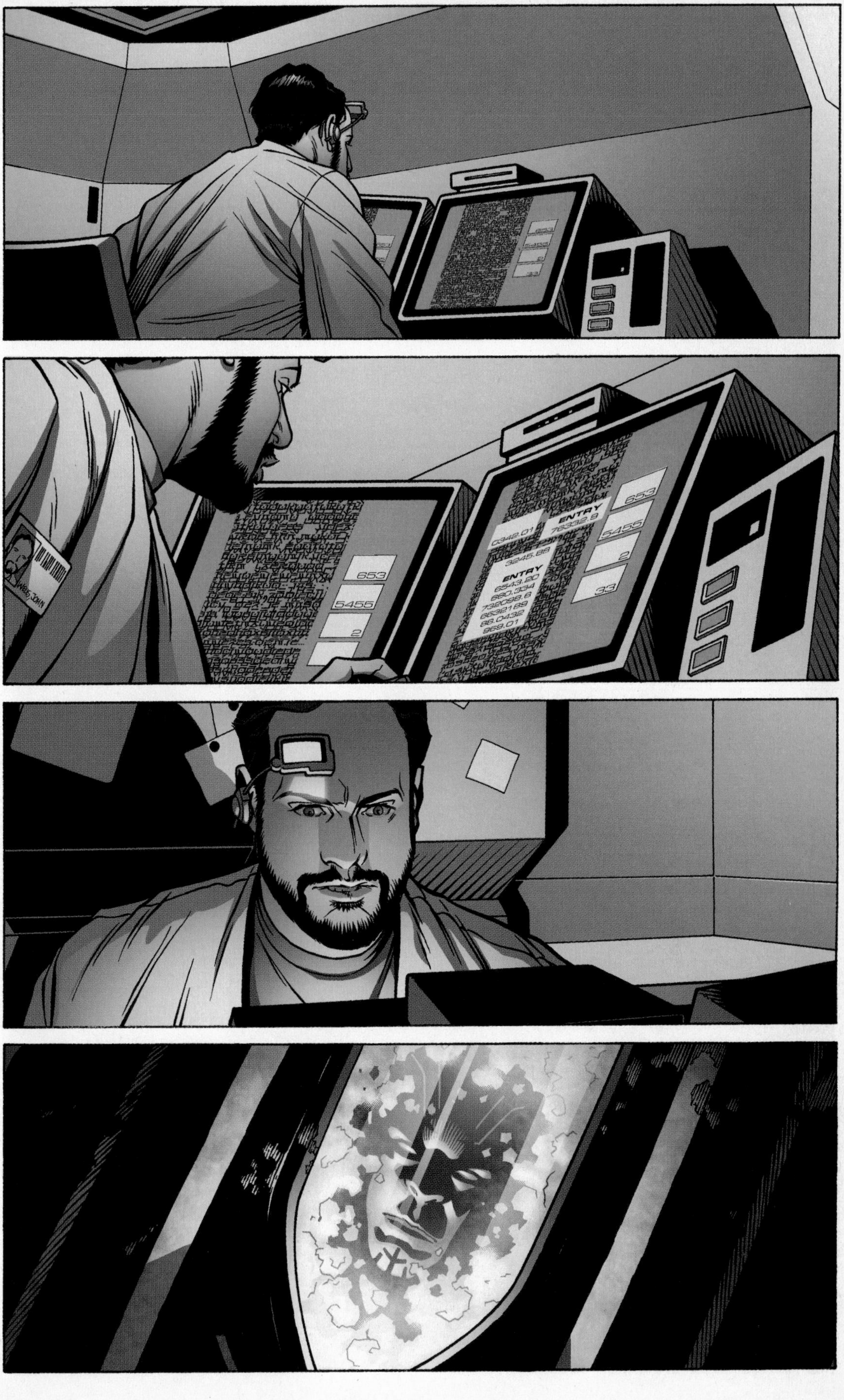
653
5455
2
653
5455
2
33
ENTRY
76332.9
0342.01
3245.88
ENTRY
6543.20
660.334
732098.6
6632189
88.0432
969.01

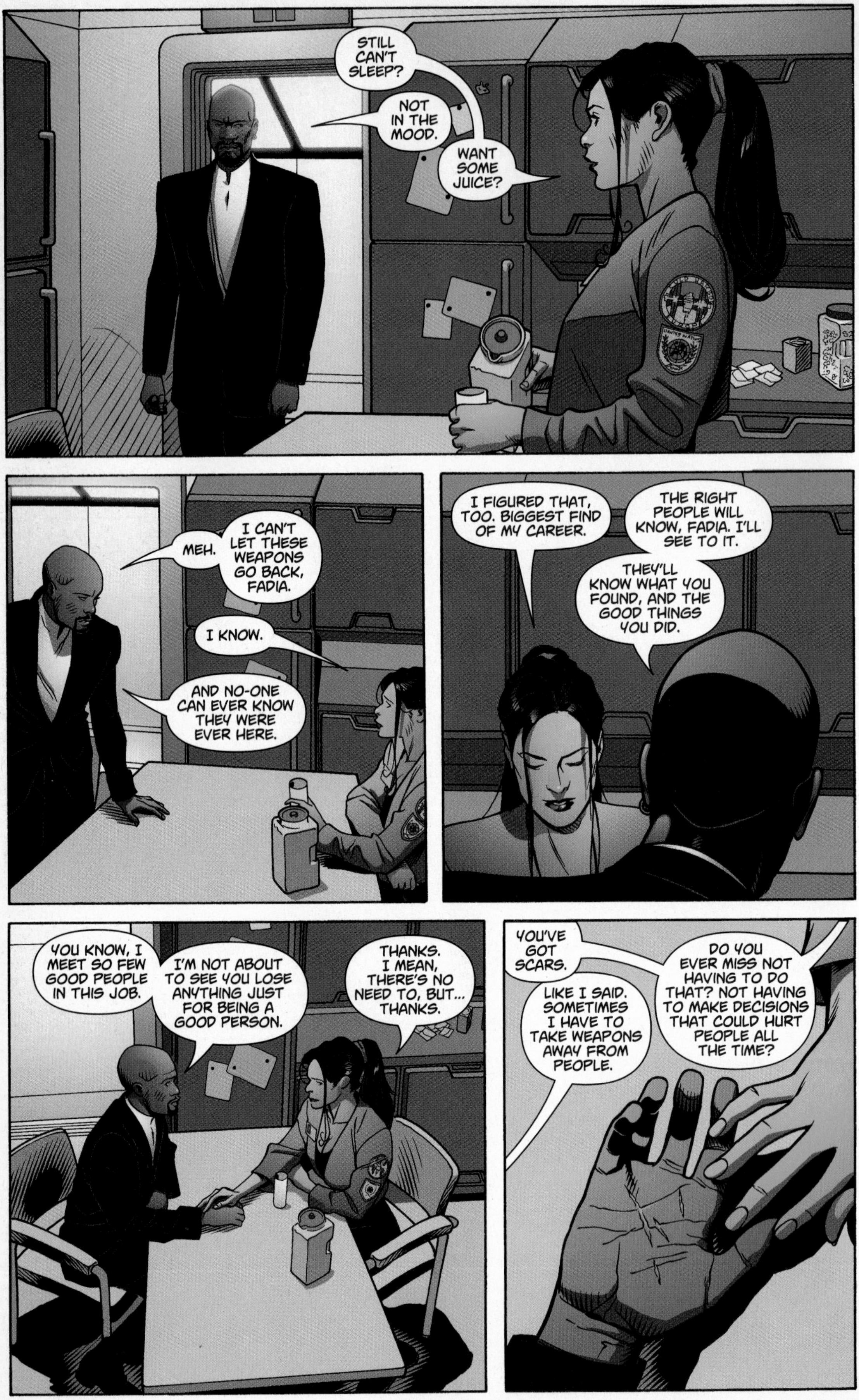
STILL CAN'T SLEEP?
NOT IN THE MOOD.
WANT SOME JUICE?
MEH.
I CAN'T LET THESE WEAPONS GO BACK, FADIA.
I KNOW.
AND NO-ONE CAN EVER KNOW THEY WERE EVER HERE.
I FIGURED THAT, TOO. BIGGEST FIND OF MY CAREER.
THE RIGHT PEOPLE WILL KNOW, FADIA. I'LL SEE TO IT.
THEY'LL KNOW WHAT YOU FOUND, AND THE GOOD THINGS YOU DID.
YOU KNOW, I MEET SO FEW GOOD PEOPLE IN THIS JOB.
I'M NOT ABOUT TO SEE YOU LOSE ANYTHING JUST FOR BEING A GOOD PERSON.
THANKS. I MEAN, THERE'S NO NEED TO, BUT... THANKS.
YOU'VE GOT SCARS.
LIKE I SAID. SOMETIMES I HAVE TO TAKE WEAPONS AWAY FROM PEOPLE.
DO YOU EVER MISS NOT HAVING TO DO THAT? NOT HAVING TO MAKE DECISIONS THAT COULD HURT PEOPLE ALL THE TIME?

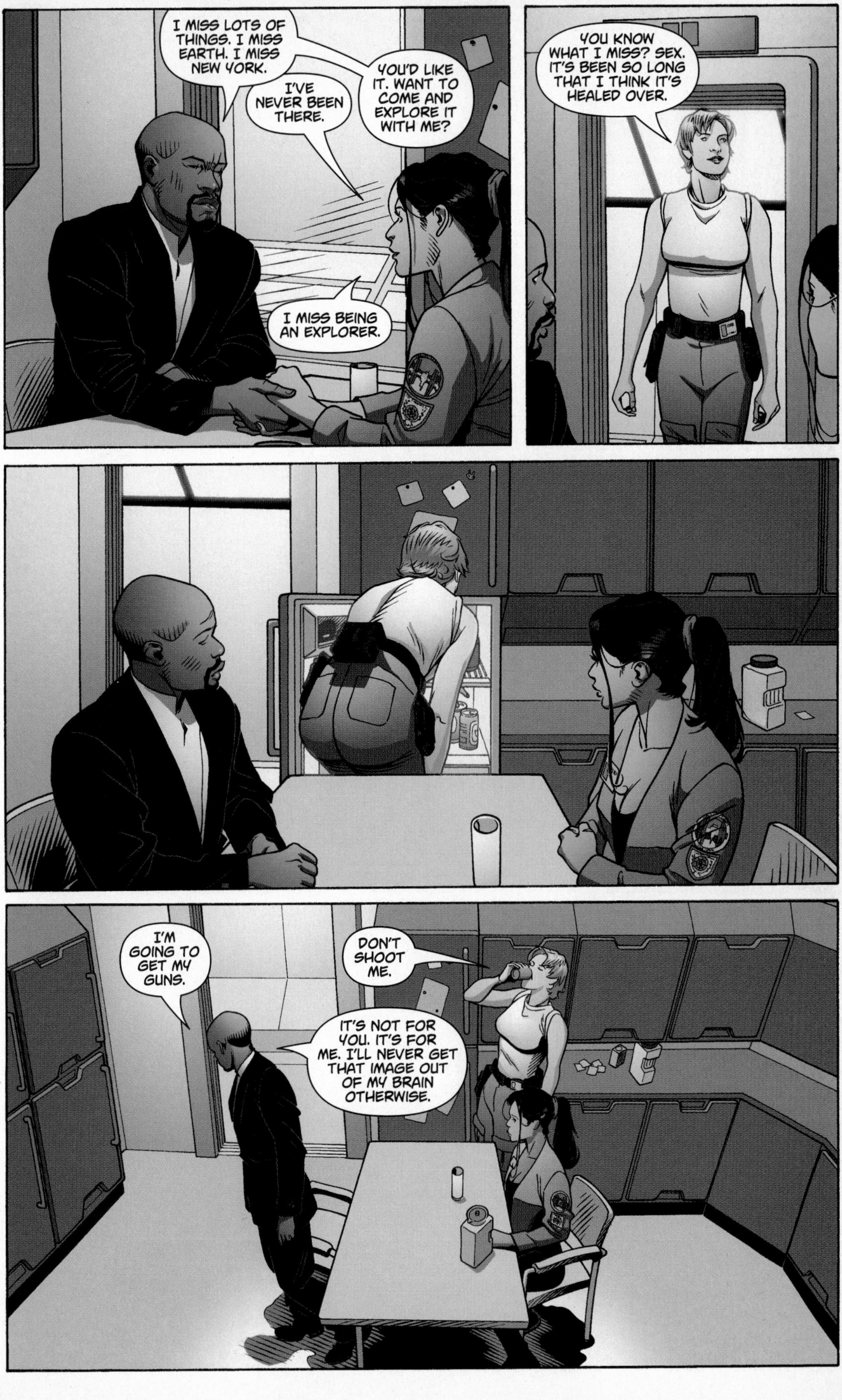
I MISS LOTS OF THINGS. I MISS EARTH. I MISS NEW YORK.
I'VE NEVER BEEN THERE.
YOU'D LIKE IT. WANT TO COME AND EXPLORE IT WITH ME?
I MISS BEING AN EXPLORER.
YOU KNOW WHAT I MISS? SEX. IT'S BEEN SO LONG THAT I THINK IT'S HEALED OVER.
I'M GOING TO GET MY GUNS.
DON'T SHOOT ME.
IT'S NOT FOR YOU. IT'S FOR ME. I'LL NEVER GET THAT IMAGE OUT OF MY BRAIN OTHERWISE.

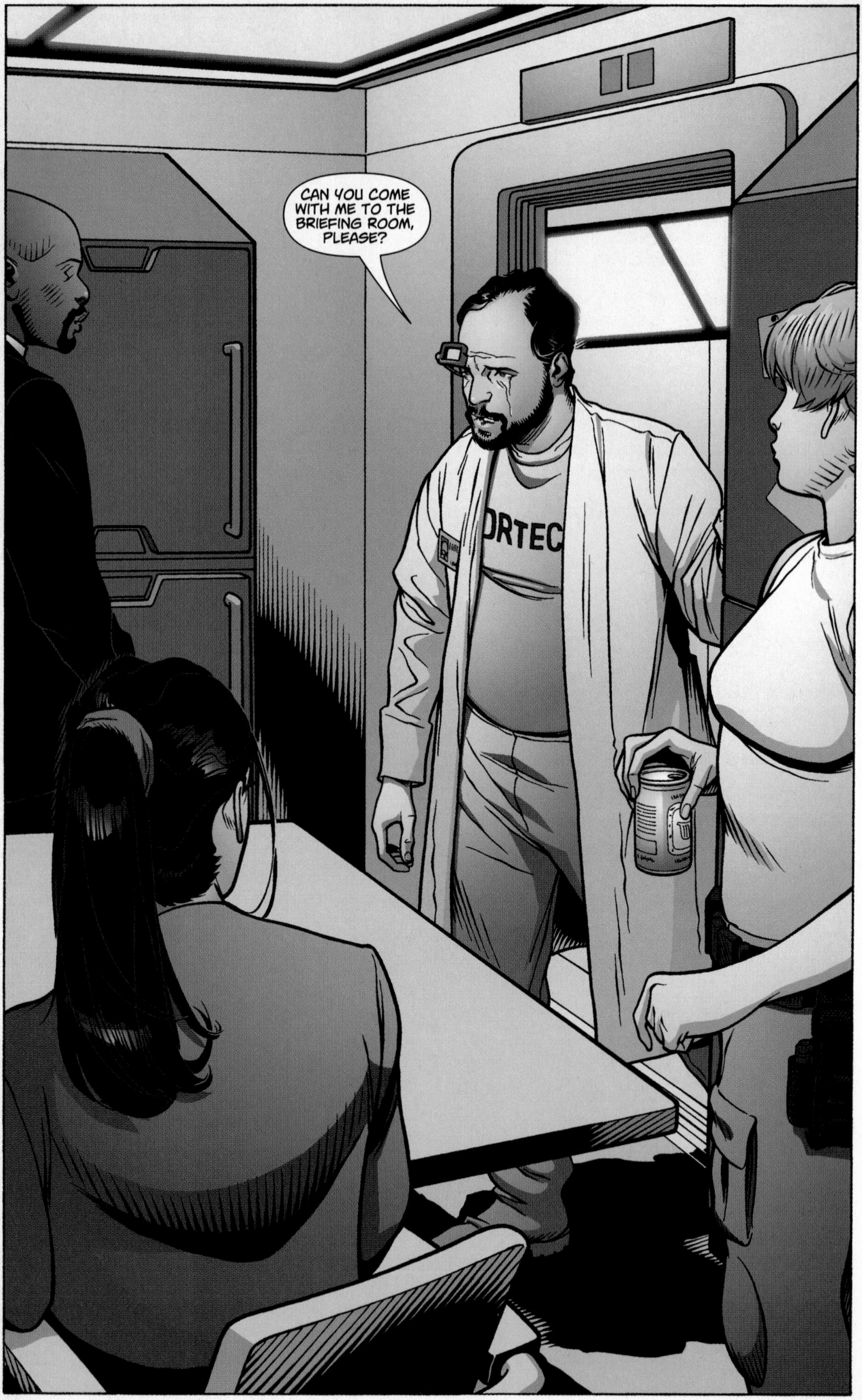
CAN YOU COME WITH ME TO THE BRIEFING ROOM, PLEASE?
ORTEC

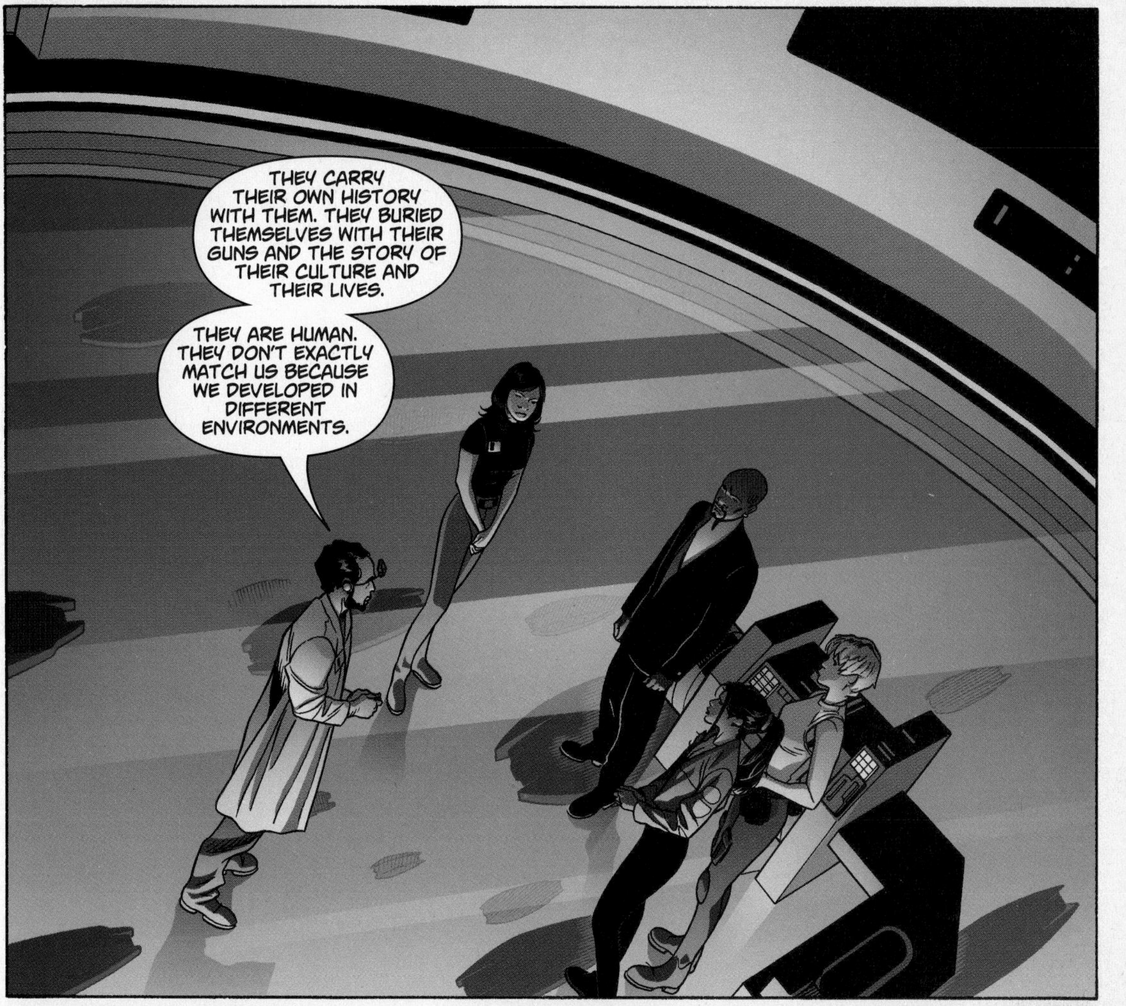
THEY CARRY THEIR OWN HISTORY WITH THEM. THEY BURIED THEMSELVES WITH THEIR GUNS AND THE STORY OF THEIR CULTURE AND THEIR LIVES.
THEY ARE HUMAN. THEY DON'T EXACTLY MATCH US BECAUSE WE DEVELOPED IN DIFFERENT ENVIRONMENTS.

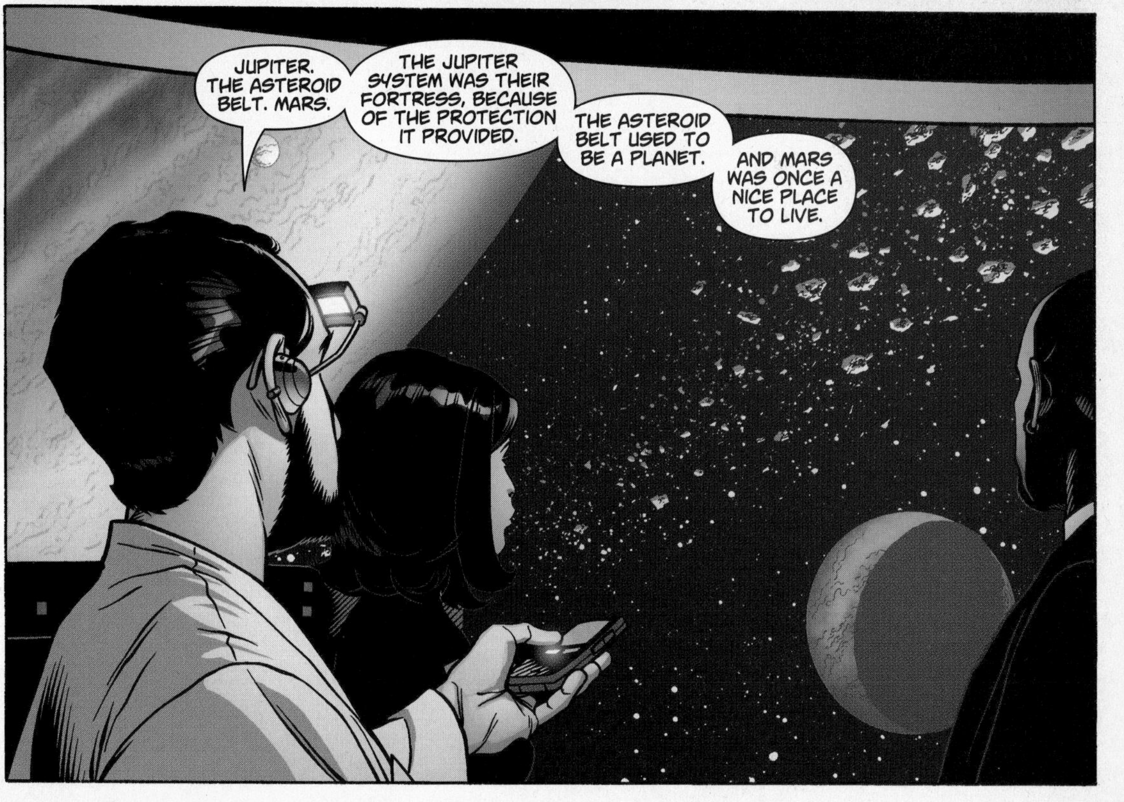
JUPITER. THE ASTEROID BELT. MARS.
THE JUPITER SYSTEM WAS THEIR FORTRESS, BECAUSE OF THE PROTECTION IT PROVIDED.
THE ASTEROID BELT USED TO BE A PLANET.
AND MARS WAS ONCE A NICE PLACE TO LIVE.

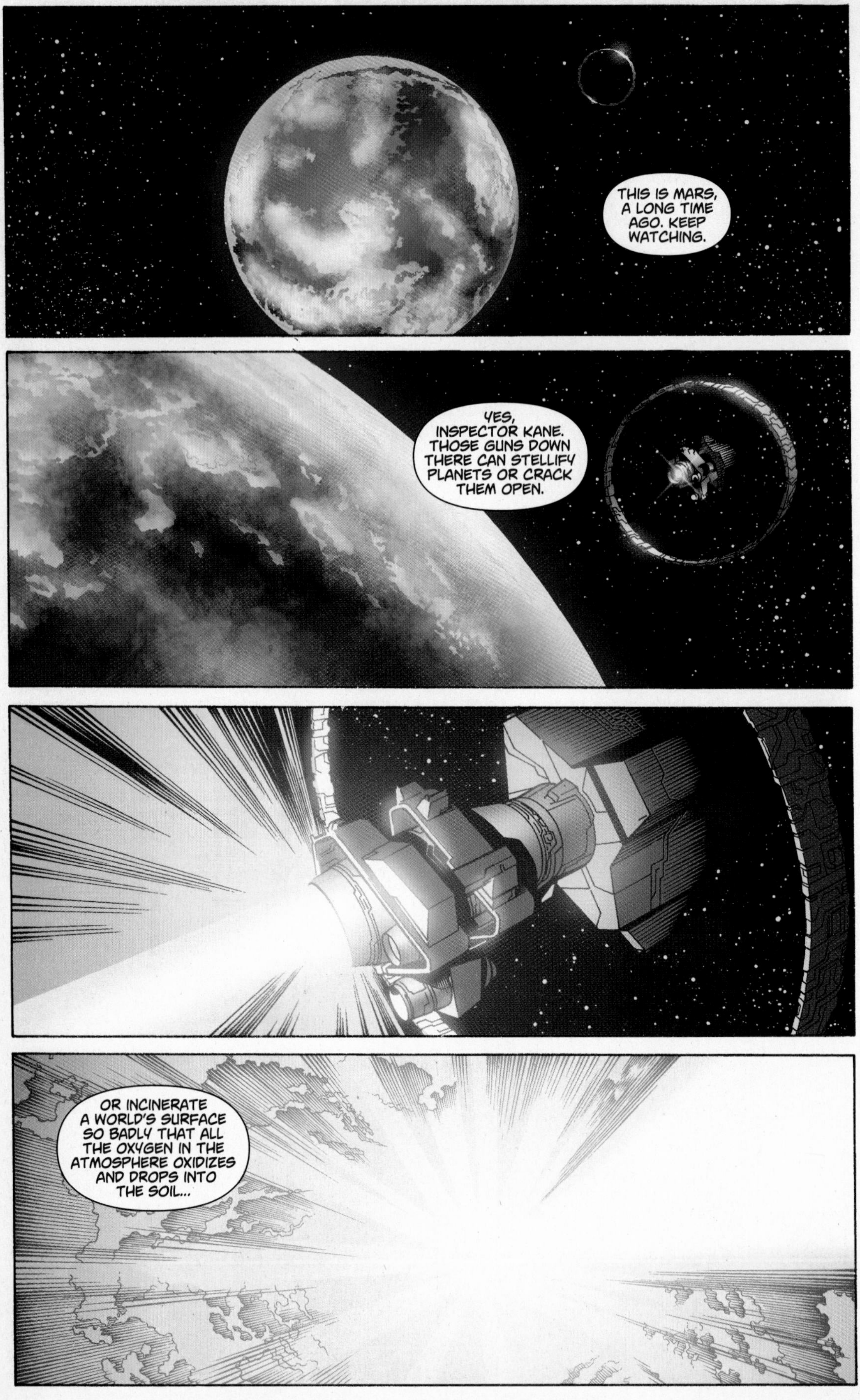
THIS IS MARS, A LONG TIME AGO. KEEP WATCHING.
YES, INSPECTOR KANE. THOSE GUNS DOWN THERE CAN STELLIFY PLANETS OR CRACK THEM OPEN.
OR INCINERATE A WORLD'S SURFACE SO BADLY THAT ALL THE OXYGEN IN THE ATMOSPHERE OXIDIZES AND DROPS INTO THE SOIL...

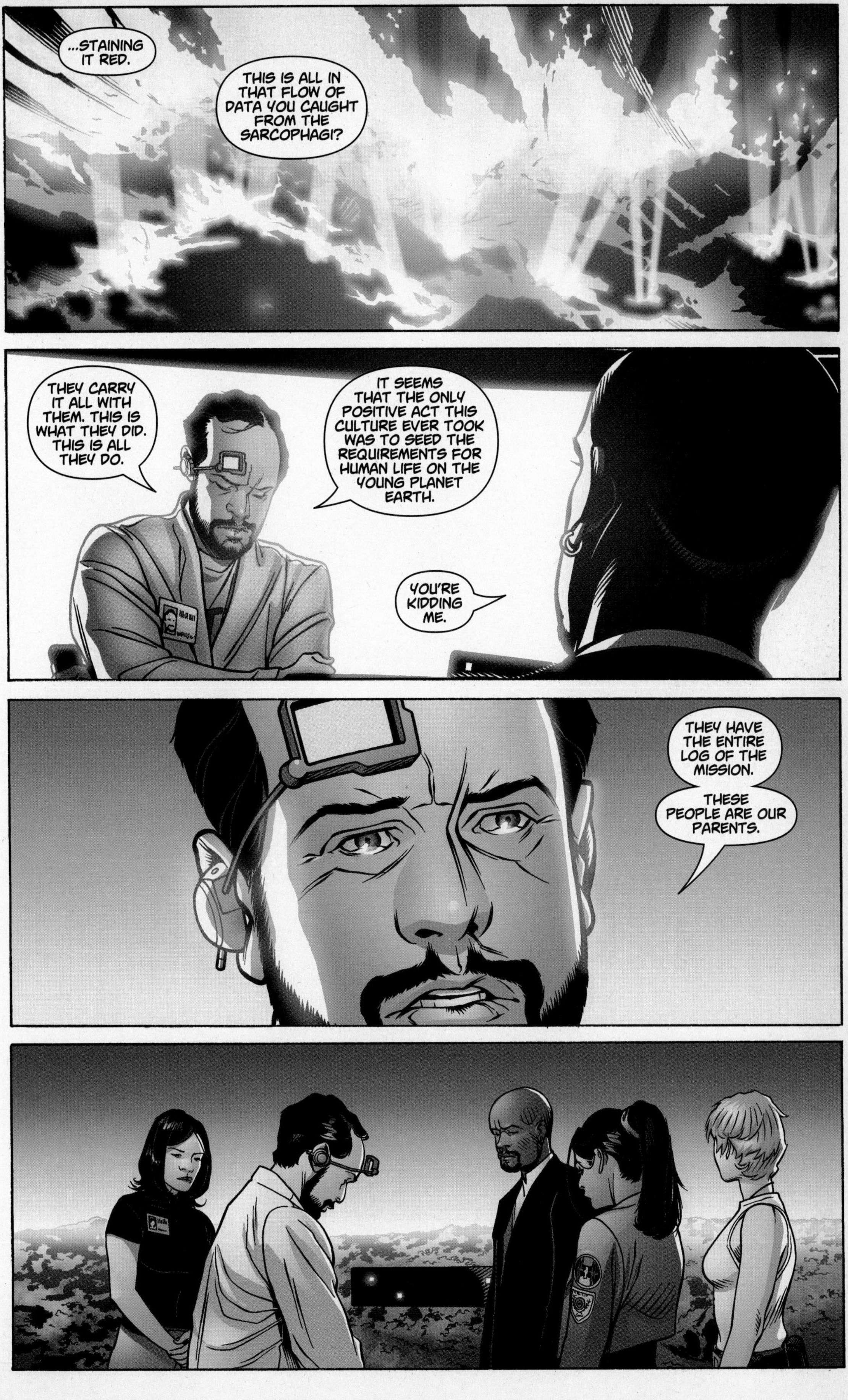
...STAINING IT RED.
THIS IS ALL IN THAT FLOW OF DATA YOU CAUGHT FROM THE SARCOPHAGI?
THEY CARRY IT ALL WITH THEM. THIS IS WHAT THEY DID. THIS IS ALL THEY DO.
IT SEEMS THAT THE ONLY POSITIVE ACT THIS CULTURE EVER TOOK WAS TO SEED THE REQUIREMENTS FOR HUMAN LIFE ON THE YOUNG PLANET EARTH.
YOU'RE KIDDING ME.
THEY HAVE THE ENTIRE LOG OF THE MISSION.
THESE PEOPLE ARE OUR PARENTS.

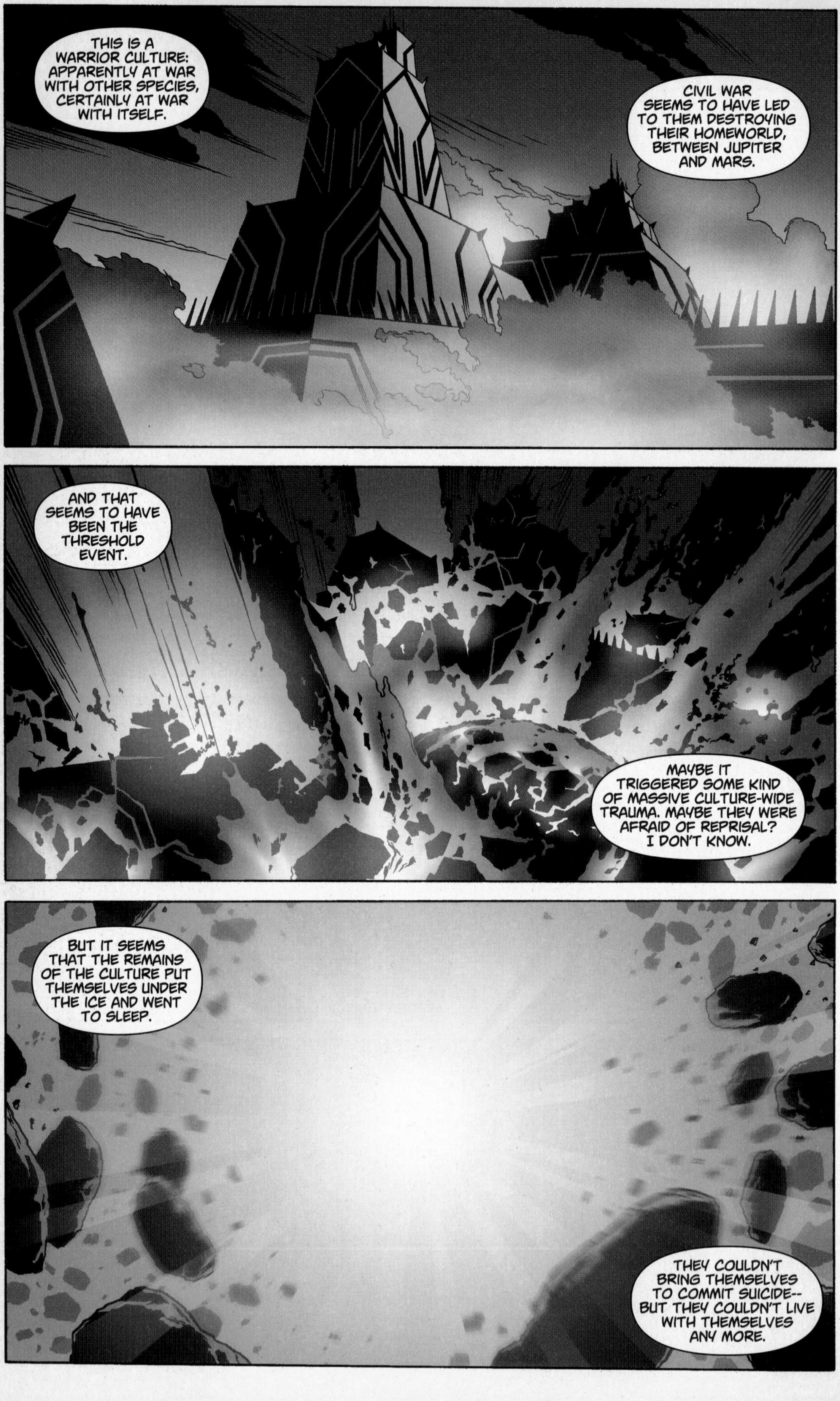
THIS IS A WARRIOR CULTURE: APPARENTLY AT WAR WITH OTHER SPECIES, CERTAINLY AT WAR WITH ITSELF.
CIVIL WAR SEEMS TO HAVE LED TO THEM DESTROYING THEIR HOMEWORLD, BETWEEN JUPITER AND MARS.
AND THAT SEEMS TO HAVE BEEN THE THRESHOLD EVENT.
MAYBE IT TRIGGERED SOME KIND OF MASSIVE CULTURE-WIDE TRAUMA. MAYBE THEY WERE AFRAID OF REPRISAL? I DON'T KNOW.
BUT IT SEEMS THAT THE REMAINS OF THE CULTURE PUT THEMSELVES UNDER THE ICE AND WENT TO SLEEP.
THEY COULDN'T BRING THEMSELVES TO COMMIT SUICIDE-- BUT THEY COULDN'T LIVE WITH THEMSELVES ANY MORE.

YOU KNOW WHAT BOTHERS ME MOST? WHATEVER'S IN THEM IS IN US. WE ARE THEIR CHILDREN.

WELL, I GUESS WHAT THEY SAY IS TRUE. YOU DON'T GET TO CHOOSE YOUR FAMILY.

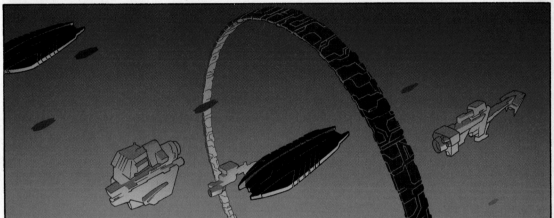

DAMN. MY STATION, RIGHT NOW.

WHAT'S HAPPENING?

THE TORUS JUST DEVELOPED A POWER FIELD.

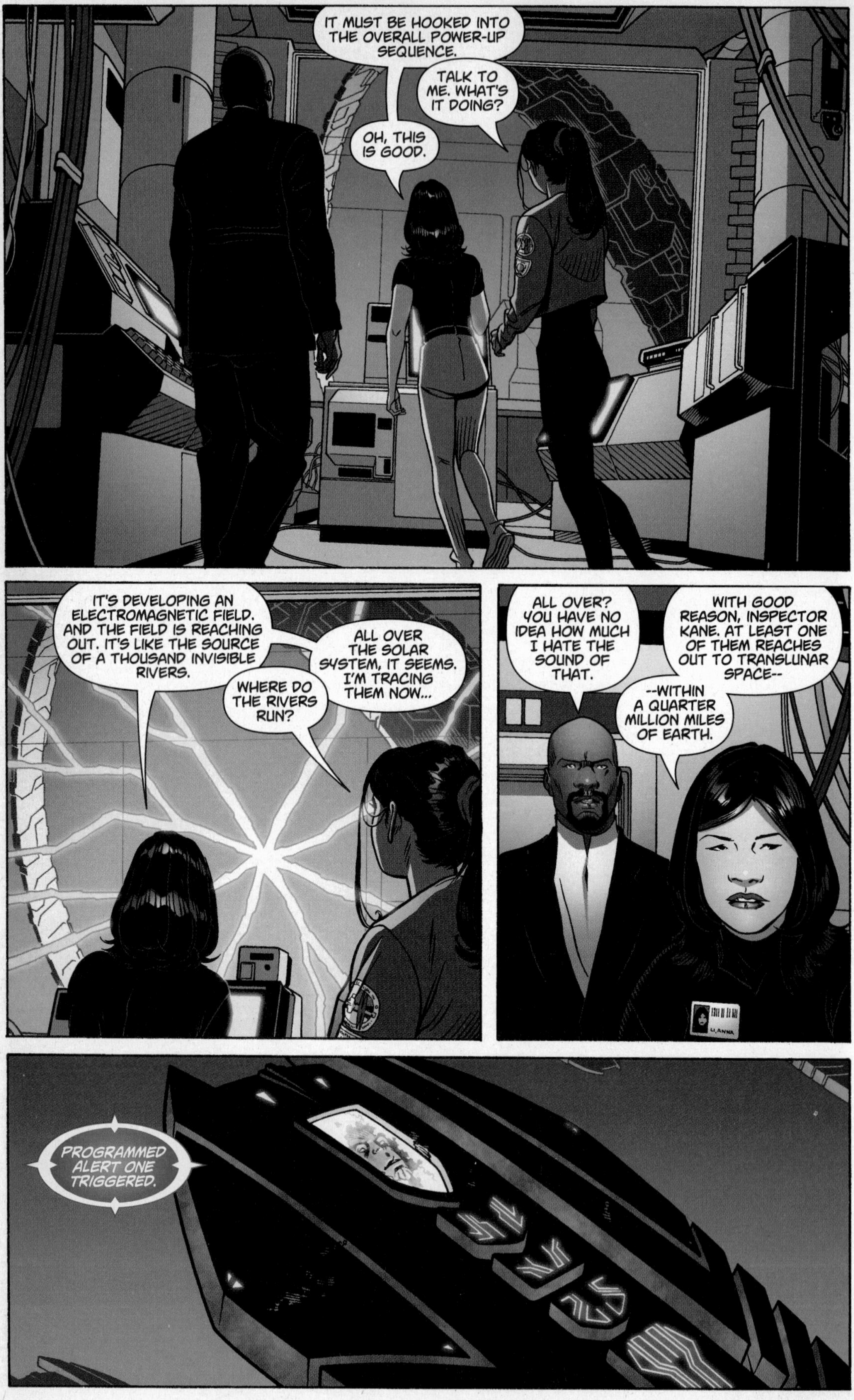
IT MUST BE HOOKED INTO THE OVERALL POWER-UP SEQUENCE.
TALK TO ME. WHAT'S IT DOING?
OH, THIS IS GOOD.
IT'S DEVELOPING AN ELECTROMAGNETIC FIELD. AND THE FIELD IS REACHING OUT. IT'S LIKE THE SOURCE OF A THOUSAND INVISIBLE RIVERS.
WHERE DO THE RIVERS RUN?
ALL OVER THE SOLAR SYSTEM, IT SEEMS. I'M TRACING THEM NOW...
ALL OVER? YOU HAVE NO IDEA HOW MUCH I HATE THE SOUND OF THAT.
WITH GOOD REASON, INSPECTOR KANE. AT LEAST ONE OF THEM REACHES OUT TO TRANSLUNAR SPACE--
--WITHIN A QUARTER MILLION MILES OF EARTH.
LI, ANNA
PROGRAMMED ALERT ONE TRIGGERED.

I'M DETECTING A COMMUNICATIONS NET DOWN THERE.

THE WEAPONS ARE AT 50% OF POWER-UP SEQUENCE. AND THEY'RE TALKING TO THE SARCOPHAGI SYSTEMS.

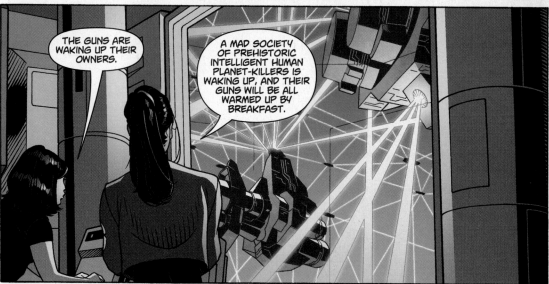

THE GUNS ARE WAKING UP THEIR OWNERS.

A MAD SOCIETY OF PREHISTORIC INTELLIGENT HUMAN PLANET-KILLERS IS WAKING UP, AND THEIR GUNS WILL BE ALL WARMED UP BY BREAKFAST.

GOD, I'M HAPPY.

HEADS UP. DOORS HAVE JUST DROPPED PROBES INTO THE OCEAN.

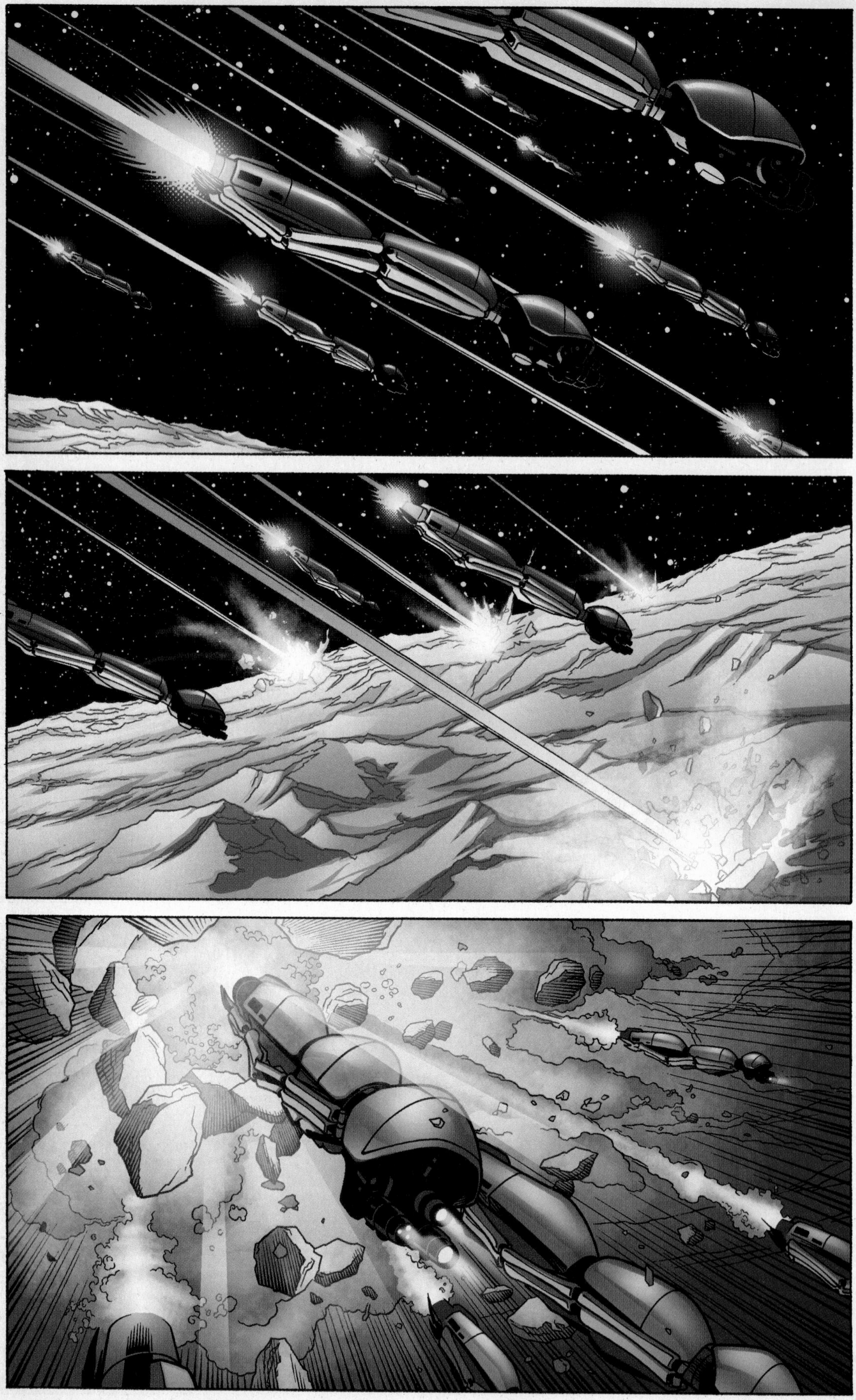

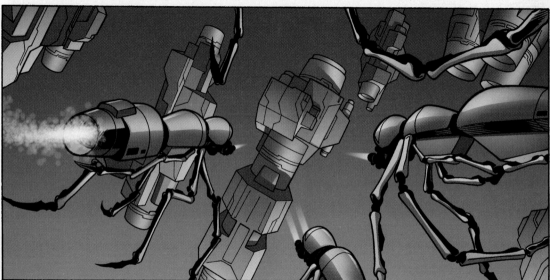

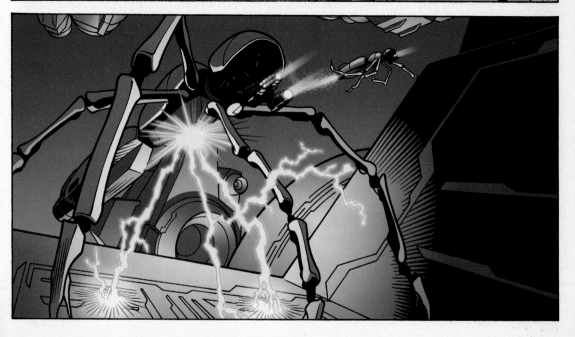

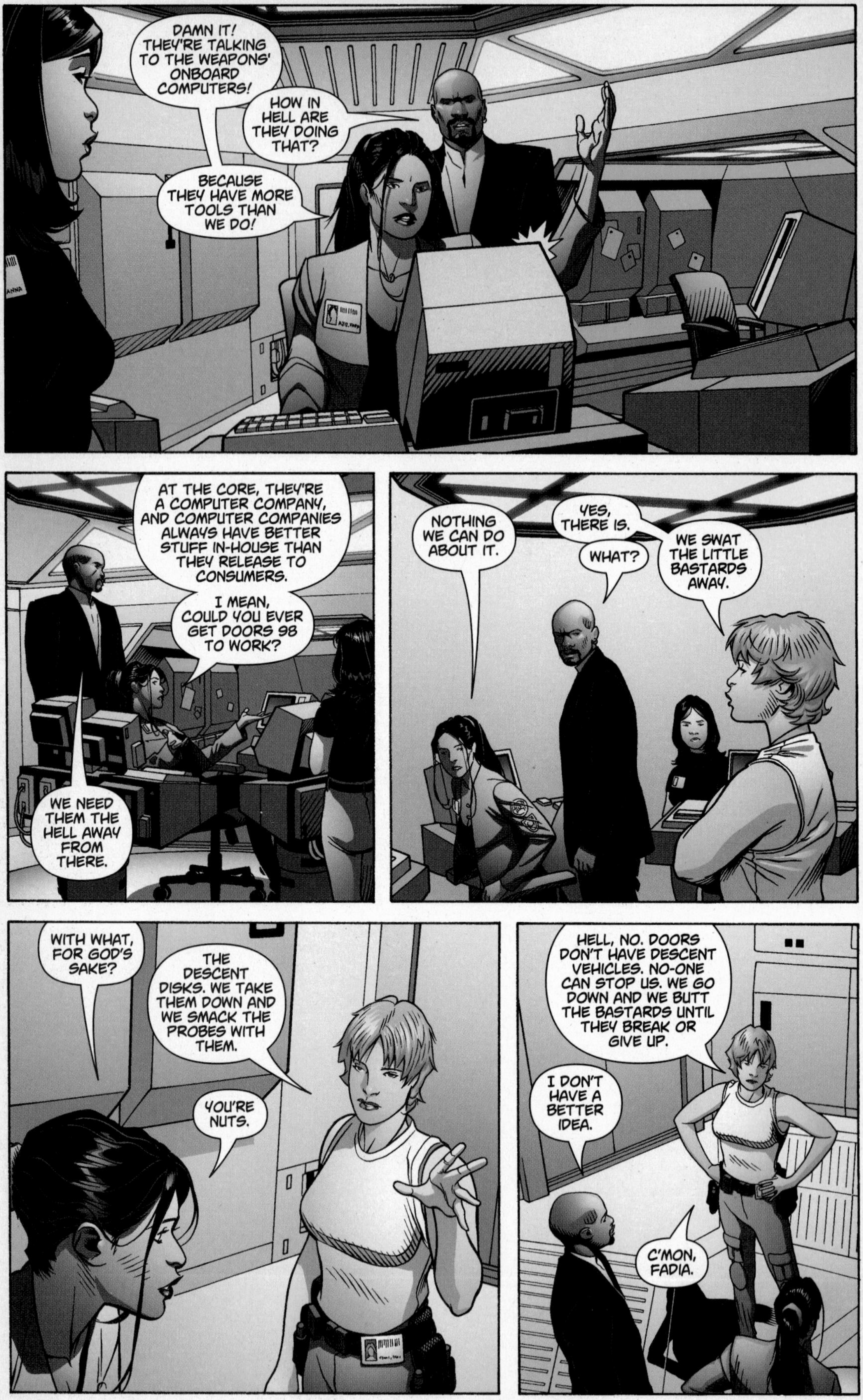
DAMN IT! THEY'RE TALKING TO THE WEAPONS' ONBOARD COMPUTERS!
HOW IN HELL ARE THEY DOING THAT?
BECAUSE THEY HAVE MORE TOOLS THAN WE DO!
AT THE CORE, THEY'RE A COMPUTER COMPANY, AND COMPUTER COMPANIES ALWAYS HAVE BETTER STUFF IN-HOUSE THAN THEY RELEASE TO CONSUMERS.
I MEAN, COULD YOU EVER GET DOORS 98 TO WORK?
WE NEED THEM THE HELL AWAY FROM THERE.
NOTHING WE CAN DO ABOUT IT.
YES, THERE IS.
WHAT?
WE SWAT THE LITTLE BASTARDS AWAY.
WITH WHAT, FOR GOD'S SAKE?
THE DESCENT DISKS. WE TAKE THEM DOWN AND WE SMACK THE PROBES WITH THEM.
YOU'RE NUTS.
HELL, NO. DOORS DON'T HAVE DESCENT VEHICLES. NO-ONE CAN STOP US. WE GO DOWN AND WE BUTT THE BASTARDS UNTIL THEY BREAK OR GIVE UP.
I DON'T HAVE A BETTER IDEA.
C'MON, FADIA.

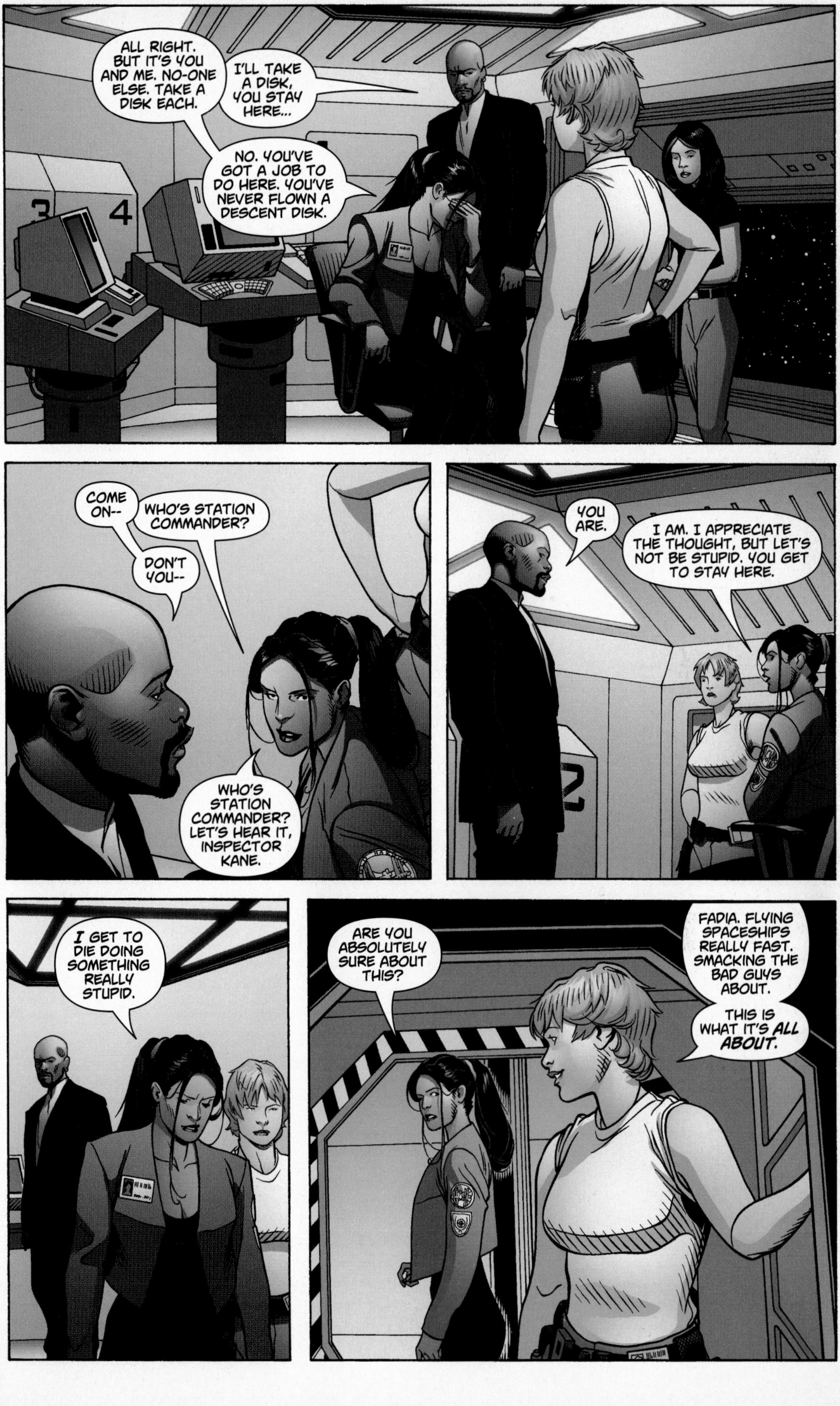
ALL RIGHT. BUT IT'S YOU AND ME. NO-ONE ELSE. TAKE A DISK EACH.
I'LL TAKE A DISK, YOU STAY HERE...
NO. YOU'VE GOT A JOB TO DO HERE. YOU'VE NEVER FLOWN A DESCENT DISK.
3
4
COME ON--
WHO'S STATION COMMANDER?
DON'T YOU--
WHO'S STATION COMMANDER? LET'S HEAR IT, INSPECTOR KANE.
YOU ARE.
I AM. I APPRECIATE THE THOUGHT, BUT LET'S NOT BE STUPID. YOU GET TO STAY HERE.
2
I GET TO DIE DOING SOMETHING REALLY STUPID.
ARE YOU ABSOLUTELY SURE ABOUT THIS?
FADIA. FLYING SPACESHIPS REALLY FAST. SMACKING THE BAD GUYS ABOUT.
THIS IS WHAT IT'S ***ALL ABOUT***.

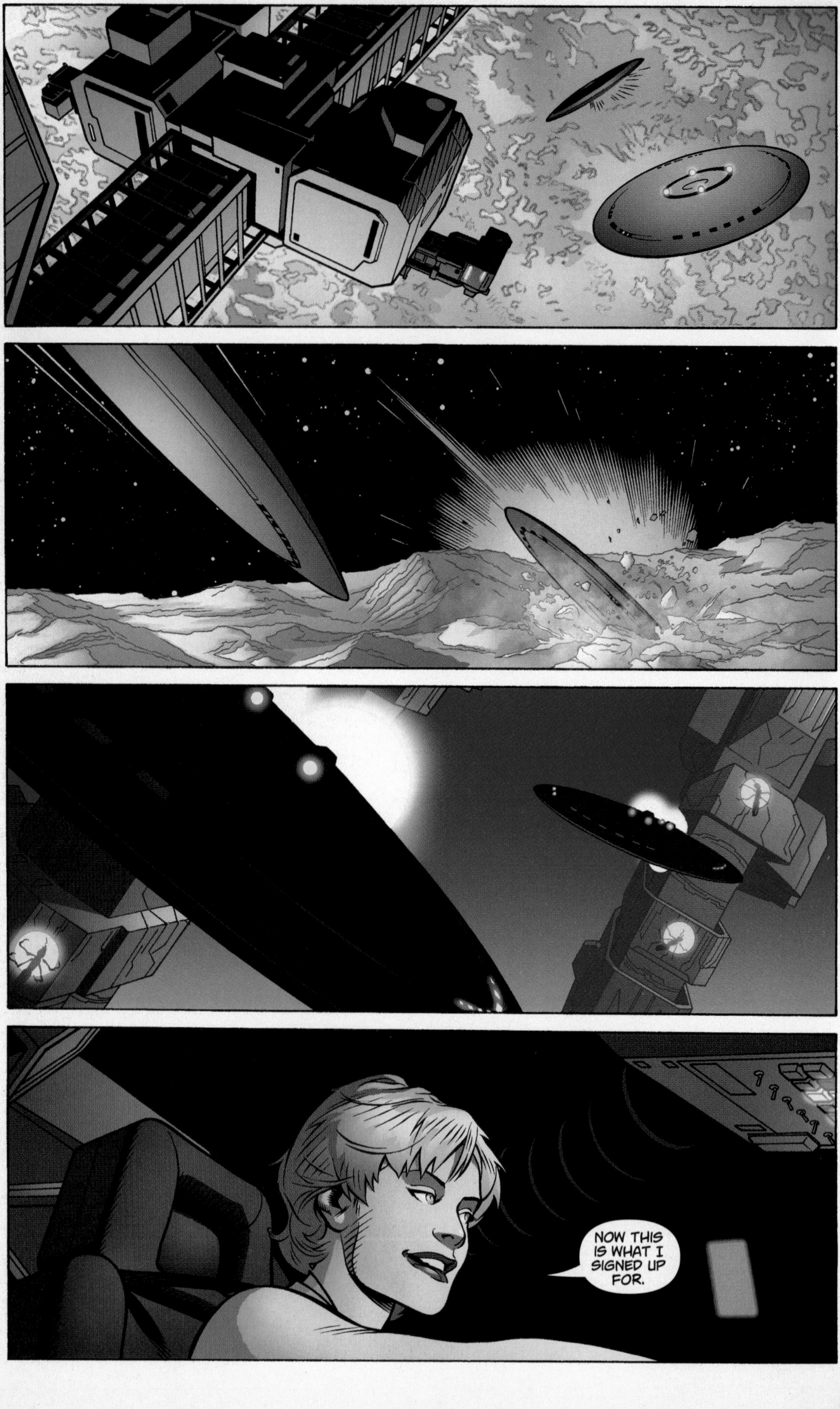
NOW THIS IS WHAT I SIGNED UP FOR.

ANNA, DO WE STILL HAVE OUR OWN PROBES DOWN THERE?

YES. WHY?

IF I CAN USE THEM TO HACK INTO ONE OF THEIR PROBES, I CAN RIDE THEIR COMMUNICATIONS BEAMS RIGHT INTO THE CONTROL SYSTEM OF ONE OF THOSE GUNS.

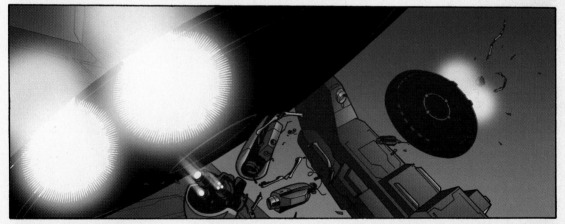

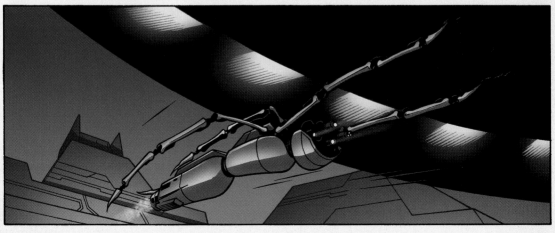

SIOBHAN, CAN YOU TAKE A LOOK UNDER MY DISK? HALF MY HULL ALARMS JUST LIT UP.

ONE OF THE BASTARDS IS HANGING ON TO YOU.

IT'S TRYING TO OPEN YOUR HATCH, FADIA...

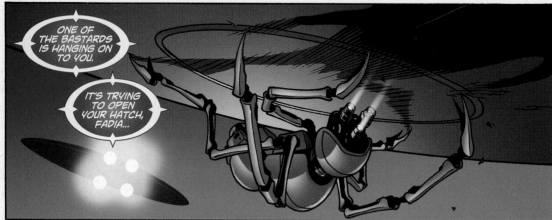

COME ON, COME ON, LET ME IN...

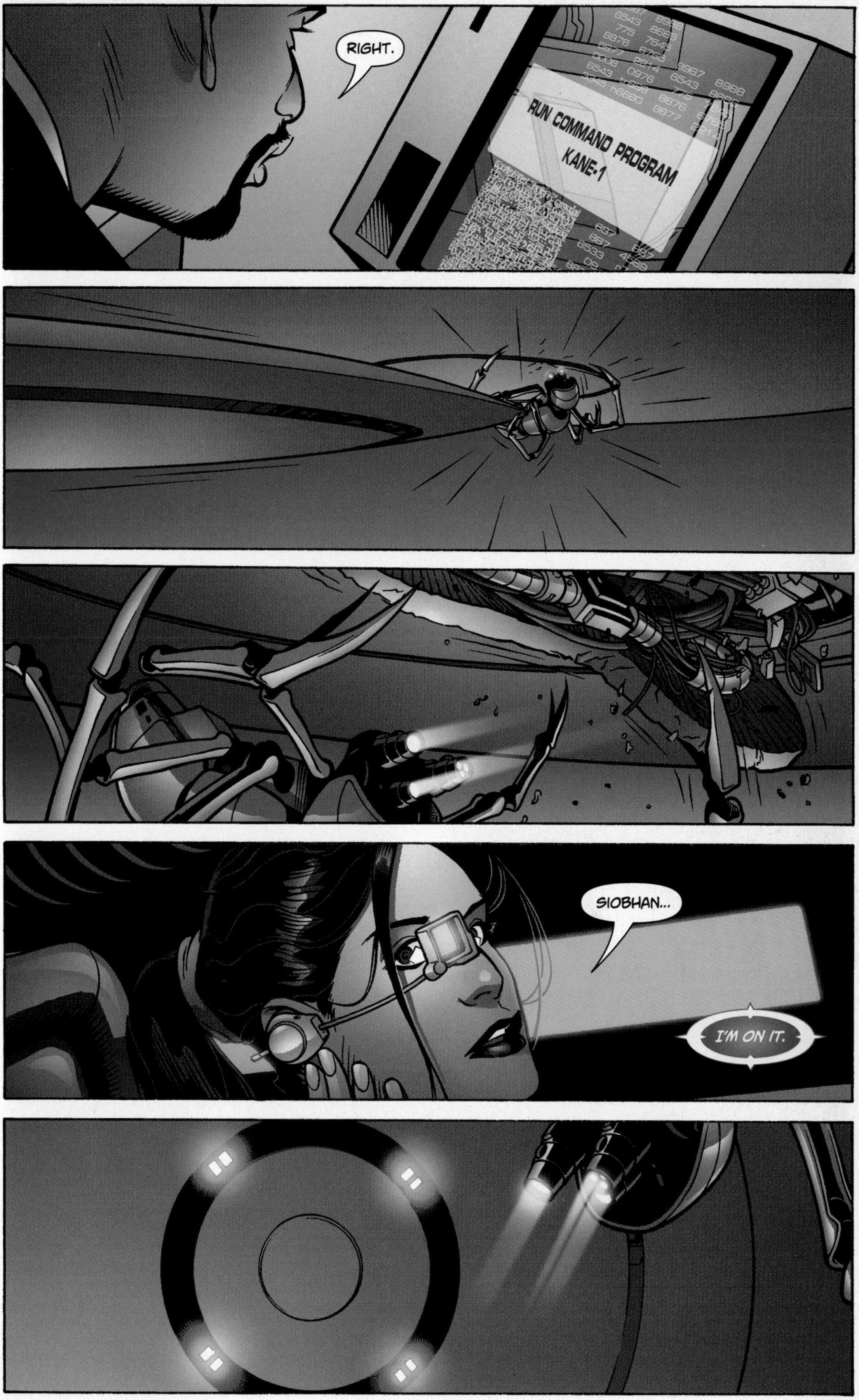
RIGHT.
RUN COMMAND PROGRAM
KANE-1
SIOBHAN...
I'M ON IT.

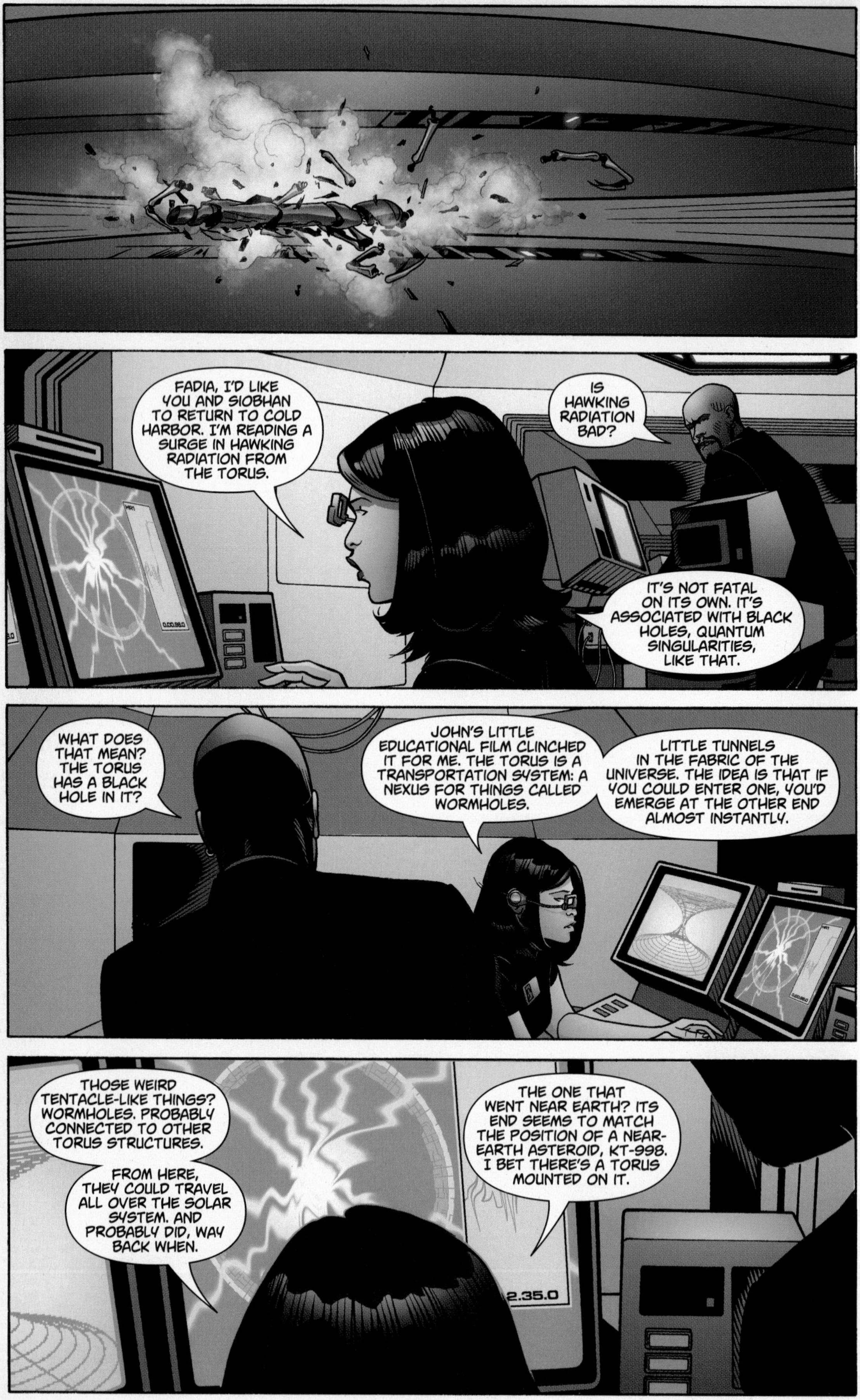
FADIA, I'D LIKE YOU AND SIOBHAN TO RETURN TO COLD HARBOR. I'M READING A SURGE IN HAWKING RADIATION FROM THE TORUS.
IS HAWKING RADIATION BAD?
IT'S NOT FATAL ON ITS OWN. IT'S ASSOCIATED WITH BLACK HOLES, QUANTUM SINGULARITIES, LIKE THAT.
WHAT DOES THAT MEAN? THE TORUS HAS A BLACK HOLE IN IT?
JOHN'S LITTLE EDUCATIONAL FILM CLINCHED IT FOR ME. THE TORUS IS A TRANSPORTATION SYSTEM: A NEXUS FOR THINGS CALLED WORMHOLES.
LITTLE TUNNELS IN THE FABRIC OF THE UNIVERSE. THE IDEA IS THAT IF YOU COULD ENTER ONE, YOU'D EMERGE AT THE OTHER END ALMOST INSTANTLY.
THOSE WEIRD TENTACLE-LIKE THINGS? WORMHOLES. PROBABLY CONNECTED TO OTHER TORUS STRUCTURES.
FROM HERE, THEY COULD TRAVEL ALL OVER THE SOLAR SYSTEM. AND PROBABLY DID, WAY BACK WHEN.
THE ONE THAT WENT NEAR EARTH? ITS END SEEMS TO MATCH THE POSITION OF A NEAR-EARTH ASTEROID, KT-998. I BET THERE'S A TORUS MOUNTED ON IT.
2.35.0

THIS IS EXTREMELY BAD NEWS.

YOU'LL NOTE I'M NOT EXACTLY DANCING.

THEY COULD WAKE UP, GRAB THEIR GUNS, AND DROP THROUGH THE TORUS INTO NEAR-EARTH SPACE TO SEE HOW THE KIDS ARE DOING.

IS IT BEING COMMANDED?

THERE WE GO... THAT'S WHY WE'RE GETTING A SURGE. IT'S COLLAPSING A NUMBER OF THE WORMHOLES DOWN.

NO, THIS LOOKS LIKE PRE-PROGRAMMED ACTION. THERE GO MORE OF THEM... BUT THE RADIATION LEVEL ISN'T DROPPING.

JESUS, LOOK AT THAT... SHOULDN'T THERE BE LESS HAWKING RADIATION IF THERE ARE LESS WORMHOLES?

YES, THERE DAMN WELL SHOULD. UNLESS... ISOLATE STREAM 088. DISPLAY.

THE OTHERS ARE COLLAPSING SO THAT THE TORUS CAN DIRECT ALL ITS POWER INTO THIS ONE AND OPEN IT RIGHT UP.

WHERE DOES IT GO?

ASTEROID KT-998. A QUARTER OF A MILLION MILES FROM EARTH. THE RELATIVES ARE COMING FOR DINNER.

088

0.02.35.0

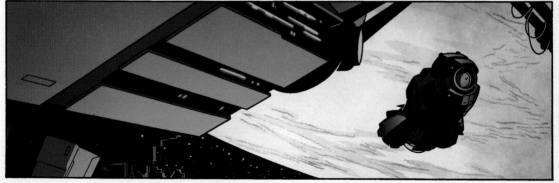

YOU OKAY?

I'M ALIVE.

SIOBHAN?

WEIRDLY HORNY.

WHAT?

WE'VE GOT A HULL BREACH ON THE NORTH SIDE.

THE BASTARDS ARE CUTTING THEIR WAY IN.

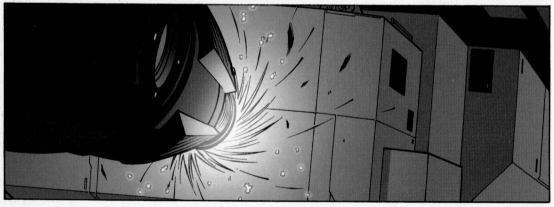

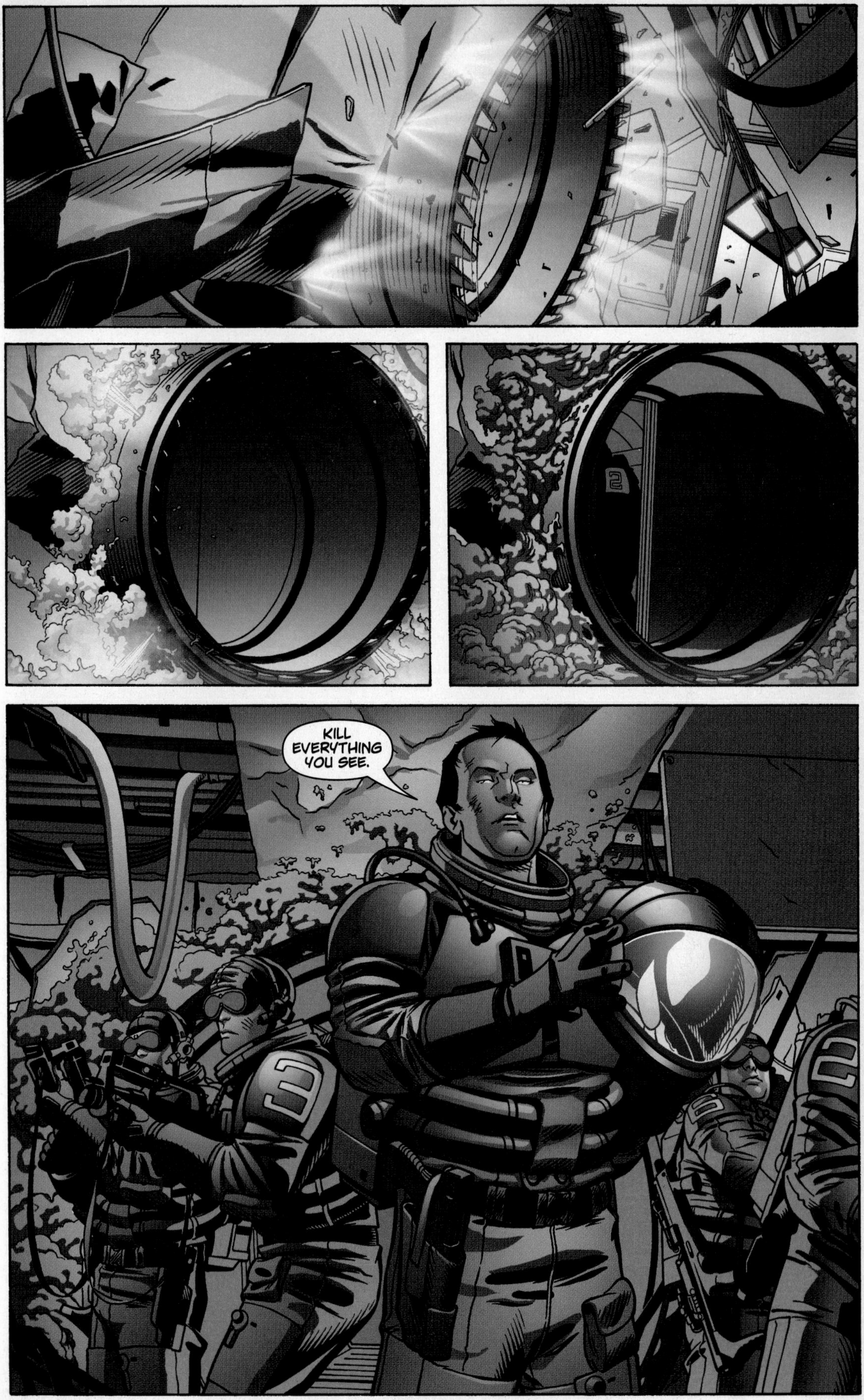
KILL EVERYTHING YOU SEE.

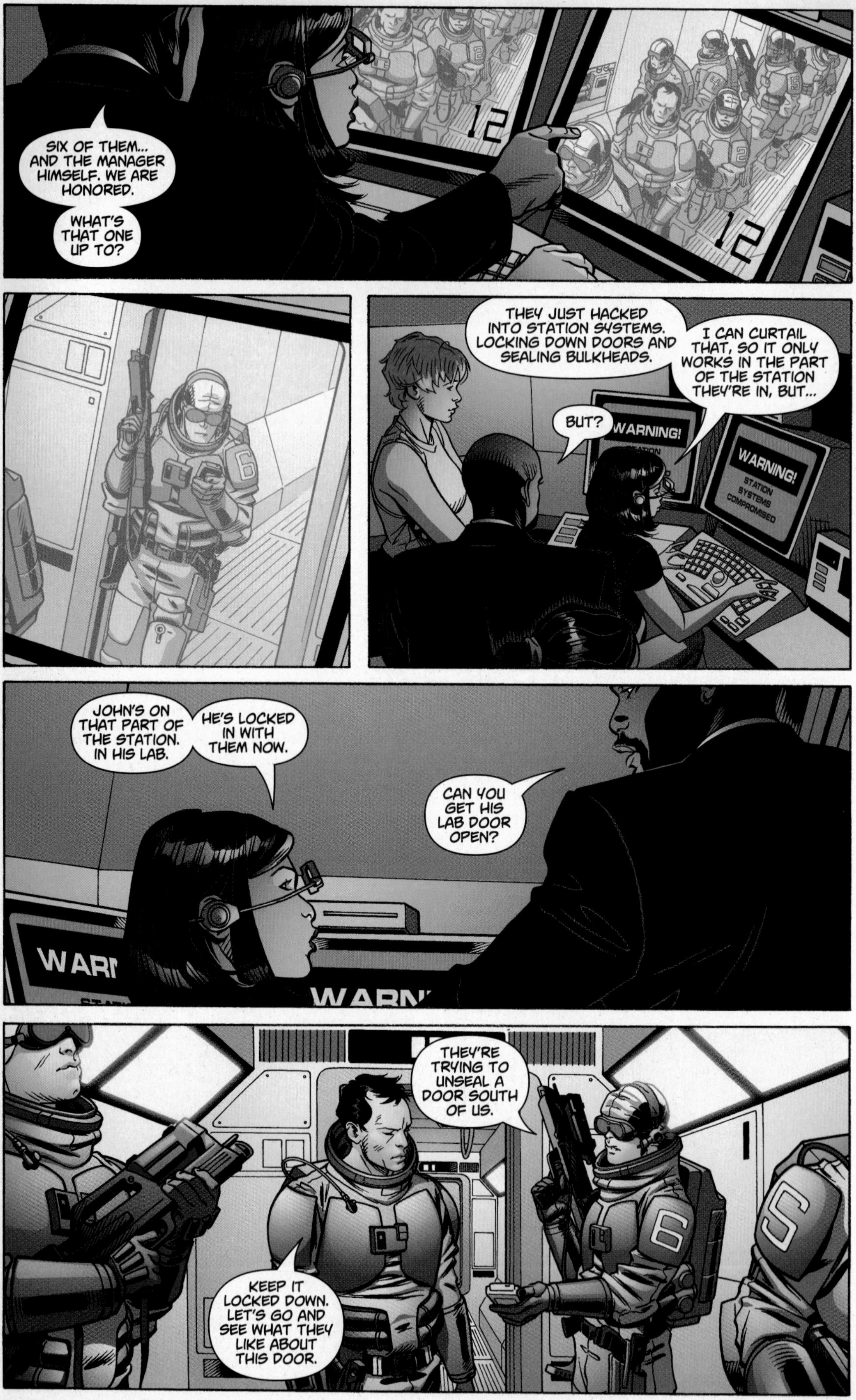
SIX OF THEM... AND THE MANAGER HIMSELF. WE ARE HONORED.
WHAT'S THAT ONE UP TO?
12
12
6
THEY JUST HACKED INTO STATION SYSTEMS. LOCKING DOWN DOORS AND SEALING BULKHEADS.
I CAN CURTAIL THAT, SO IT ONLY WORKS IN THE PART OF THE STATION THEY'RE IN, BUT...
BUT?
WARNING!
WARNING! STATION SYSTEMS COMPROMISED
JOHN'S ON THAT PART OF THE STATION. IN HIS LAB.
HE'S LOCKED IN WITH THEM NOW.
CAN YOU GET HIS LAB DOOR OPEN?
THEY'RE TRYING TO UNSEAL A DOOR SOUTH OF US.
KEEP IT LOCKED DOWN. LET'S GO AND SEE WHAT THEY LIKE ABOUT THIS DOOR.

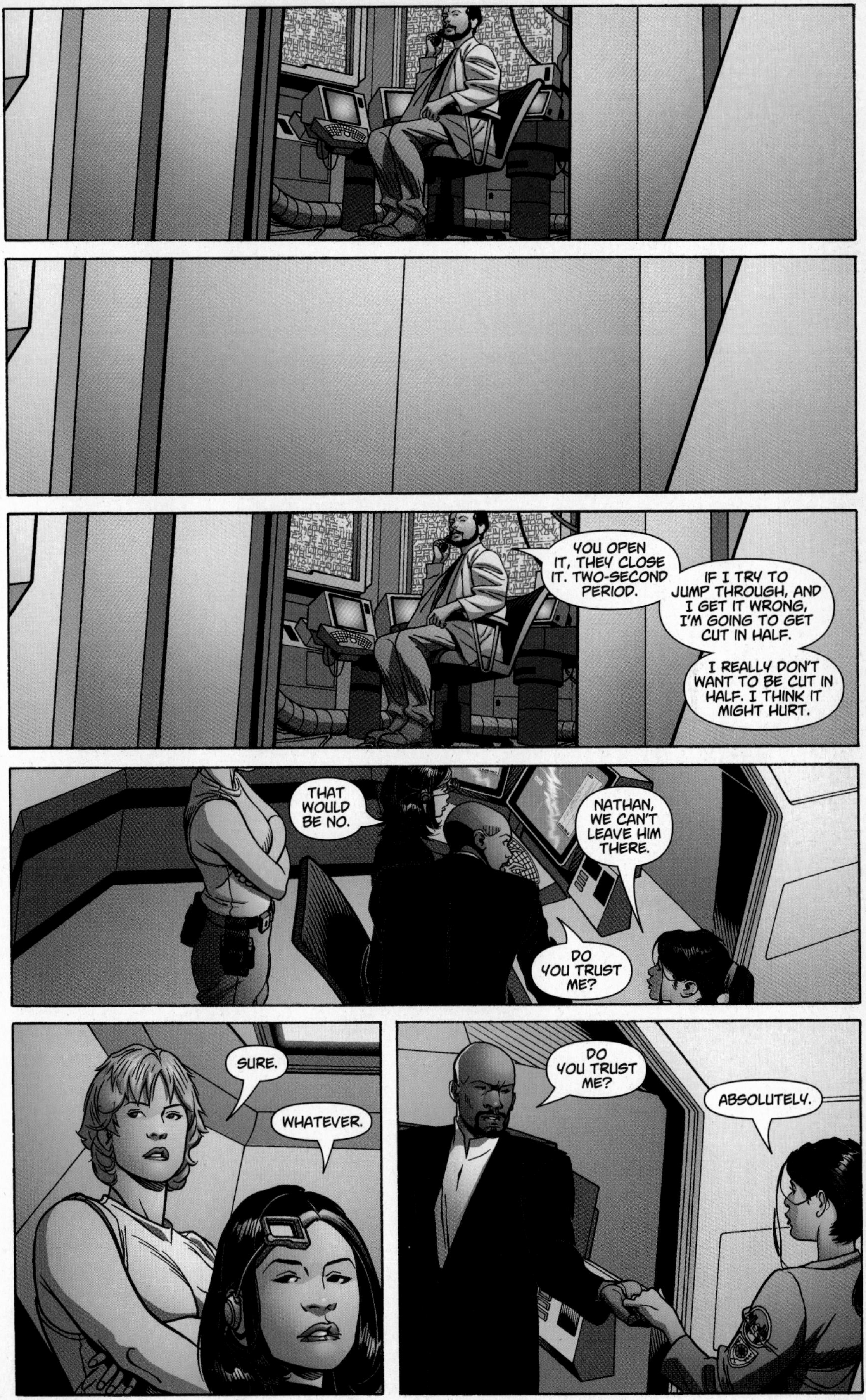
YOU OPEN IT, THEY CLOSE IT. TWO-SECOND PERIOD.
IF I TRY TO JUMP THROUGH, AND I GET IT WRONG, I'M GOING TO GET CUT IN HALF.
I REALLY DON'T WANT TO BE CUT IN HALF. I THINK IT MIGHT HURT.
THAT WOULD BE NO.
NATHAN, WE CAN'T LEAVE HIM THERE.
DO YOU TRUST ME?
SURE.
WHATEVER.
DO YOU TRUST ME?
ABSOLUTELY.

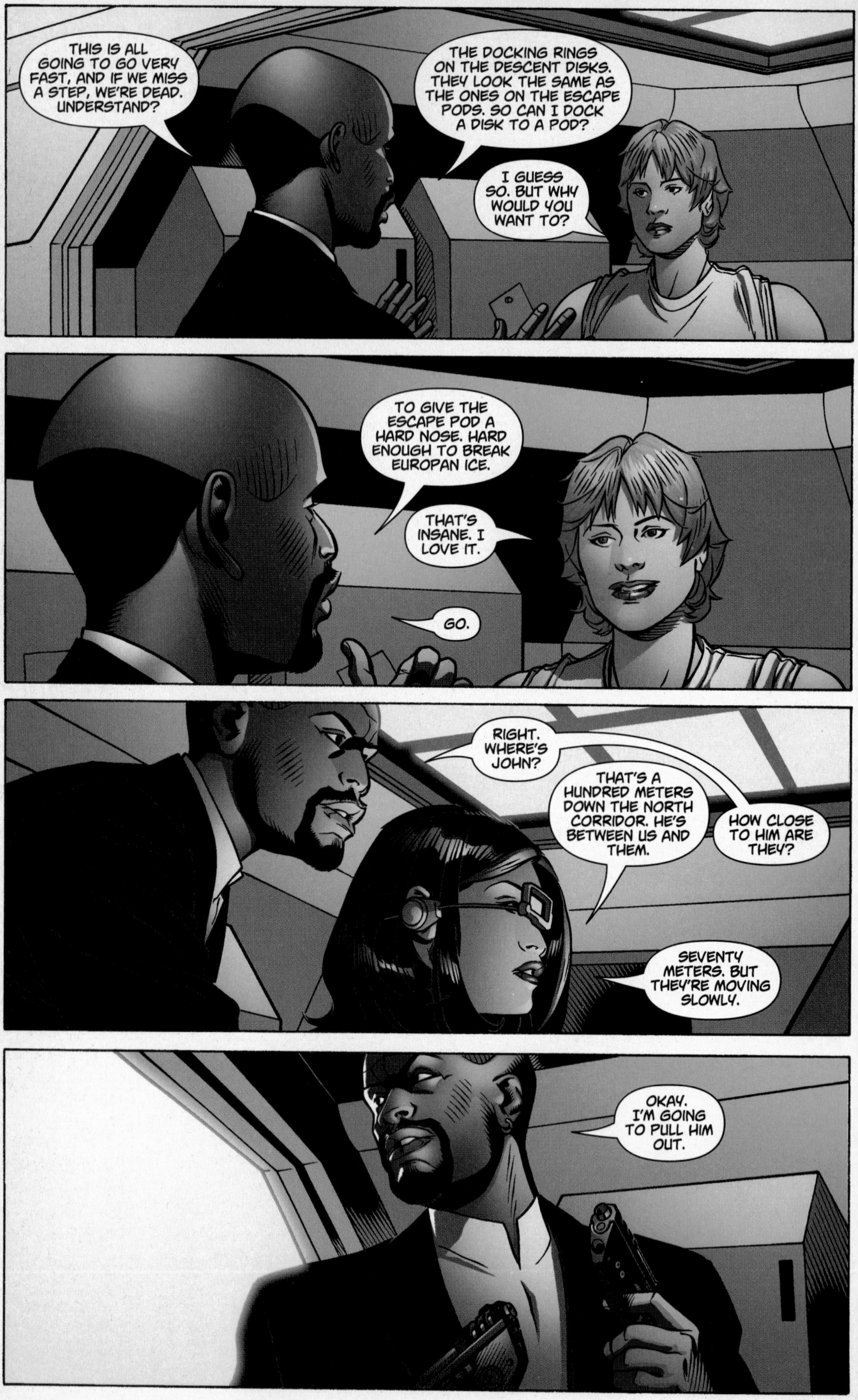
THIS IS ALL GOING TO GO VERY FAST, AND IF WE MISS A STEP, WE'RE DEAD. UNDERSTAND?
THE DOCKING RINGS ON THE DESCENT DISKS. THEY LOOK THE SAME AS THE ONES ON THE ESCAPE PODS. SO CAN I DOCK A DISK TO A POD?
I GUESS SO. BUT WHY WOULD YOU WANT TO?
TO GIVE THE ESCAPE POD A HARD NOSE. HARD ENOUGH TO BREAK EUROPAN ICE.
THAT'S INSANE. I LOVE IT.
GO.
RIGHT. WHERE'S JOHN?
THAT'S A HUNDRED METERS DOWN THE NORTH CORRIDOR. HE'S BETWEEN US AND THEM.
HOW CLOSE TO HIM ARE THEY?
SEVENTY METERS. BUT THEY'RE MOVING SLOWLY.
OKAY. I'M GOING TO PULL HIM OUT.

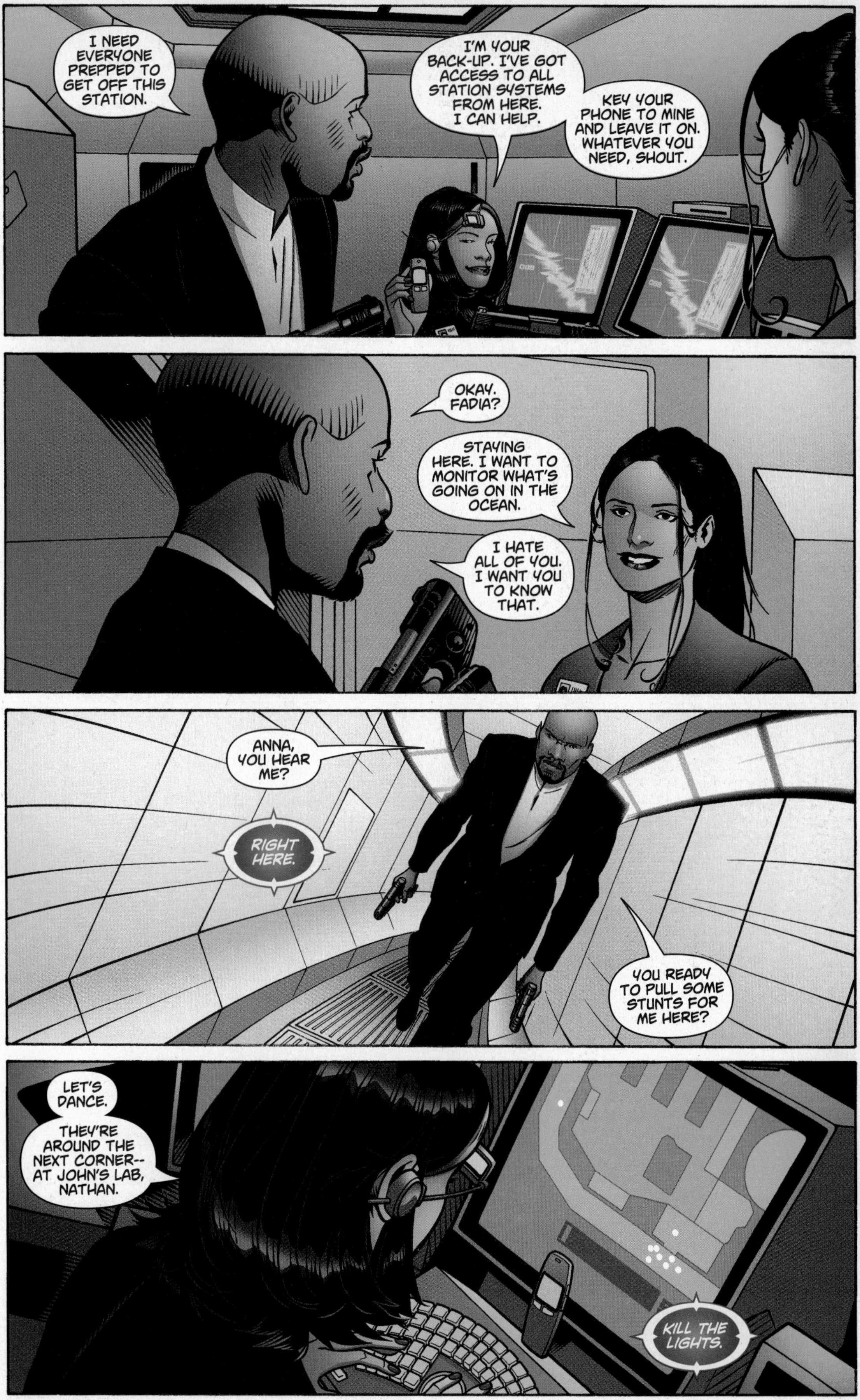

I NEED EVERYONE PREPPED TO GET OFF THIS STATION.
I'M YOUR BACK-UP. I'VE GOT ACCESS TO ALL STATION SYSTEMS FROM HERE. I CAN HELP.
KEY YOUR PHONE TO MINE AND LEAVE IT ON. WHATEVER YOU NEED, SHOUT.
OKAY. FADIA?
STAYING HERE. I WANT TO MONITOR WHAT'S GOING ON IN THE OCEAN.
I HATE ALL OF YOU. I WANT YOU TO KNOW THAT.
ANNA, YOU HEAR ME?
RIGHT HERE.
YOU READY TO PULL SOME STUNTS FOR ME HERE?
LET'S DANCE.
THEY'RE AROUND THE NEXT CORNER-- AT JOHN'S LAB, NATHAN.
KILL THE LIGHTS.

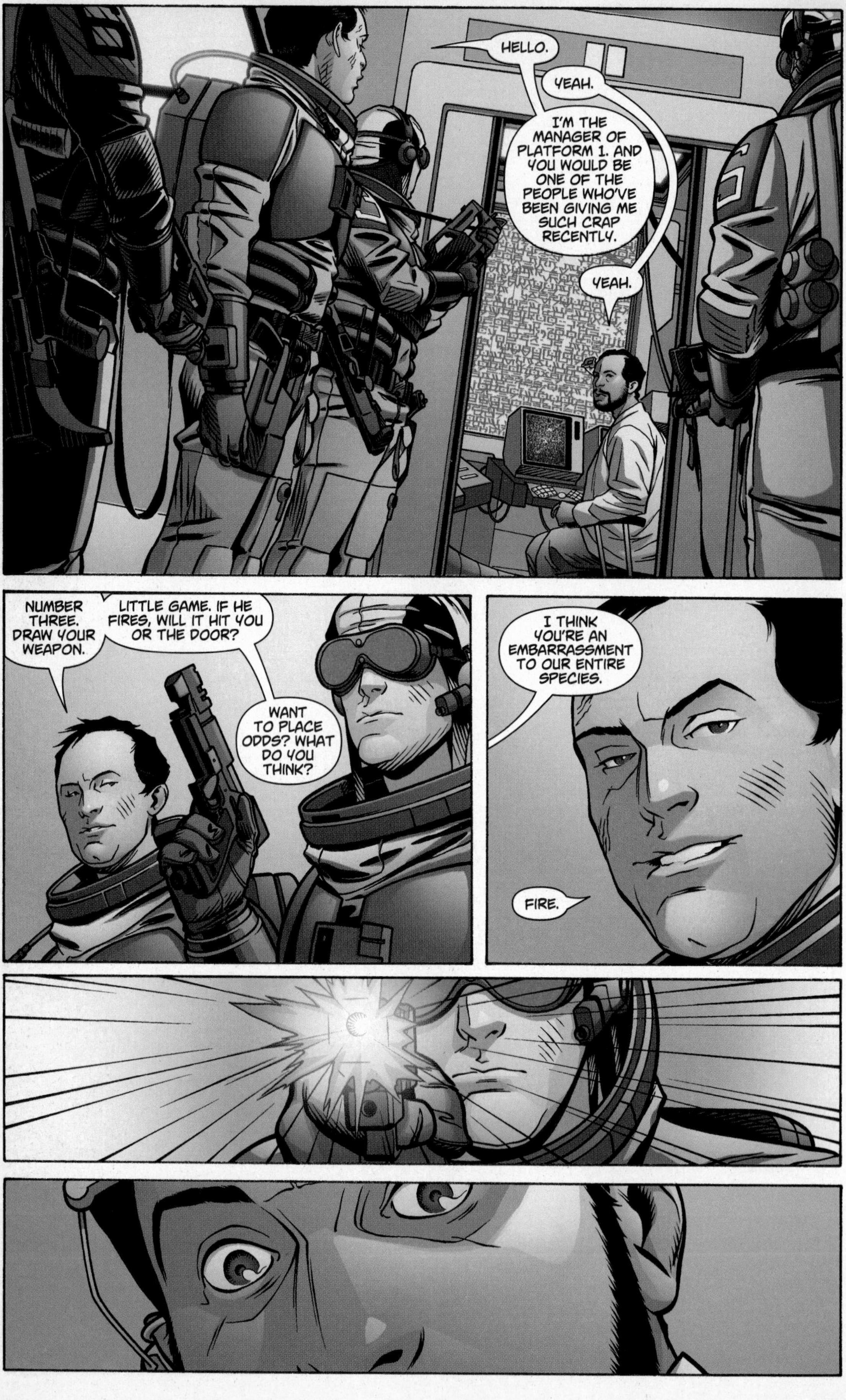
HELLO.
YEAH.
I'M THE MANAGER OF PLATFORM 1. AND YOU WOULD BE ONE OF THE PEOPLE WHO'VE BEEN GIVING ME SUCH CRAP RECENTLY.
YEAH.
NUMBER THREE. DRAW YOUR WEAPON.
LITTLE GAME. IF HE FIRES, WILL IT HIT YOU OR THE DOOR?
WANT TO PLACE ODDS? WHAT DO YOU THINK?
I THINK YOU'RE AN EMBARRASSMENT TO OUR ENTIRE SPECIES.
FIRE.

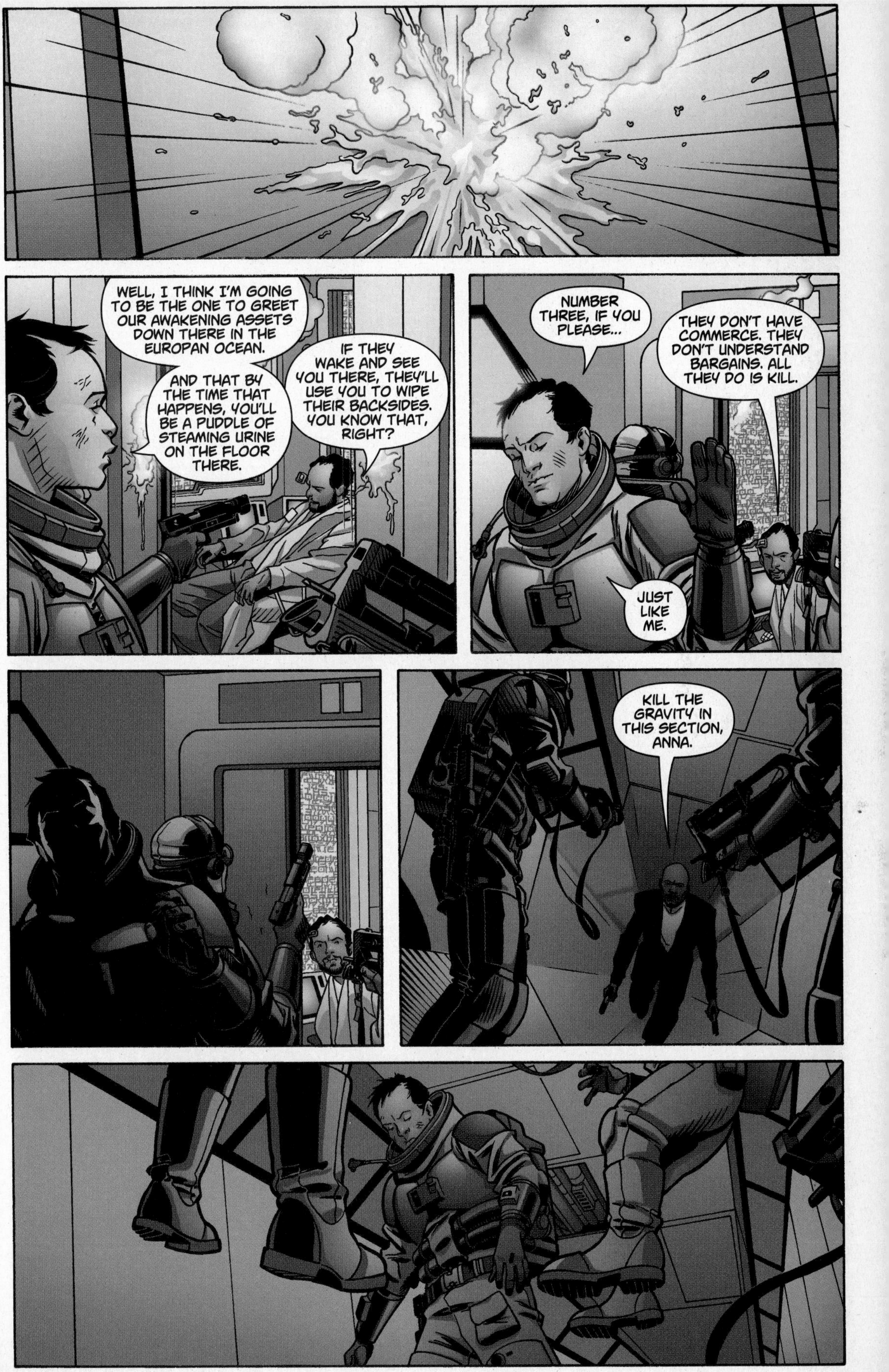
WELL, I THINK I'M GOING TO BE THE ONE TO GREET OUR AWAKENING ASSETS DOWN THERE IN THE EUROPAN OCEAN.
AND THAT BY THE TIME THAT HAPPENS, YOU'LL BE A PUDDLE OF STEAMING URINE ON THE FLOOR THERE.
IF THEY WAKE AND SEE YOU THERE, THEY'LL USE YOU TO WIPE THEIR BACKSIDES. YOU KNOW THAT, RIGHT?
NUMBER THREE, IF YOU PLEASE...
THEY DON'T HAVE COMMERCE. THEY DON'T UNDERSTAND BARGAINS. ALL THEY DO IS KILL.
JUST LIKE ME.
KILL THE GRAVITY IN THIS SECTION, ANNA.

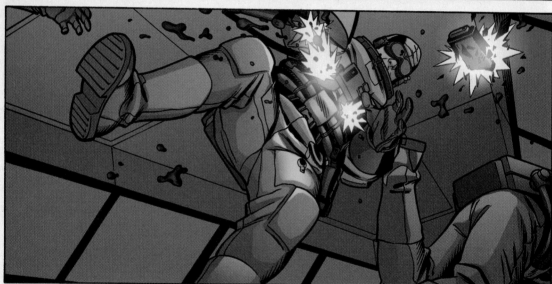

ANNA: GRAVITY.

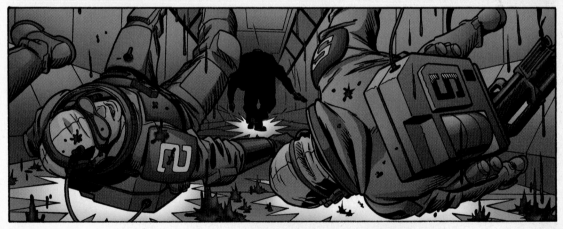

LIGHTS.

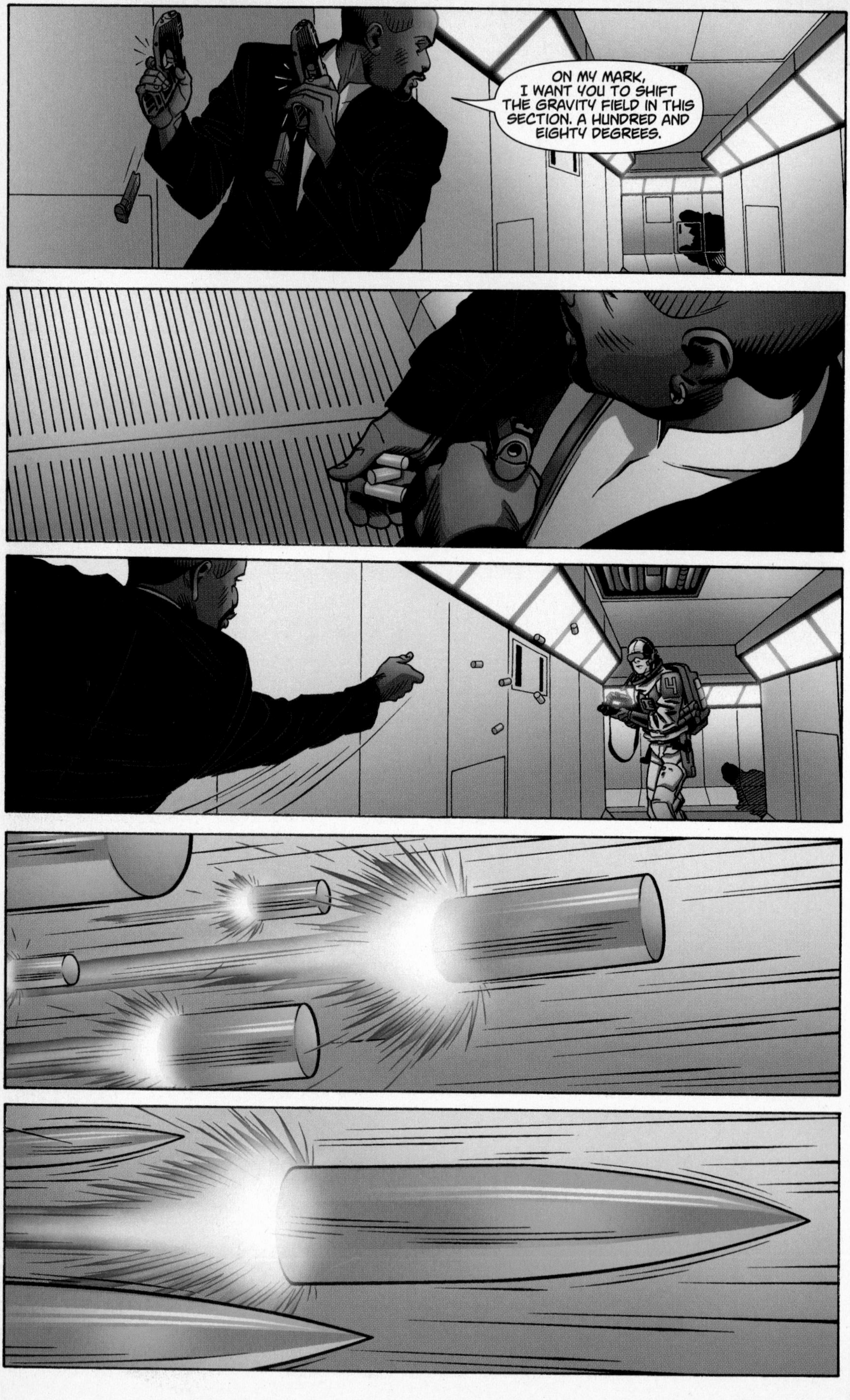
ON MY MARK, I WANT YOU TO SHIFT THE GRAVITY FIELD IN THIS SECTION. A HUNDRED AND EIGHTY DEGREES.

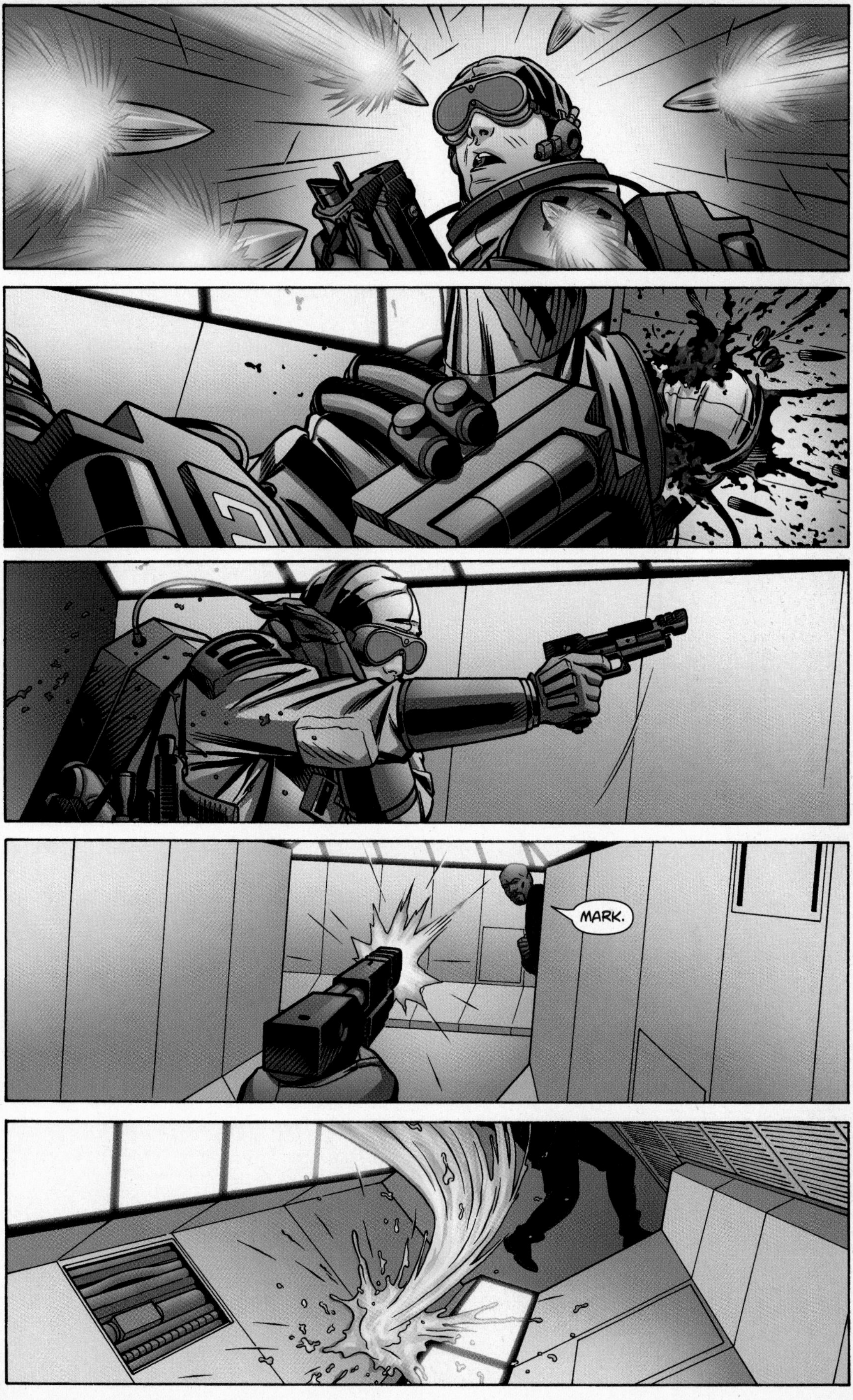
MARK.

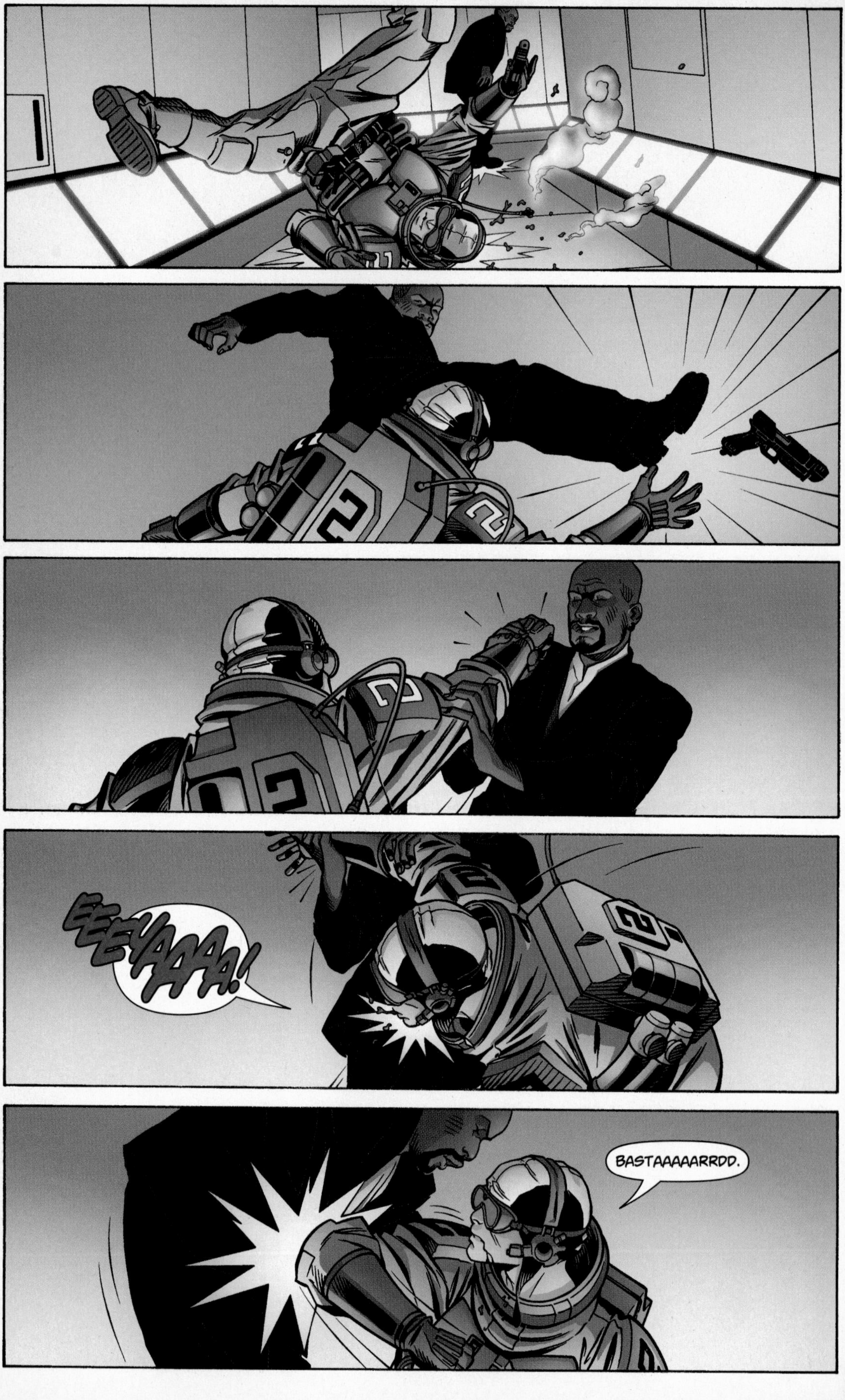
EEEYAAAA!
BASTAAAAARRDD.

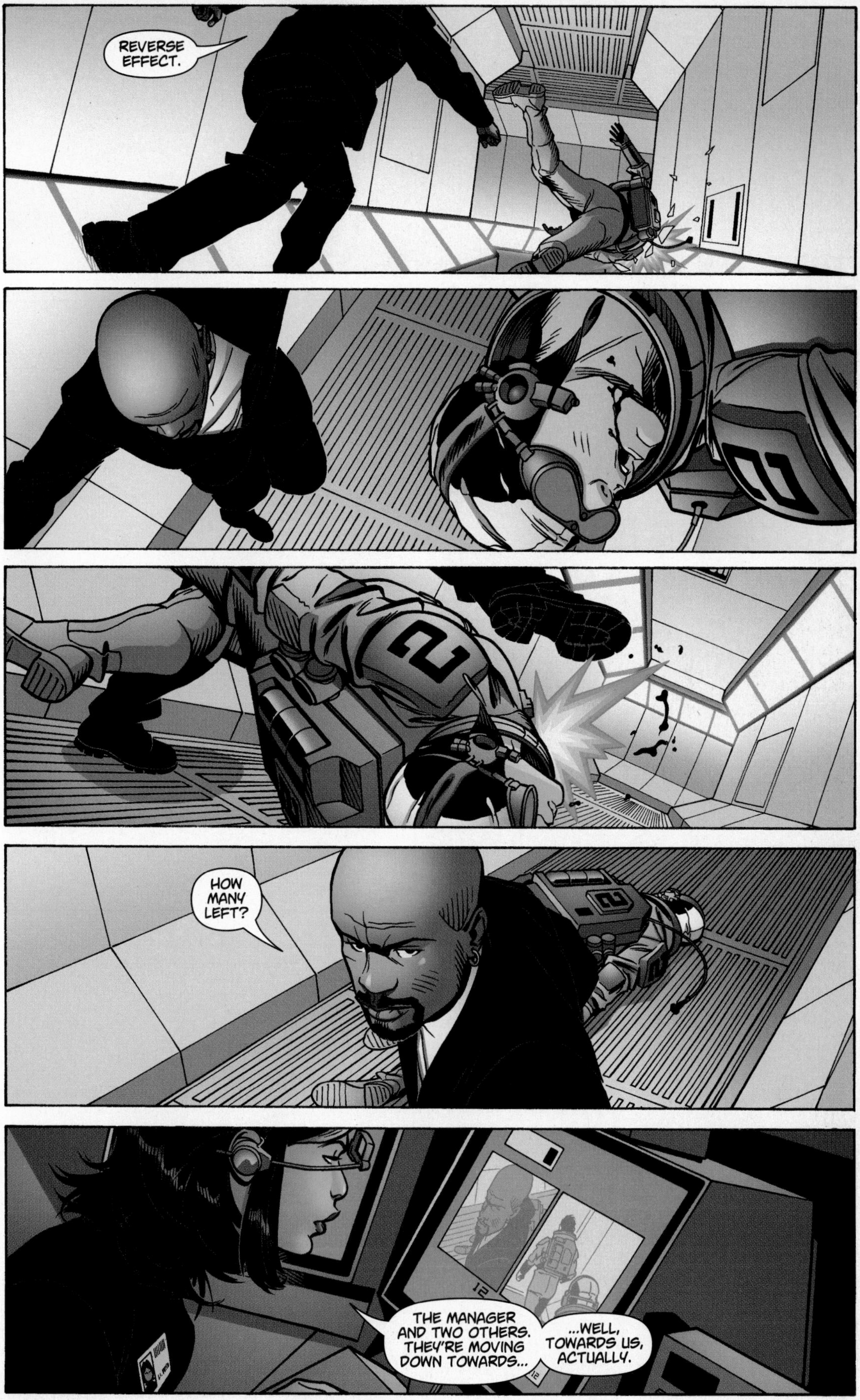
REVERSE EFFECT.
HOW MANY LEFT?
THE MANAGER AND TWO OTHERS. THEY'RE MOVING DOWN TOWARDS...
...WELL, TOWARDS US, ACTUALLY.

TAKE A COUPLE OF STEPS BACK, JOHN.

NOW WHAT?

NOW WE TRY NOT TO DIE SOME MORE.

NATHAN; THE GUNS ARE POWERED UP.

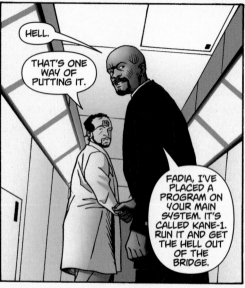

HELL.

THAT'S ONE WAY OF PUTTING IT.

FADIA, I'VE PLACED A PROGRAM ON YOUR MAIN SYSTEM. IT'S CALLED KANE-1. RUN IT AND GET THE HELL OUT OF THE BRIDGE.

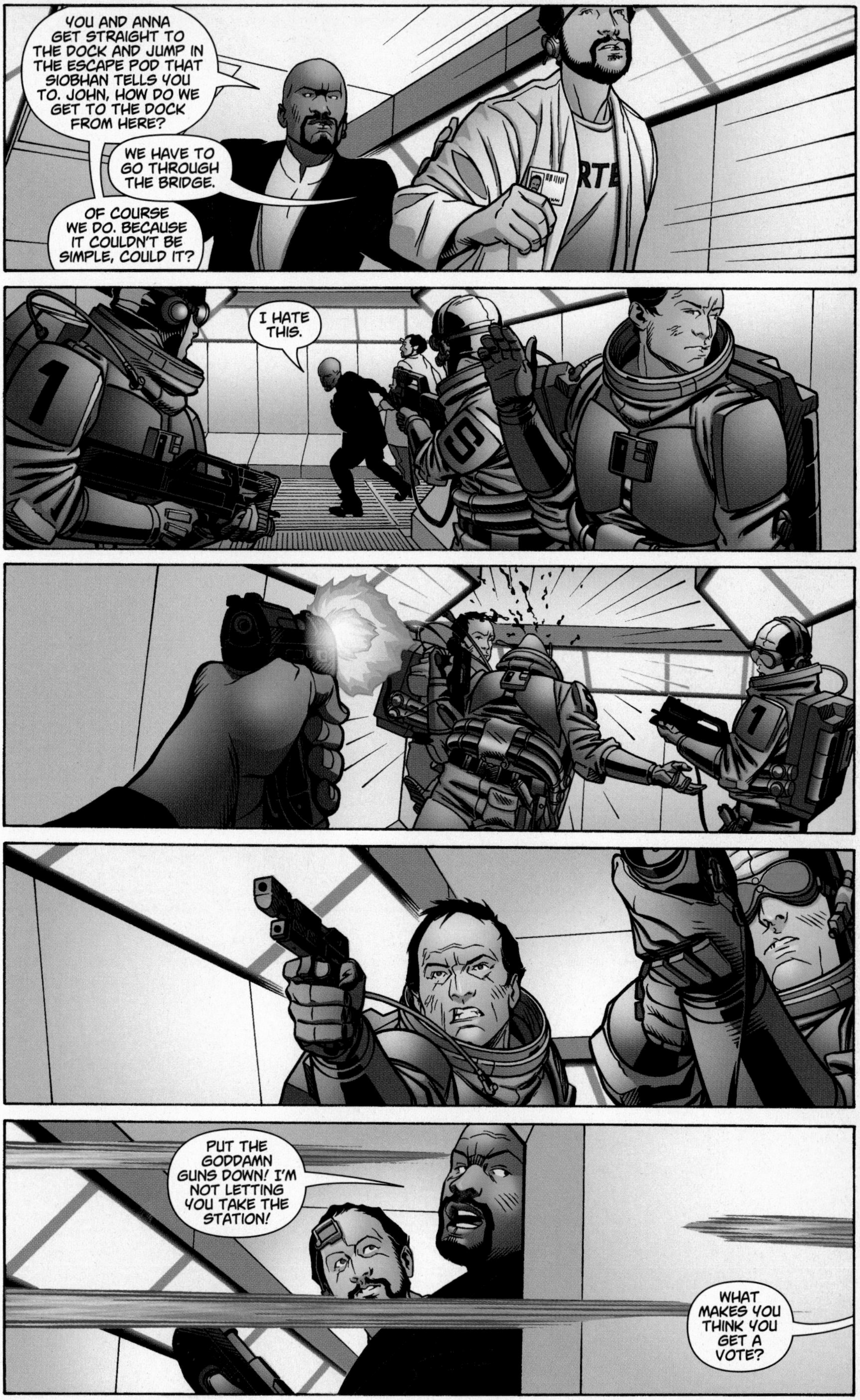
YOU AND ANNA GET STRAIGHT TO THE DOCK AND JUMP IN THE ESCAPE POD THAT SIOBHAN TELLS YOU TO. JOHN, HOW DO WE GET TO THE DOCK FROM HERE?
WE HAVE TO GO THROUGH THE BRIDGE.
OF COURSE WE DO. BECAUSE IT COULDN'T BE SIMPLE, COULD IT?
I HATE THIS.
PUT THE GODDAMN GUNS DOWN! I'M NOT LETTING YOU TAKE THE STATION!
WHAT MAKES YOU THINK YOU GET A VOTE?

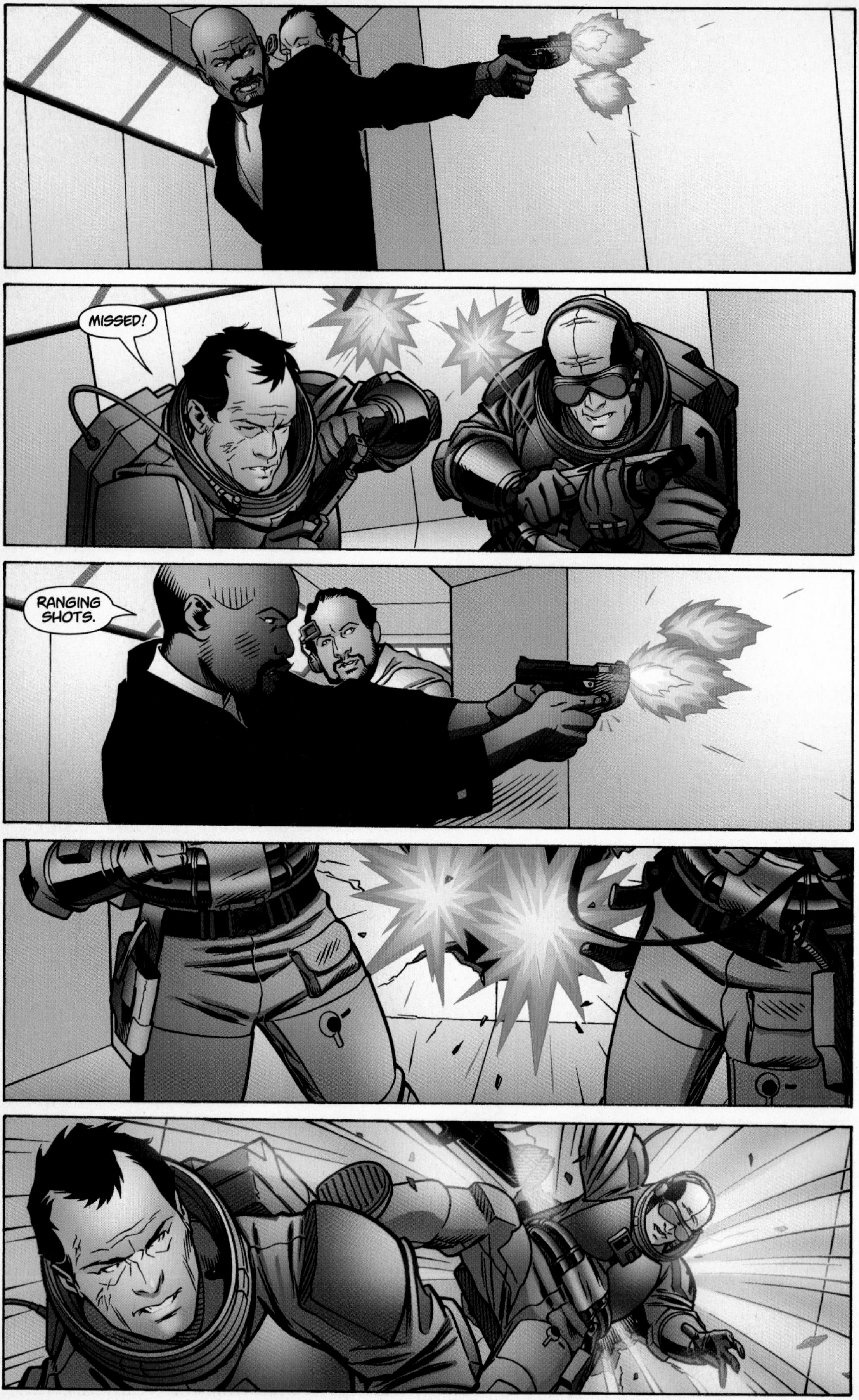
MISSED!
RANGING SHOTS.

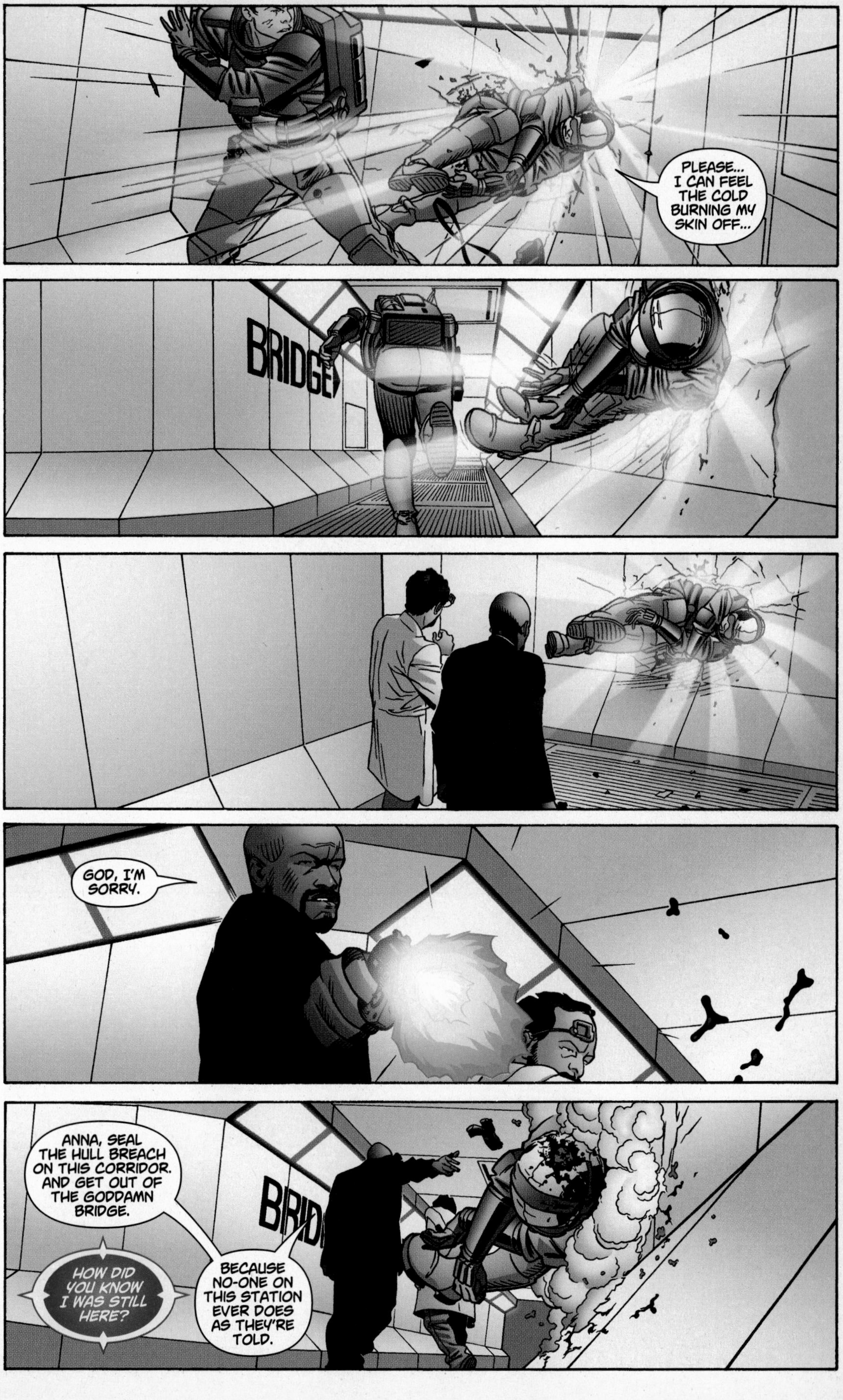
PLEASE... I CAN FEEL THE COLD BURNING MY SKIN OFF...
BRIDGE
GOD, I'M SORRY.
ANNA, SEAL THE HULL BREACH ON THIS CORRIDOR. AND GET OUT OF THE GODDAMN BRIDGE.
HOW DID YOU KNOW I WAS STILL HERE?
BECAUSE NO-ONE ON THIS STATION EVER DOES AS THEY'RE TOLD.

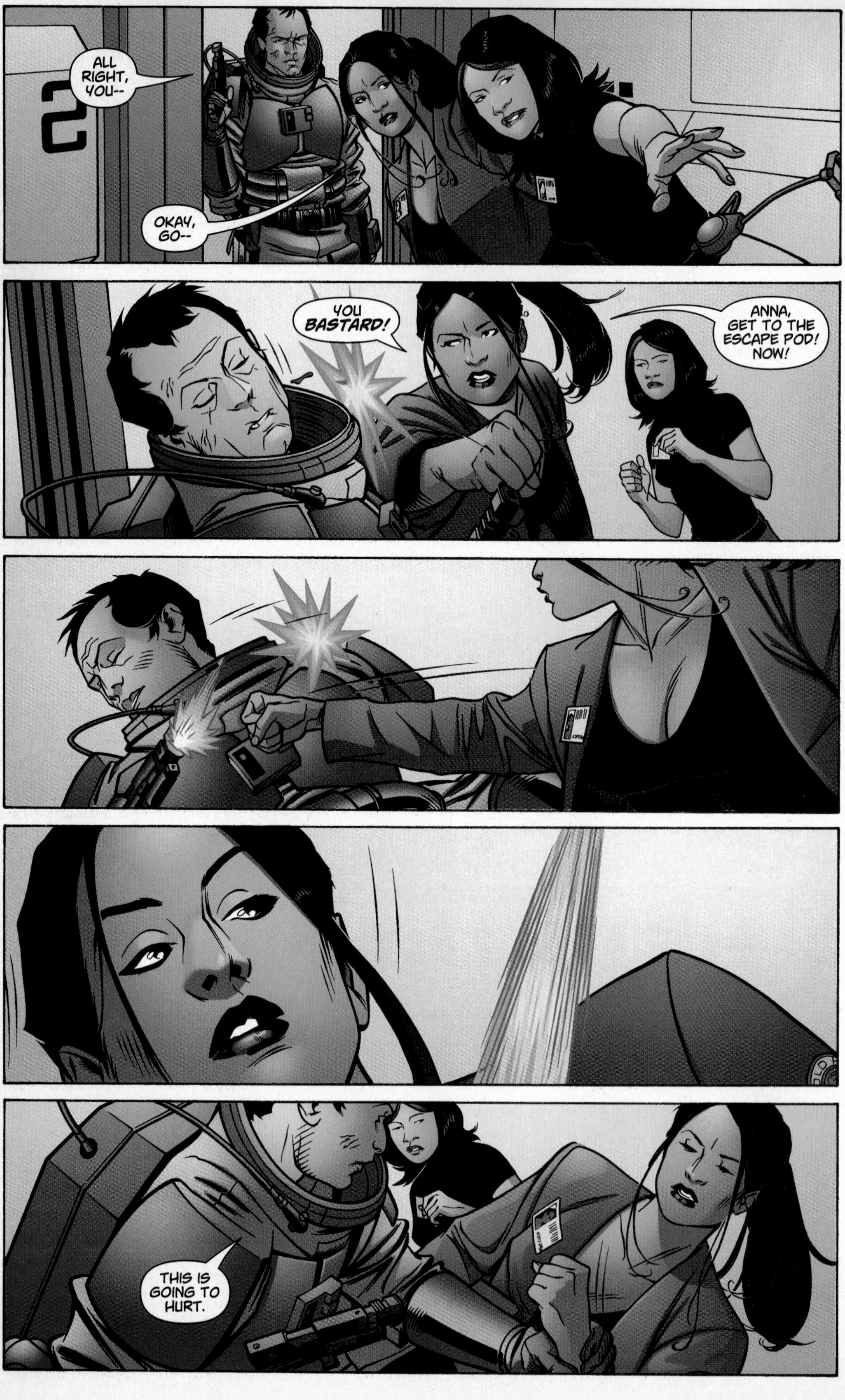
ALL RIGHT, YOU--
OKAY, GO--
YOU BASTARD!
ANNA, GET TO THE ESCAPE POD! NOW!
THIS IS GOING TO HURT.

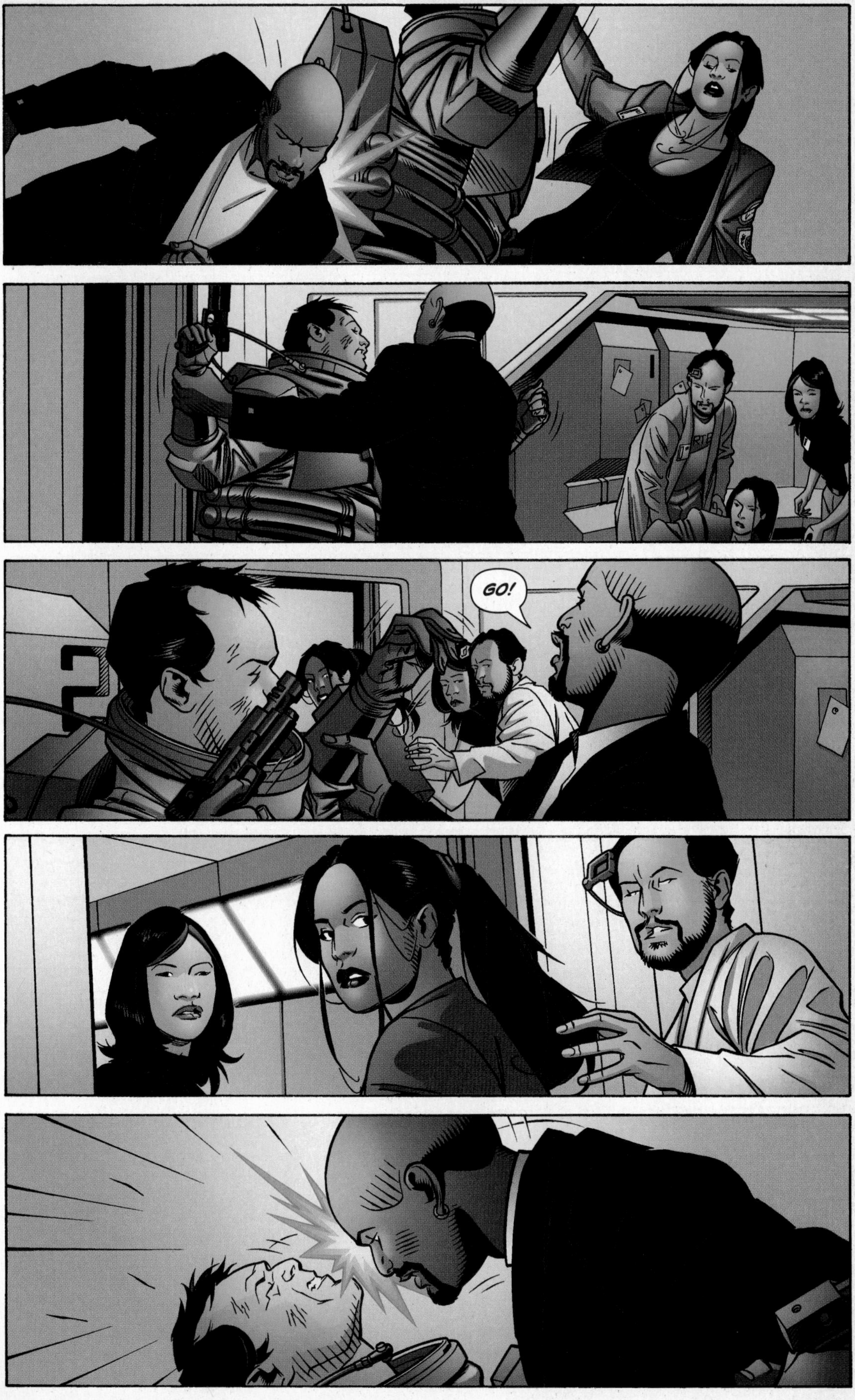
GO!

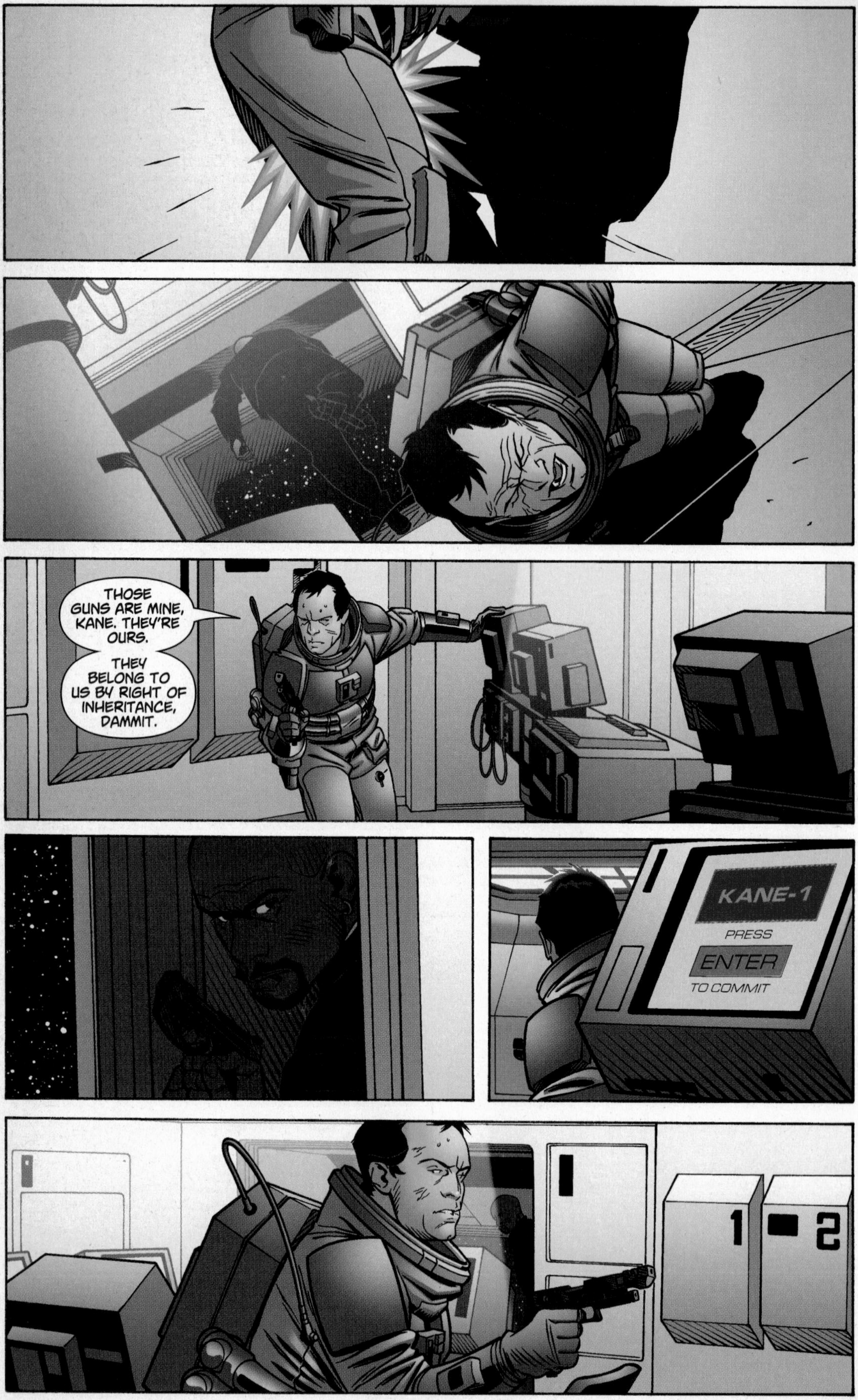
THOSE GUNS ARE MINE, KANE. THEY'RE OURS.
THEY BELONG TO US BY RIGHT OF INHERITANCE, DAMMIT.
KANE-1
PRESS
ENTER
TO COMMIT
1
2

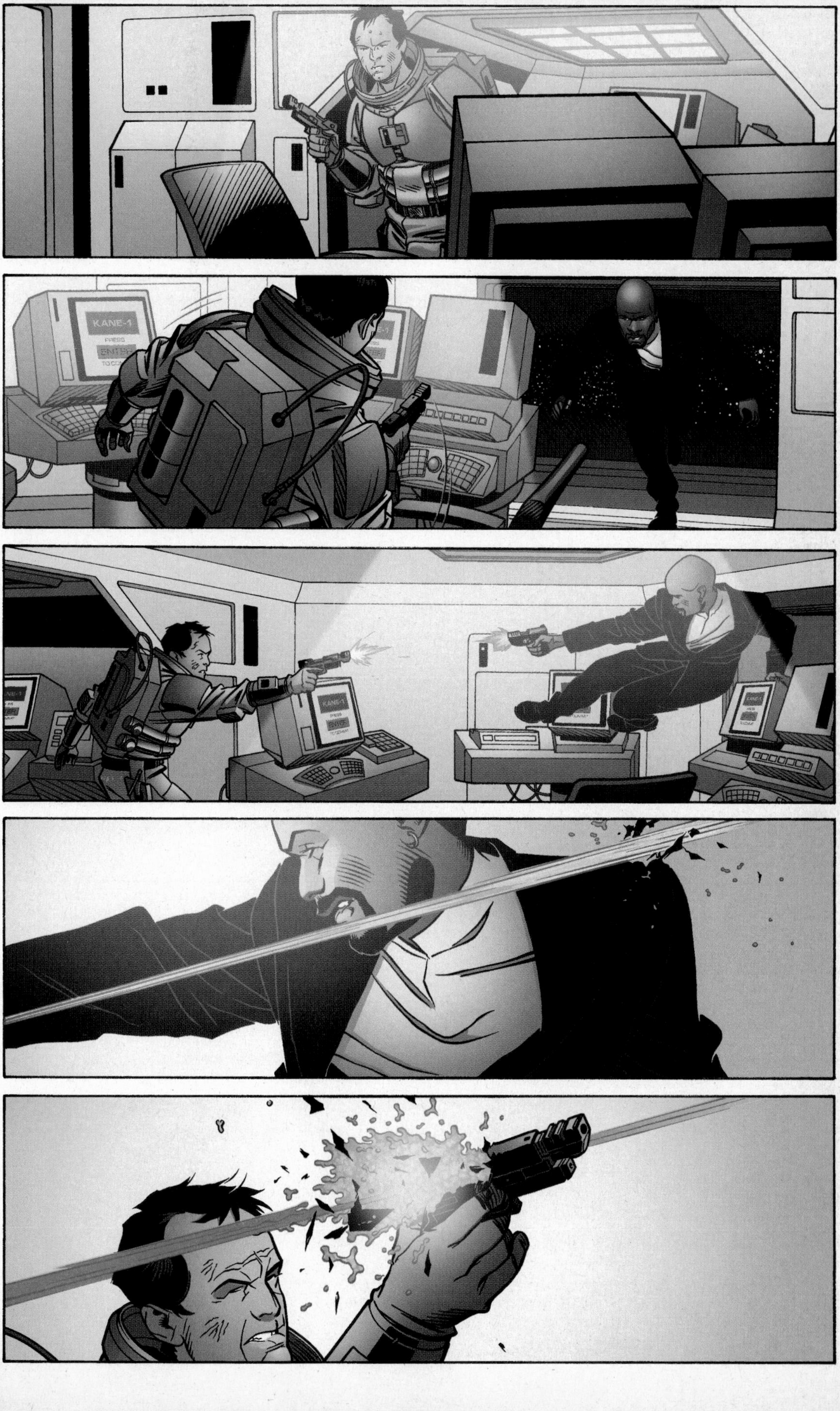
KANE-1

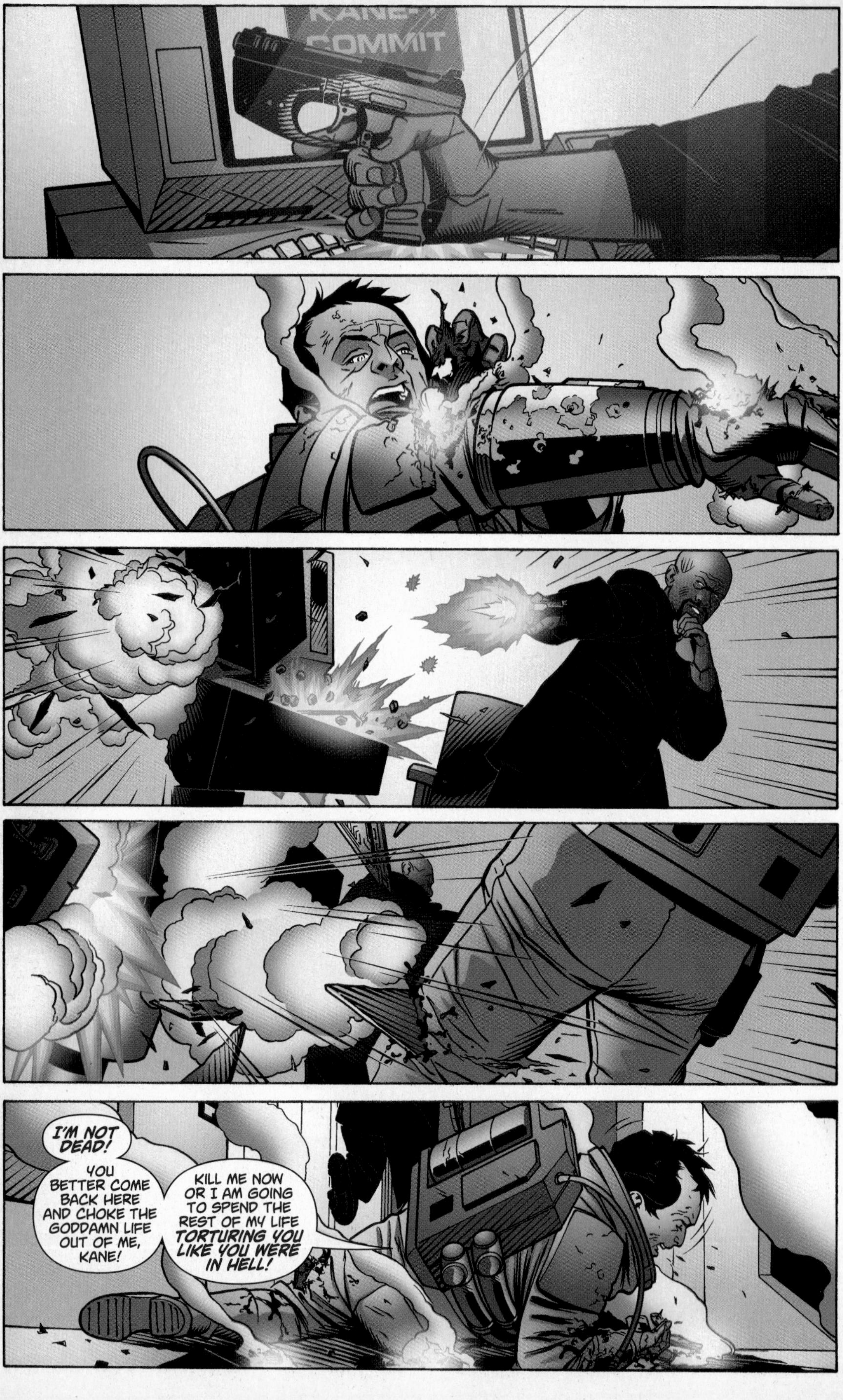
KANE-
COMMIT
I'M NOT DEAD!
YOU BETTER COME BACK HERE AND CHOKE THE GODDAMN LIFE OUT OF ME, KANE!
KILL ME NOW OR I AM GOING TO SPEND THE REST OF MY LIFE TORTURING YOU LIKE YOU WERE IN HELL!

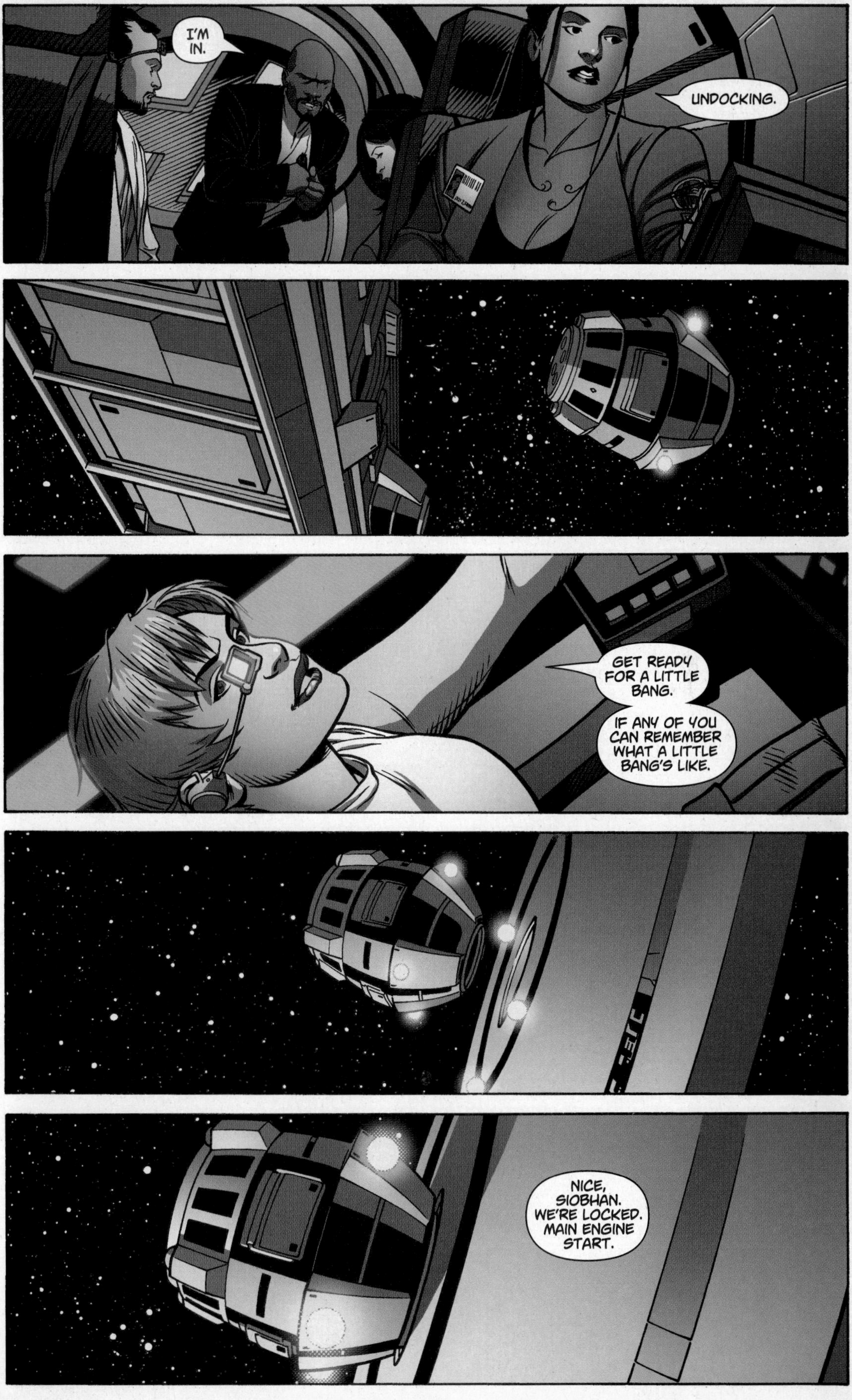
I'M IN.
UNDOCKING.
GET READY FOR A LITTLE BANG.
IF ANY OF YOU CAN REMEMBER WHAT A LITTLE BANG'S LIKE.
NICE, SIOBHAN. WE'RE LOCKED. MAIN ENGINE START.

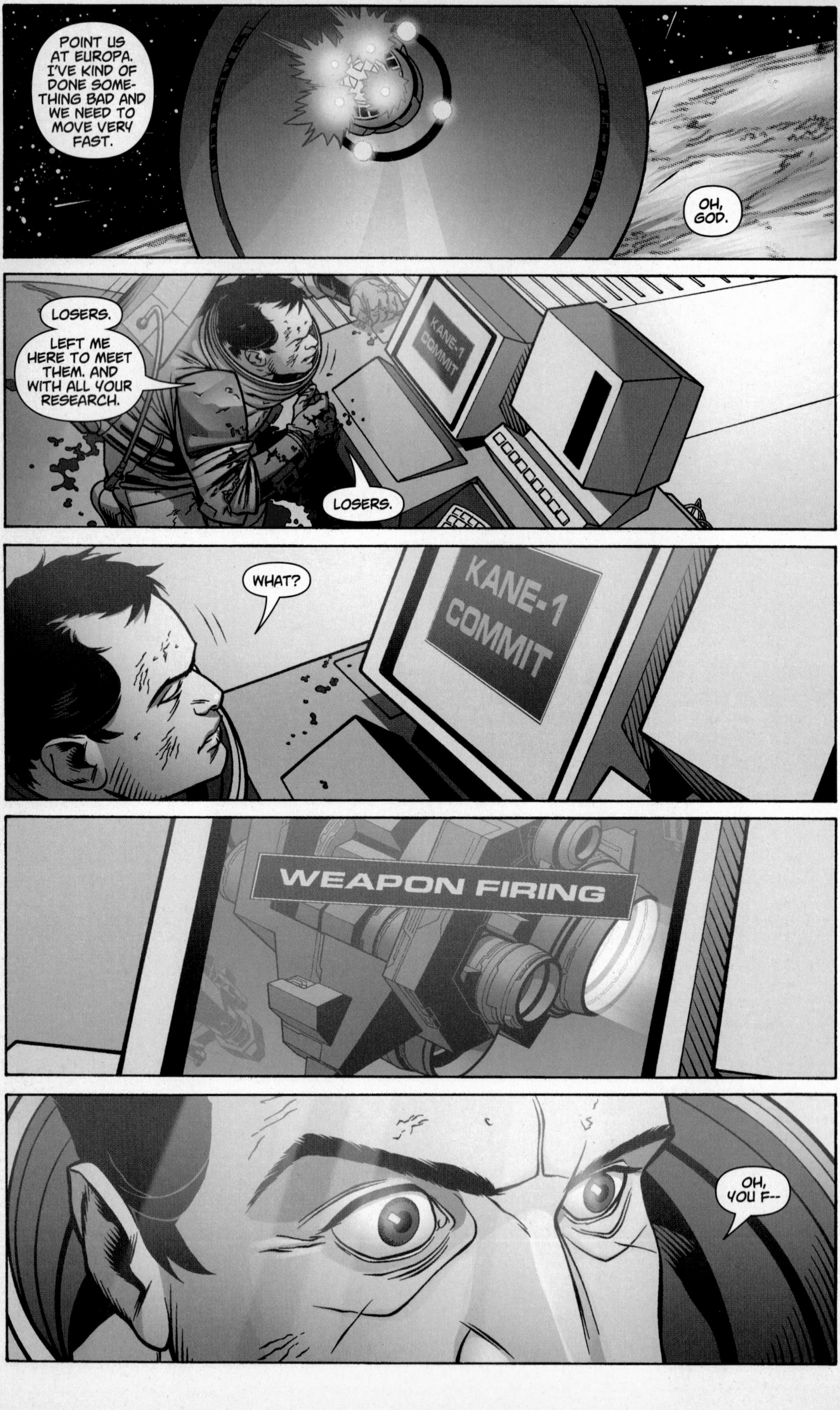

POINT US AT EUROPA. I'VE KIND OF DONE SOMETHING BAD AND WE NEED TO MOVE VERY FAST.
OH, GOD.
LOSERS.
LEFT ME HERE TO MEET THEM. AND WITH ALL YOUR RESEARCH.
KANE-1 COMMIT
LOSERS.
WHAT?
KANE-1 COMMIT
WEAPON FIRING
OH, YOU F--

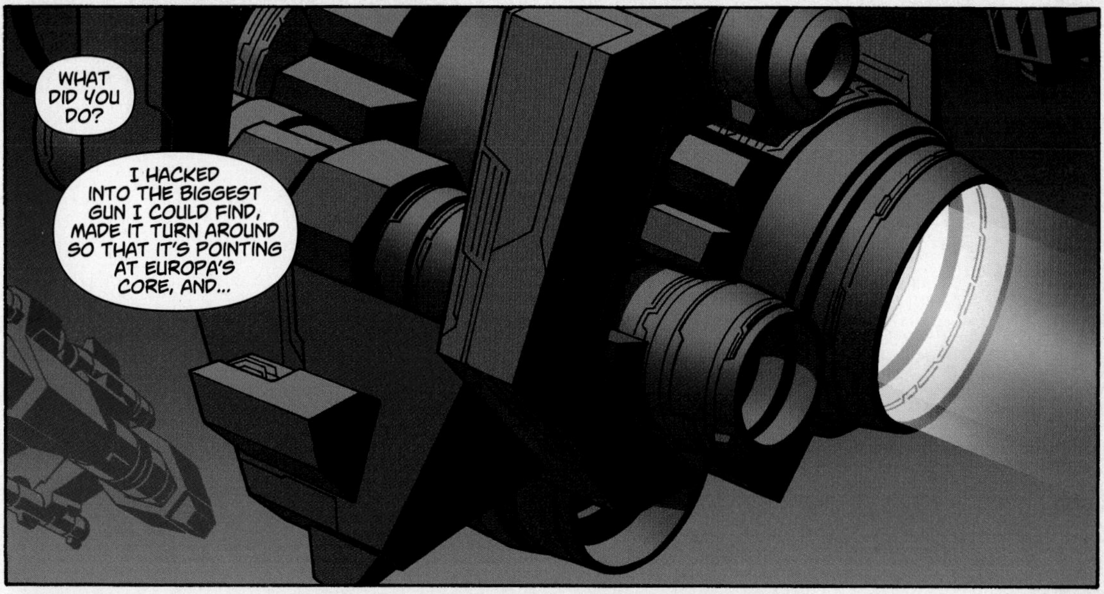
WHAT DID YOU DO?
I HACKED INTO THE BIGGEST GUN I COULD FIND, MADE IT TURN AROUND SO THAT IT'S POINTING AT EUROPA'S CORE, AND...

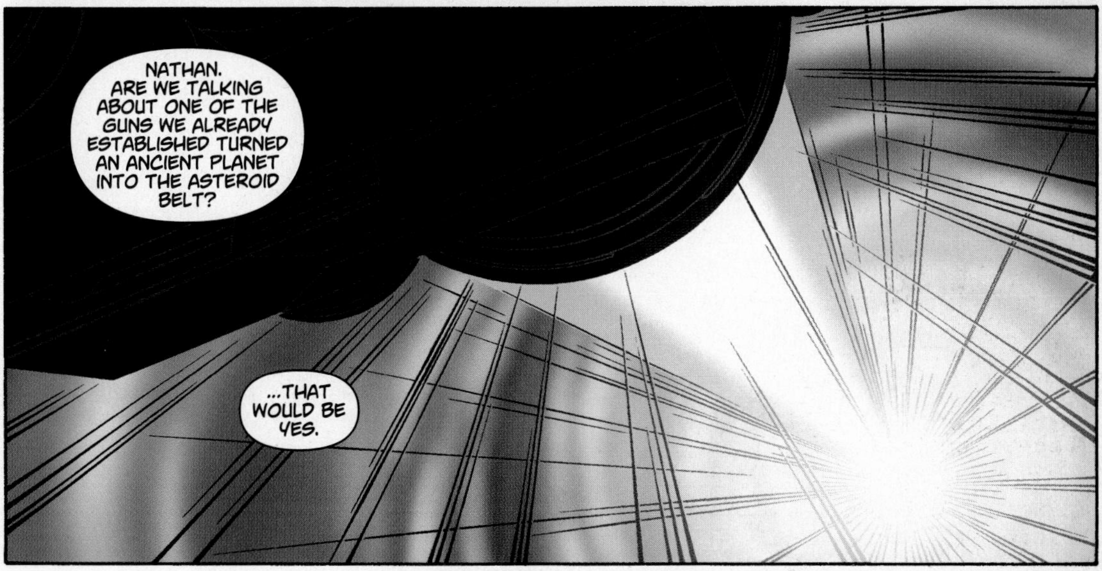
NATHAN. ARE WE TALKING ABOUT ONE OF THE GUNS WE ALREADY ESTABLISHED TURNED AN ANCIENT PLANET INTO THE ASTEROID BELT?
...THAT WOULD BE YES.

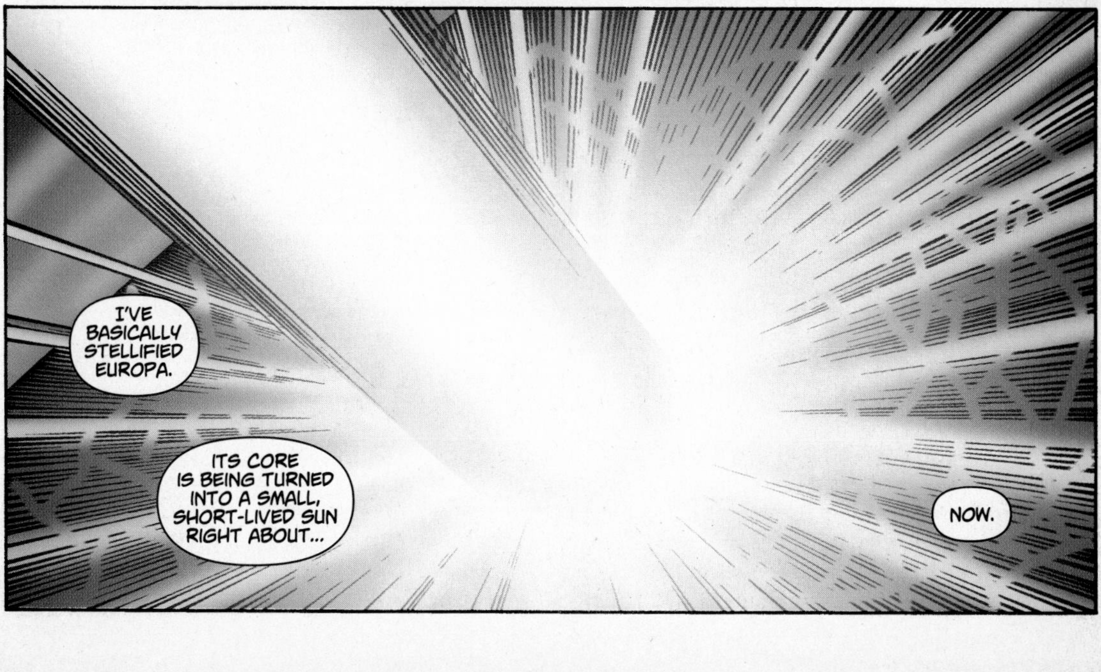
I'VE BASICALLY STELLIFIED EUROPA.
ITS CORE IS BEING TURNED INTO A SMALL, SHORT-LIVED SUN RIGHT ABOUT...
NOW.

IT'S REALLY NOT AS BAD AS IT SOUNDS.

EXCEPT THAT WE HAVE LESS THAN TWO MINUTES TO REACH THE TORUS BEFORE WE ALL DIE.

STRAP YOURSELF DOWN QUICKLY. THIS IS GOING TO BE EXTRAORDINARILY PAINFUL.

WILL THE STRAPS HELP WITH THAT?

NO.

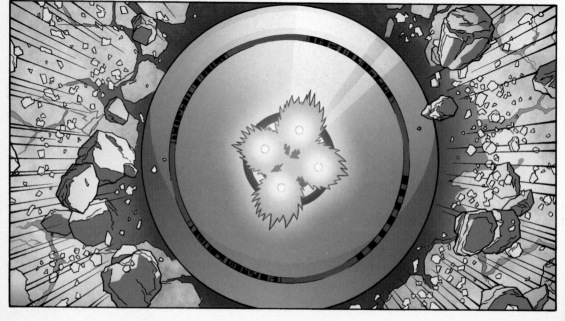

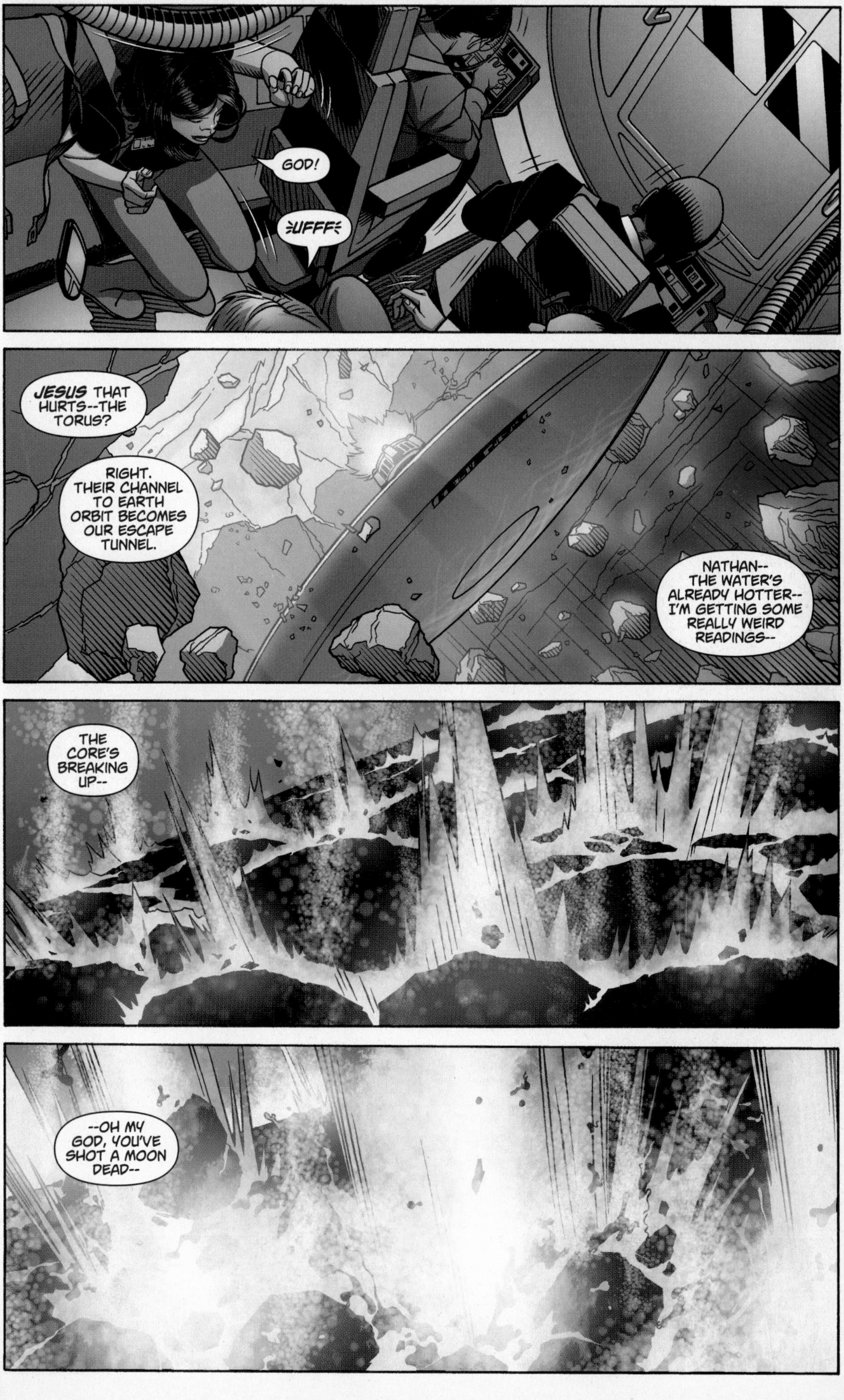
GOD!
UFFF
JESUS THAT HURTS--THE TORUS?
RIGHT. THEIR CHANNEL TO EARTH ORBIT BECOMES OUR ESCAPE TUNNEL.
NATHAN-- THE WATER'S ALREADY HOTTER-- I'M GETTING SOME REALLY WEIRD READINGS--
THE CORE'S BREAKING UP--
--OH MY GOD, YOU'VE SHOT A MOON DEAD--

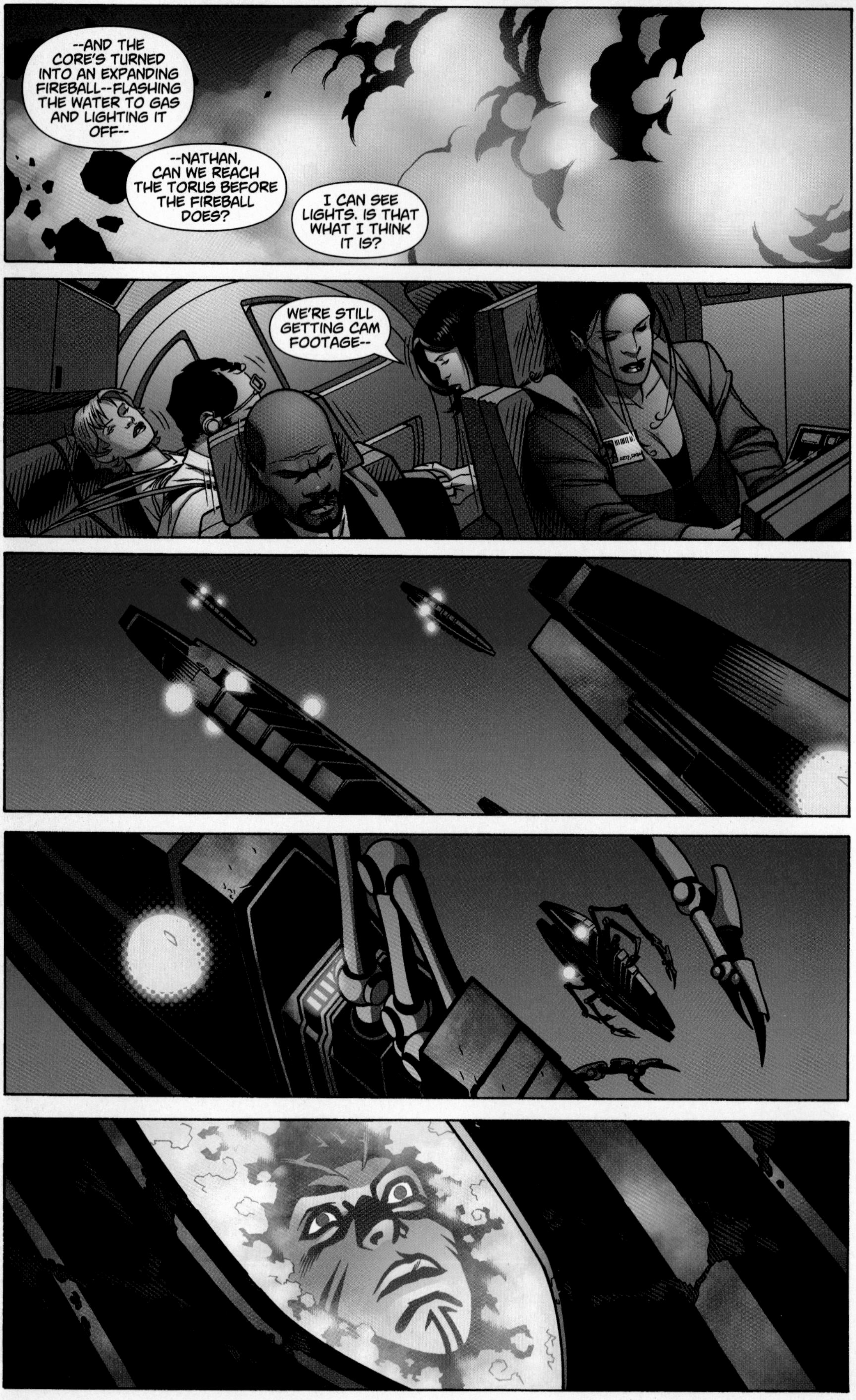
--AND THE CORE'S TURNED INTO AN EXPANDING FIREBALL--FLASHING THE WATER TO GAS AND LIGHTING IT OFF--
--NATHAN, CAN WE REACH THE TORUS BEFORE THE FIREBALL DOES?
I CAN SEE LIGHTS. IS THAT WHAT I THINK IT IS?
WE'RE STILL GETTING CAM FOOTAGE--

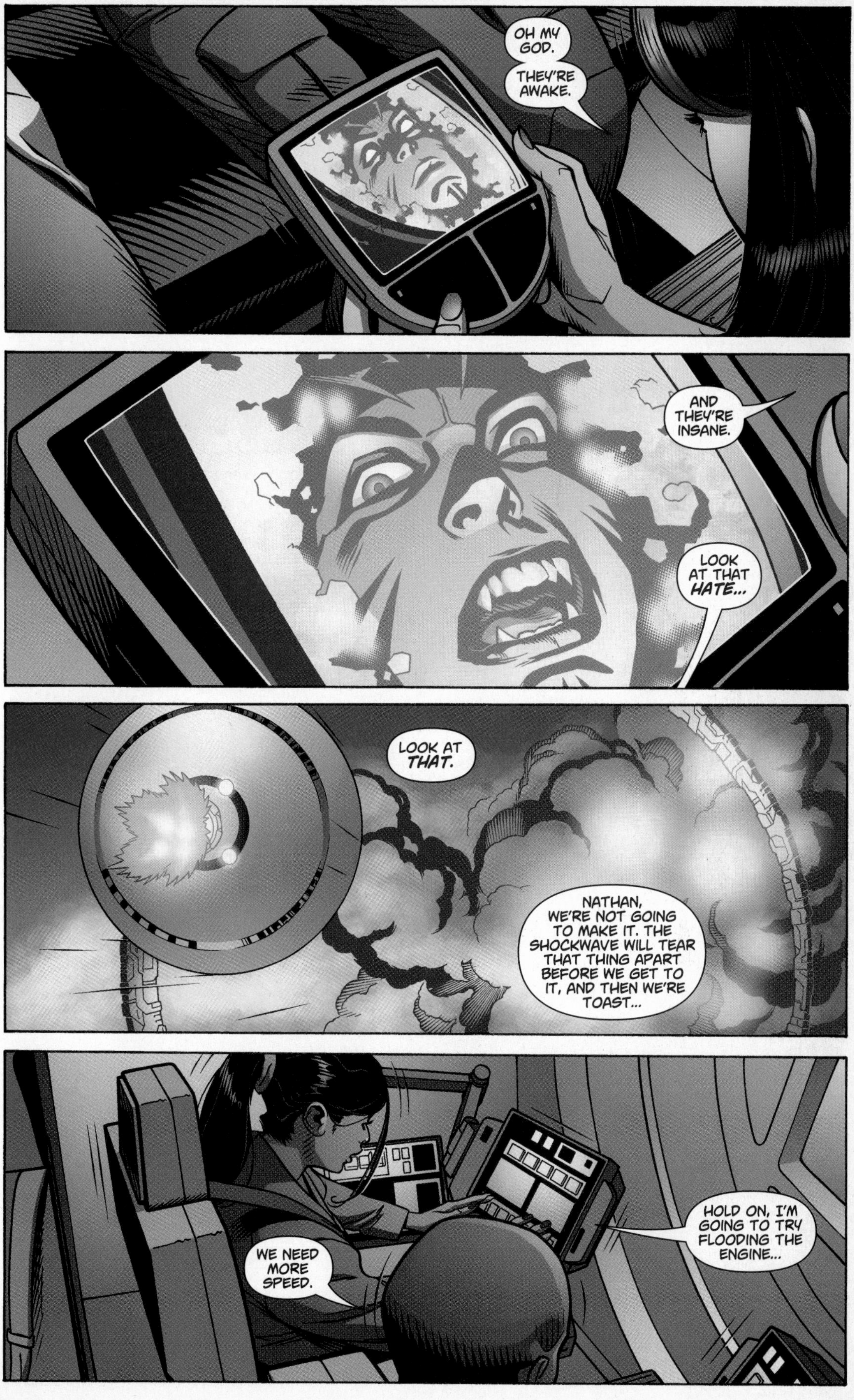
OH MY GOD.
THEY'RE AWAKE.
AND THEY'RE INSANE.
LOOK AT THAT HATE...
LOOK AT THAT.
NATHAN, WE'RE NOT GOING TO MAKE IT. THE SHOCKWAVE WILL TEAR THAT THING APART BEFORE WE GET TO IT, AND THEN WE'RE TOAST...
WE NEED MORE SPEED.
HOLD ON, I'M GOING TO TRY FLOODING THE ENGINE...

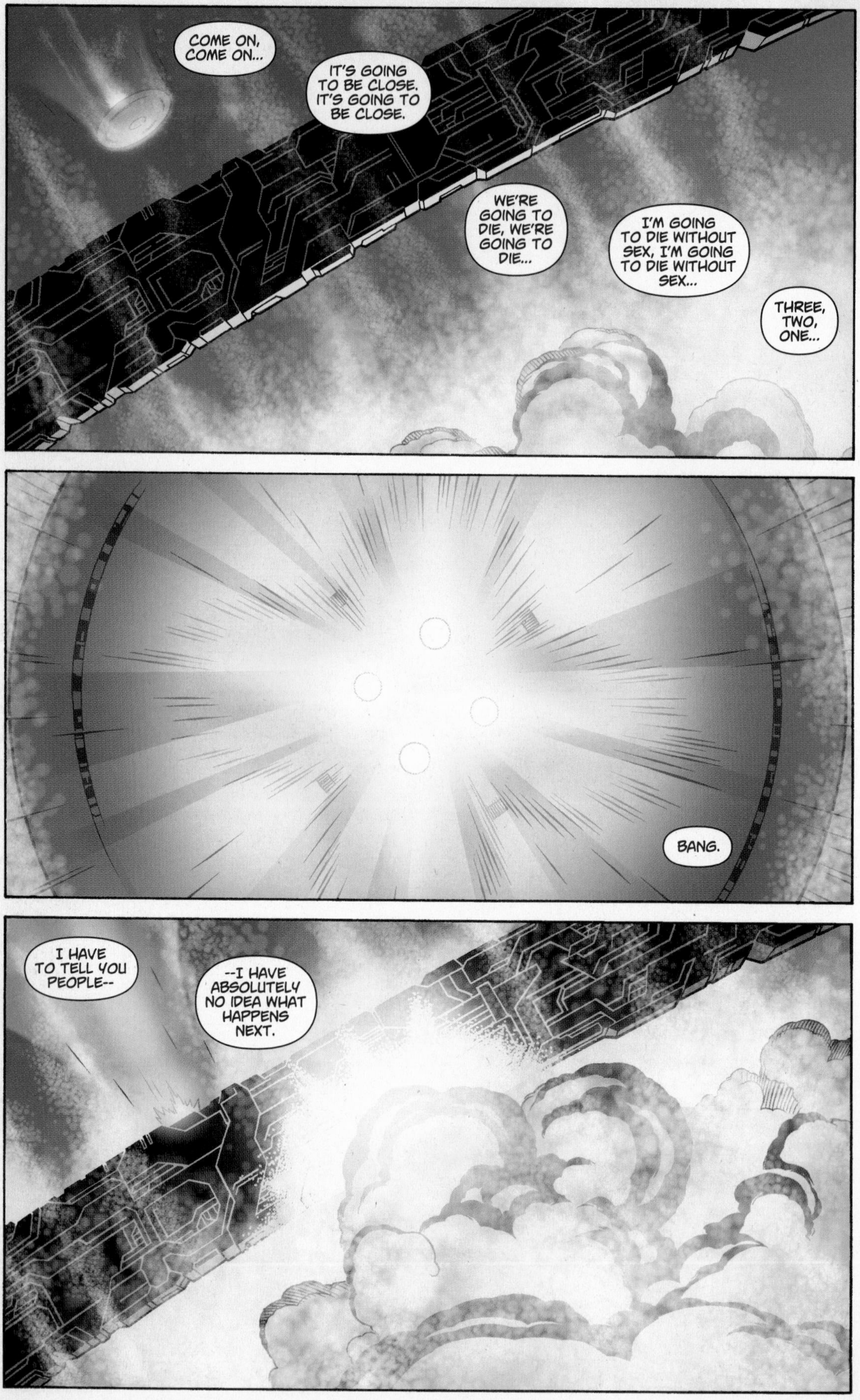
COME ON, COME ON...
IT'S GOING TO BE CLOSE. IT'S GOING TO BE CLOSE.
WE'RE GOING TO DIE, WE'RE GOING TO DIE...
I'M GOING TO DIE WITHOUT SEX, I'M GOING TO DIE WITHOUT SEX...
THREE, TWO, ONE...
BANG.
I HAVE TO TELL YOU PEOPLE--
--I HAVE ABSOLUTELY NO IDEA WHAT HAPPENS NEXT.

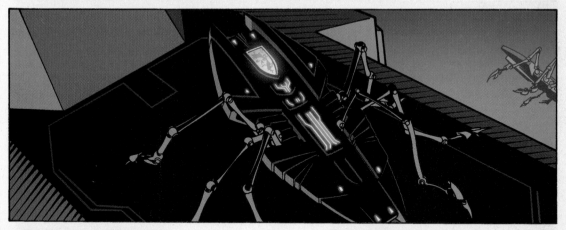

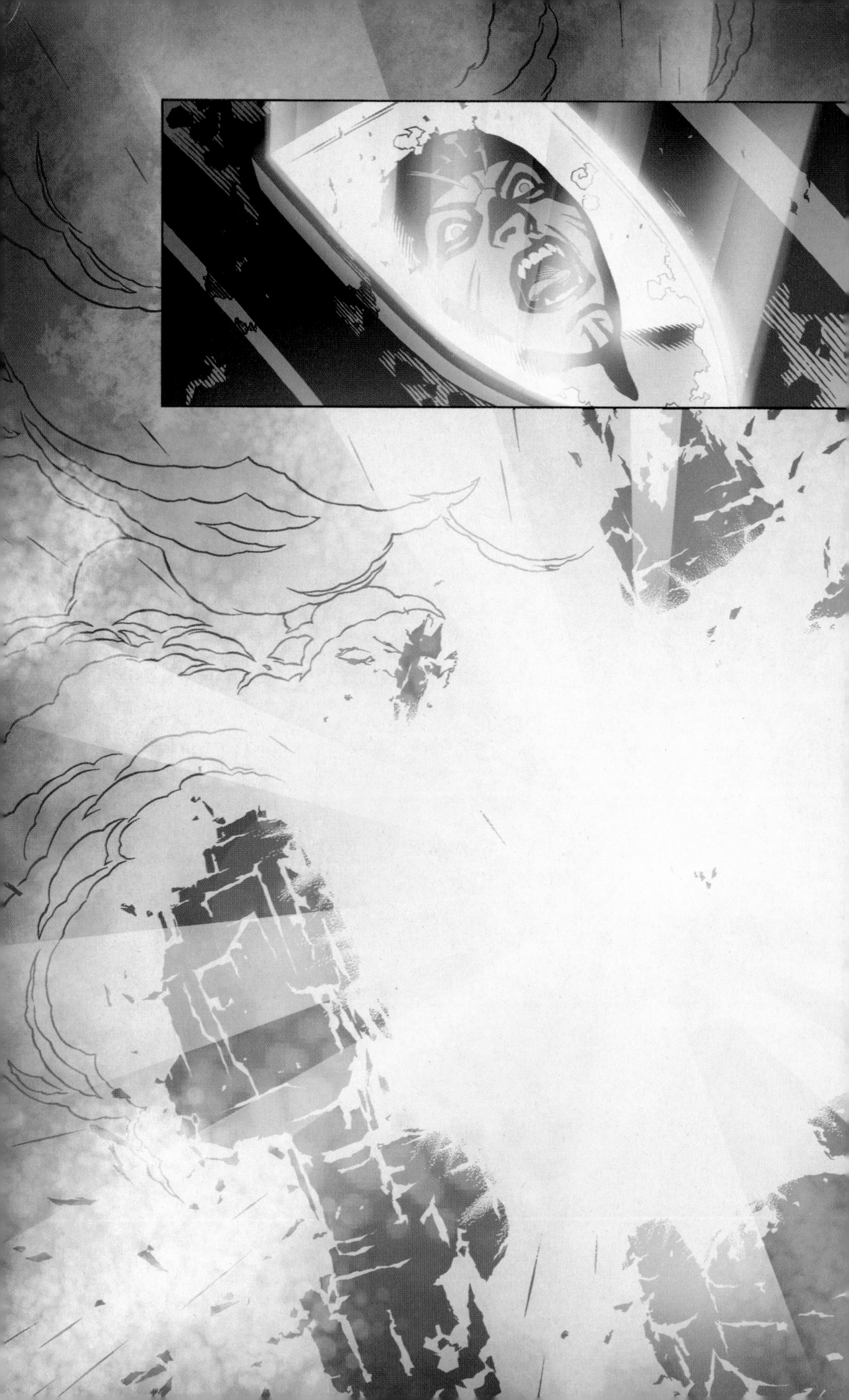

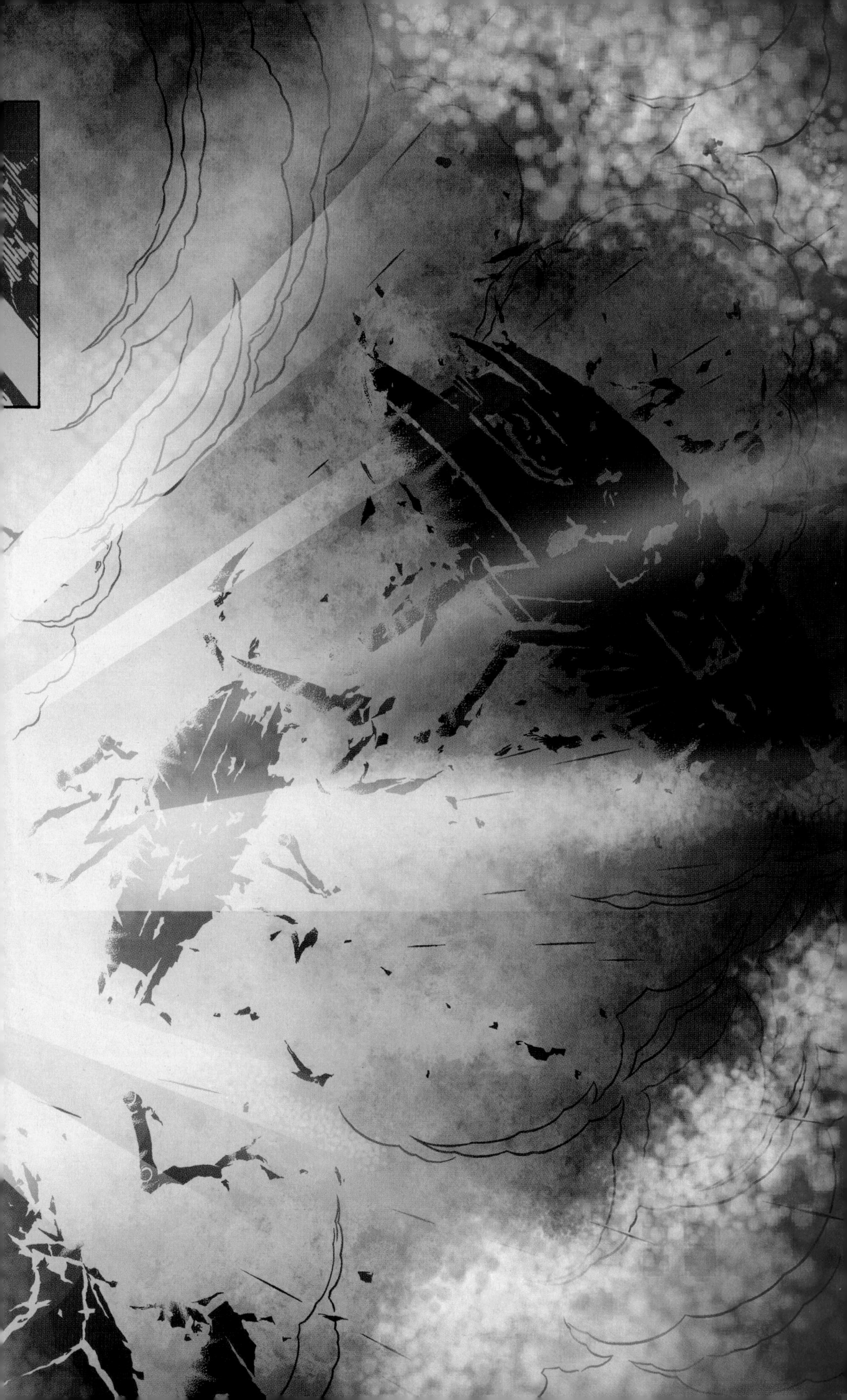

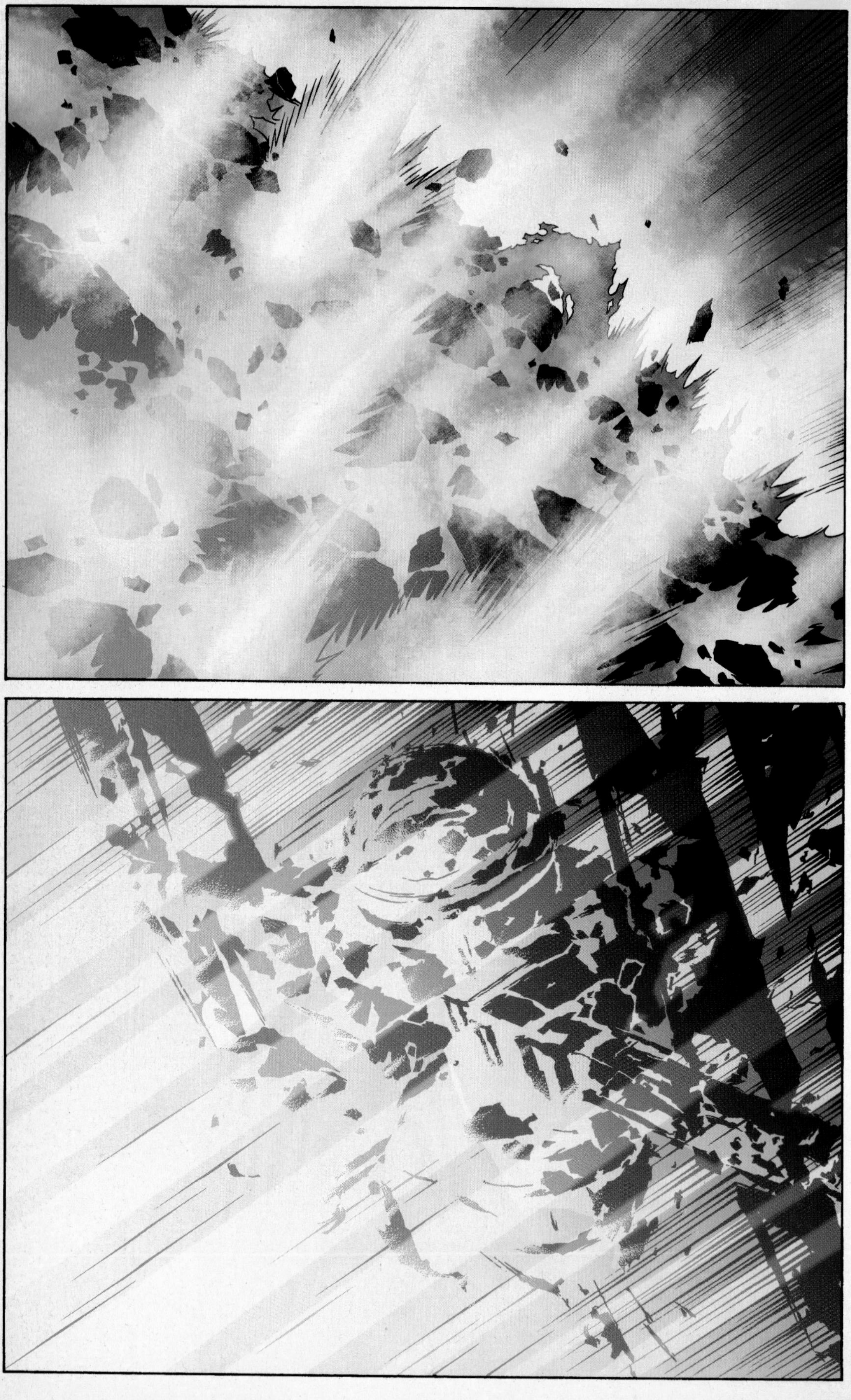

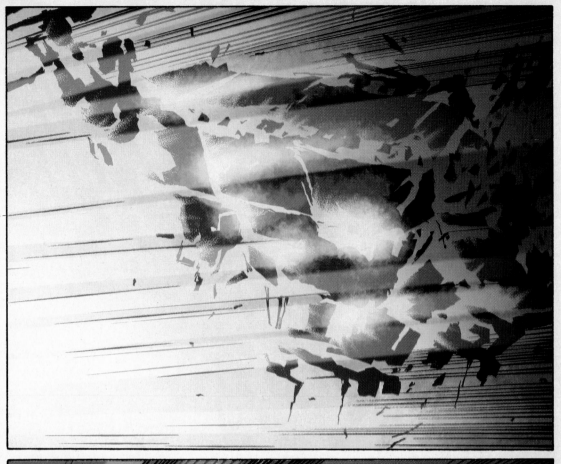

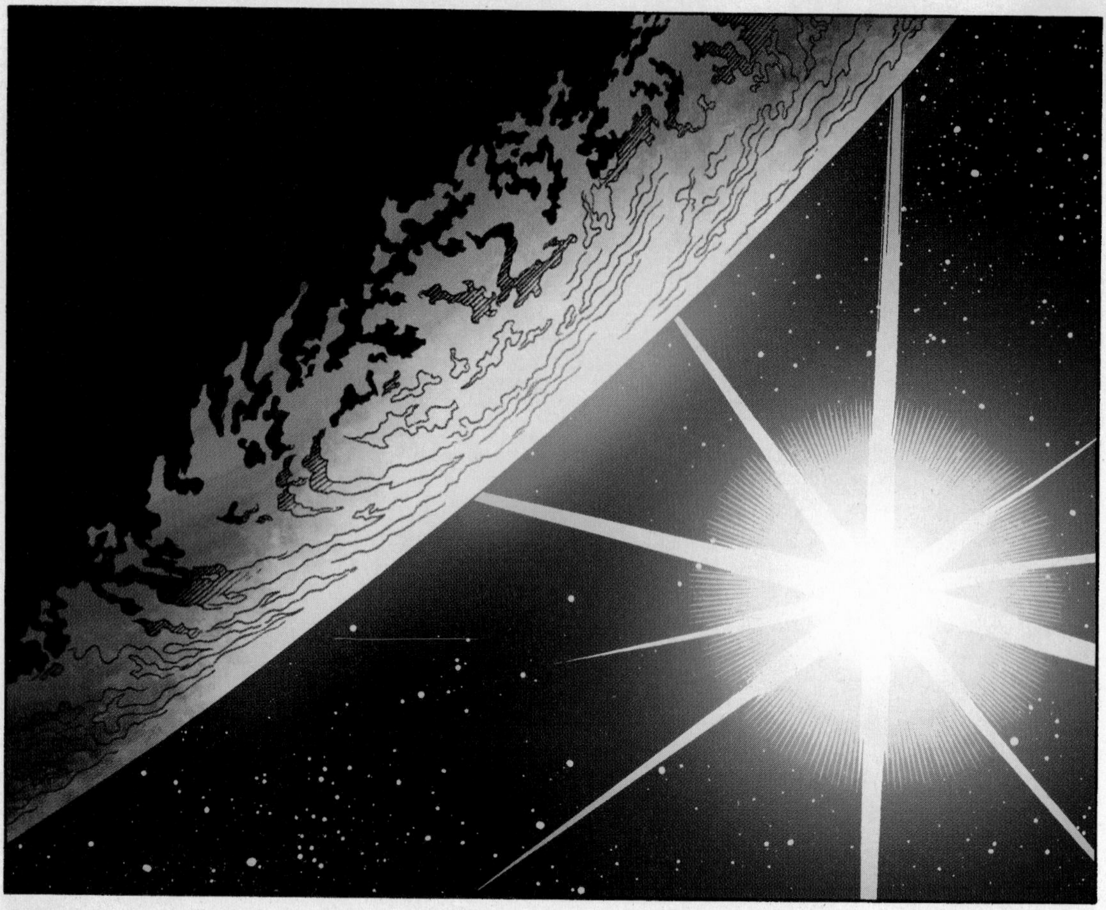
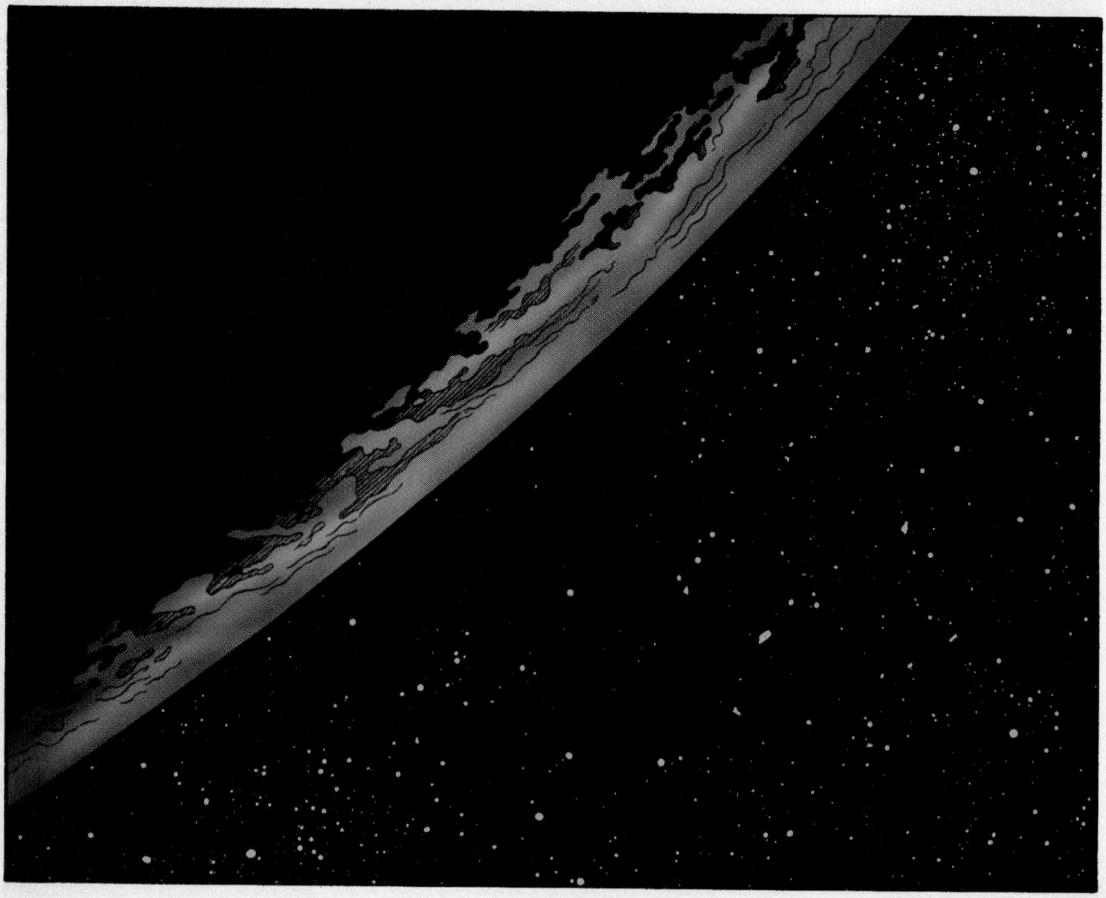

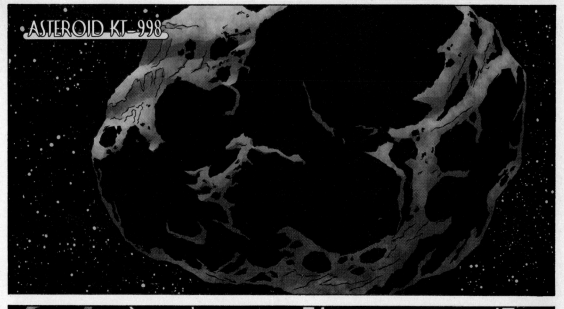

ASTEROID KT-998

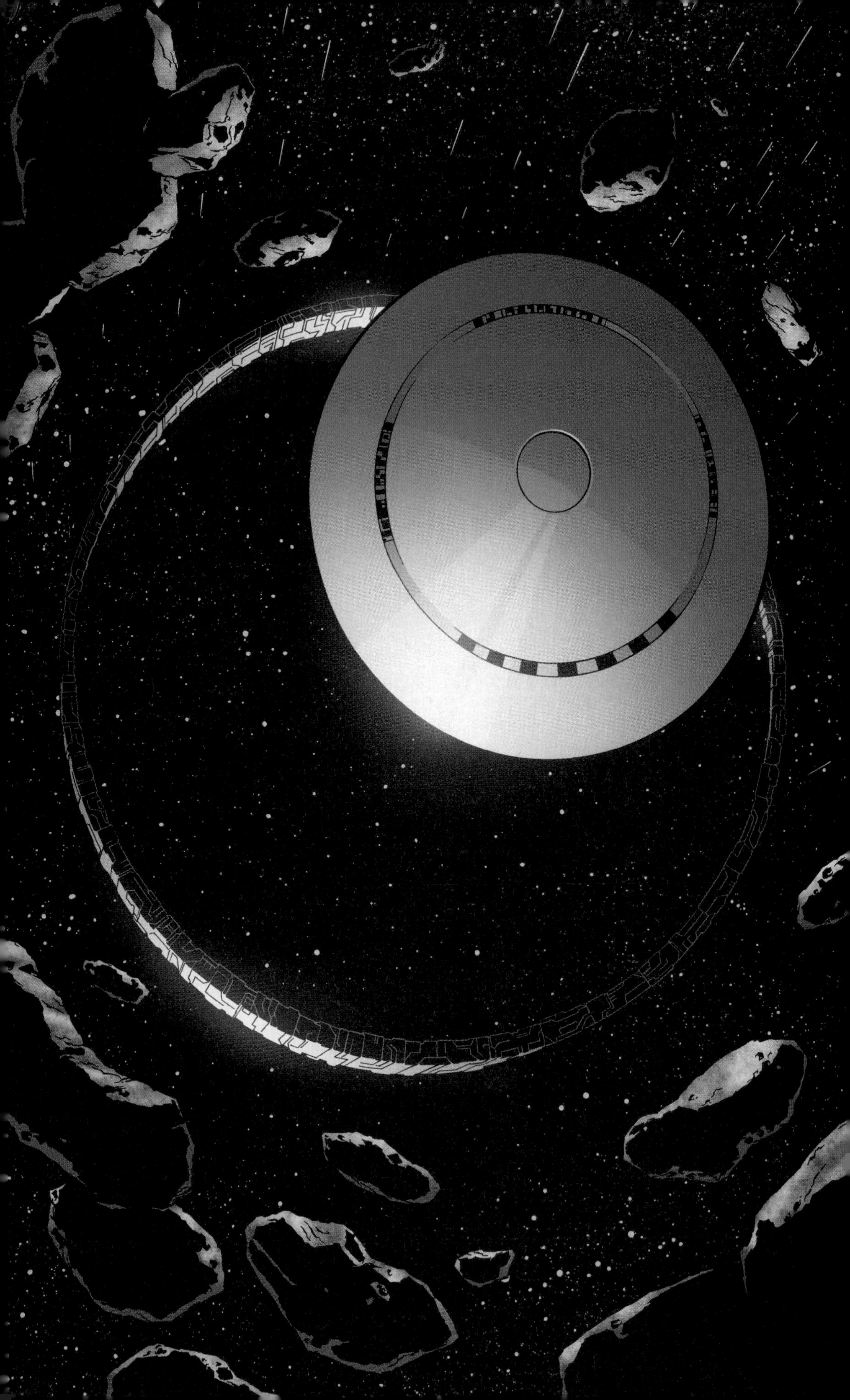

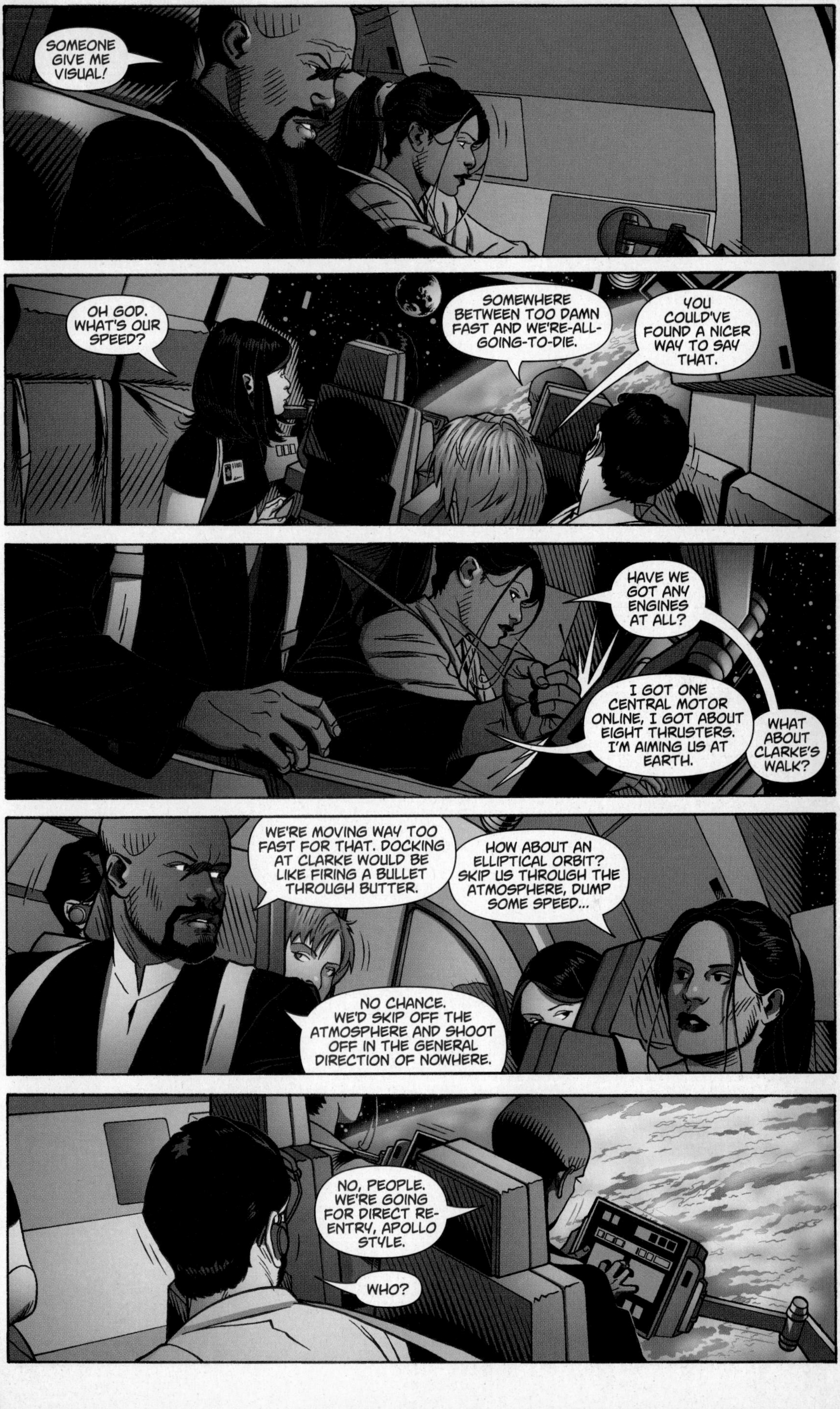
SOMEONE GIVE ME VISUAL!
OH GOD. WHAT'S OUR SPEED?
SOMEWHERE BETWEEN TOO DAMN FAST AND WE'RE-ALL-GOING-TO-DIE.
YOU COULD'VE FOUND A NICER WAY TO SAY THAT.
HAVE WE GOT ANY ENGINES AT ALL?
I GOT ONE CENTRAL MOTOR ONLINE, I GOT ABOUT EIGHT THRUSTERS. I'M AIMING US AT EARTH.
WHAT ABOUT CLARKE'S WALK?
WE'RE MOVING WAY TOO FAST FOR THAT. DOCKING AT CLARKE WOULD BE LIKE FIRING A BULLET THROUGH BUTTER.
HOW ABOUT AN ELLIPTICAL ORBIT? SKIP US THROUGH THE ATMOSPHERE, DUMP SOME SPEED...
NO CHANCE. WE'D SKIP OFF THE ATMOSPHERE AND SHOOT OFF IN THE GENERAL DIRECTION OF NOWHERE.
NO, PEOPLE. WE'RE GOING FOR DIRECT RE-ENTRY, APOLLO STYLE.
WHO?

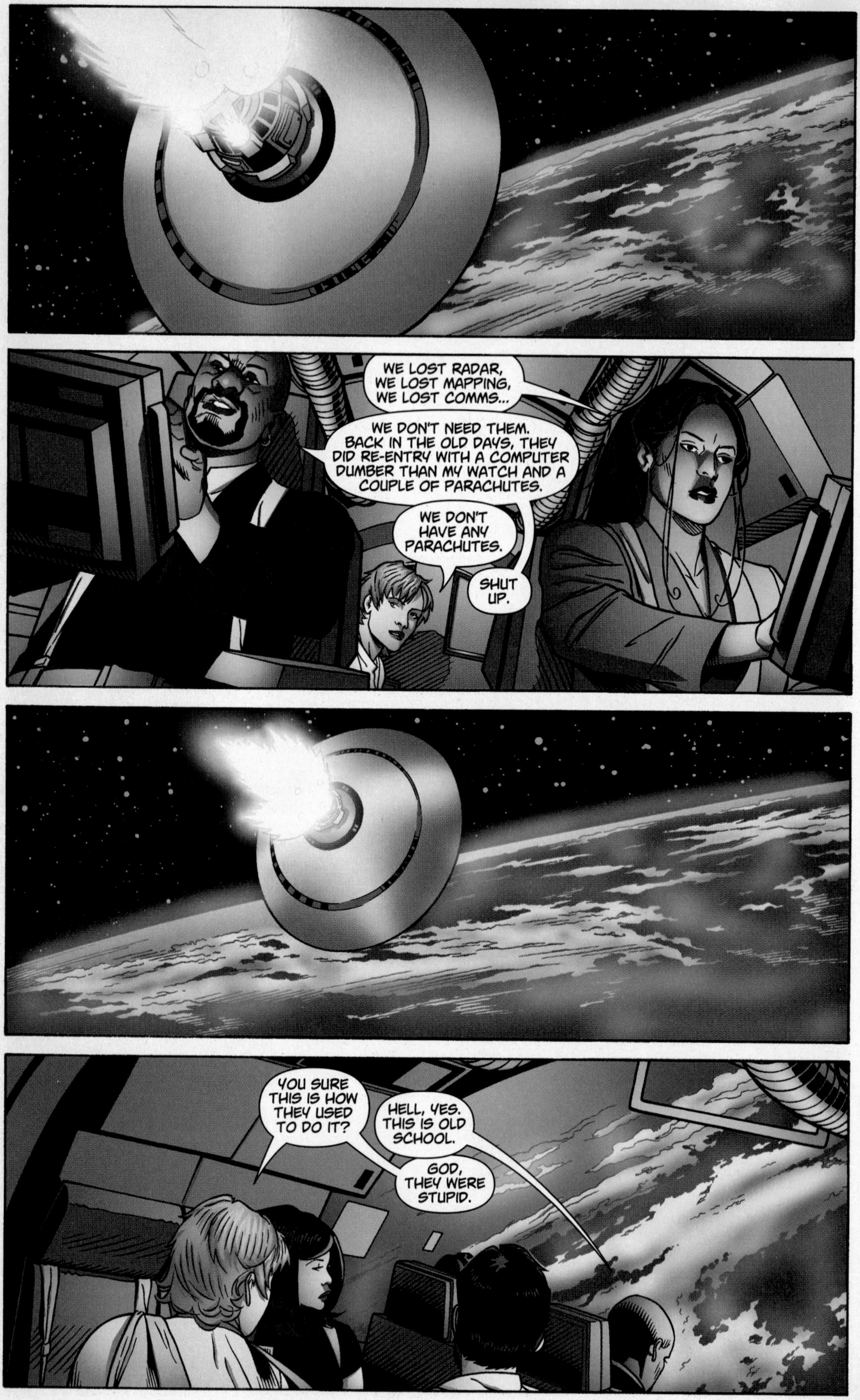
WE LOST RADAR, WE LOST MAPPING, WE LOST COMMS...
WE DON'T NEED THEM. BACK IN THE OLD DAYS, THEY DID RE-ENTRY WITH A COMPUTER DUMBER THAN MY WATCH AND A COUPLE OF PARACHUTES.
WE DON'T HAVE ANY PARACHUTES.
SHUT UP.
YOU SURE THIS IS HOW THEY USED TO DO IT?
HELL, YES. THIS IS OLD SCHOOL.
GOD, THEY WERE STUPID.

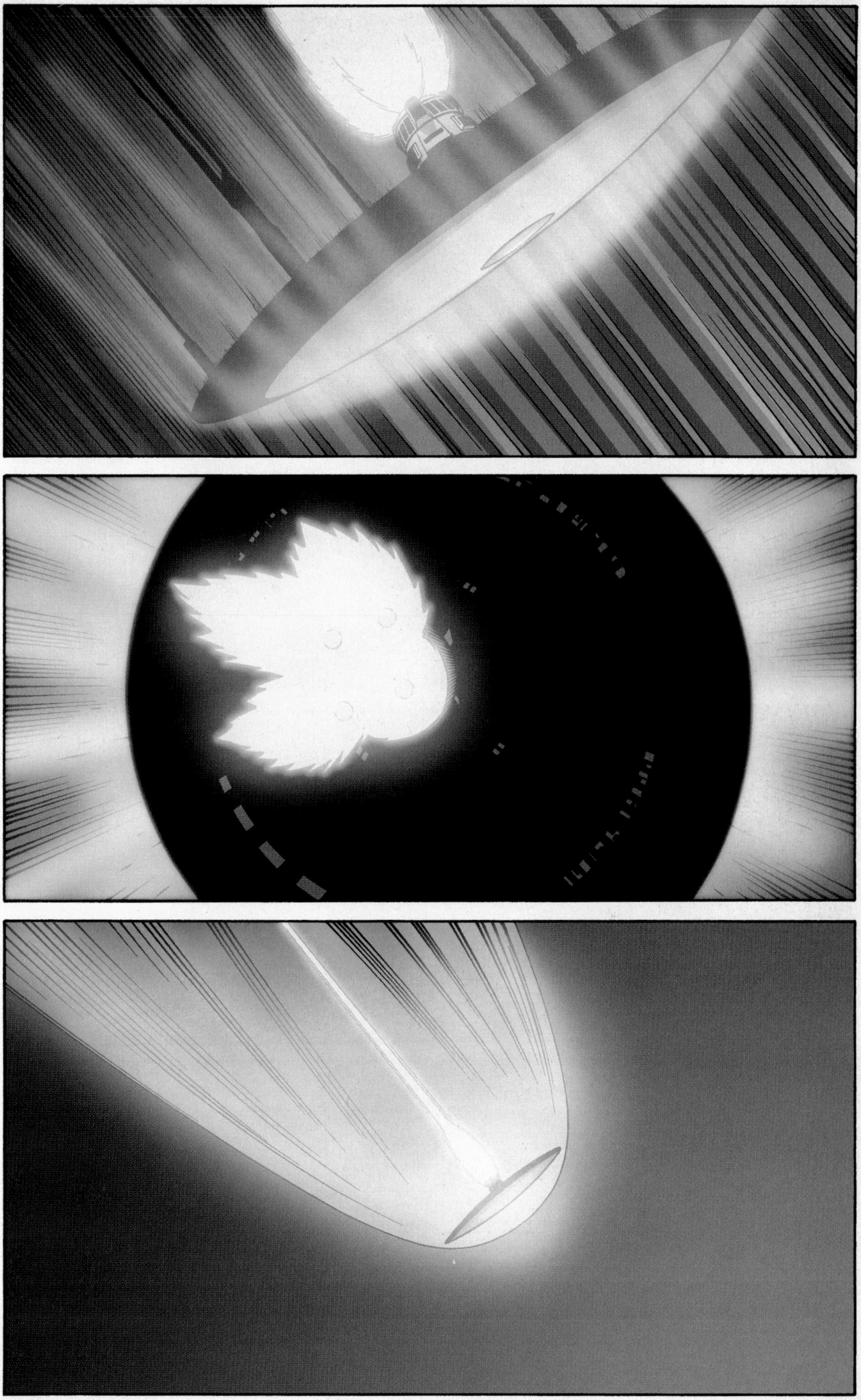

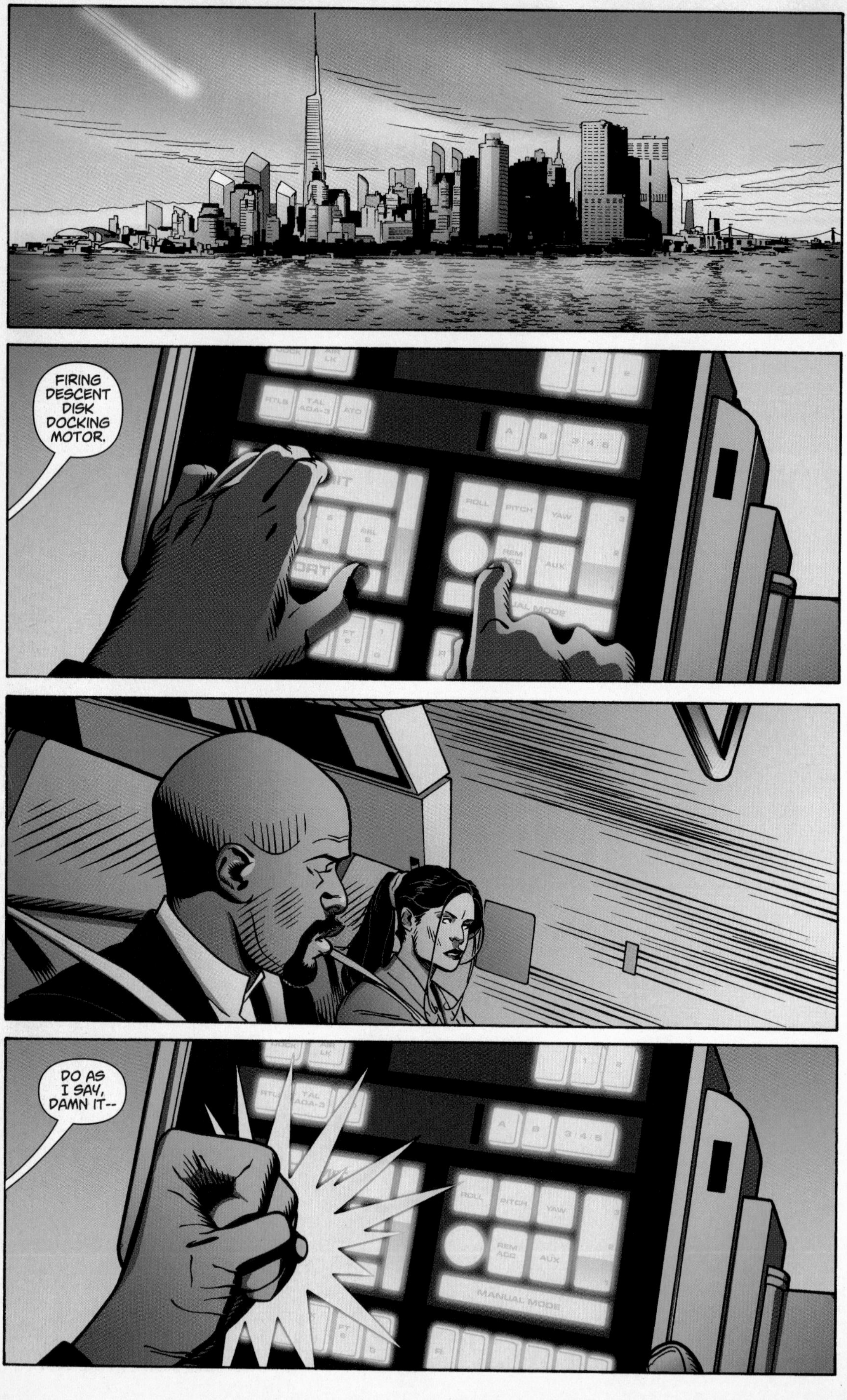
FIRING DESCENT DISK DOCKING MOTOR.
DO AS I SAY, DAMN IT--

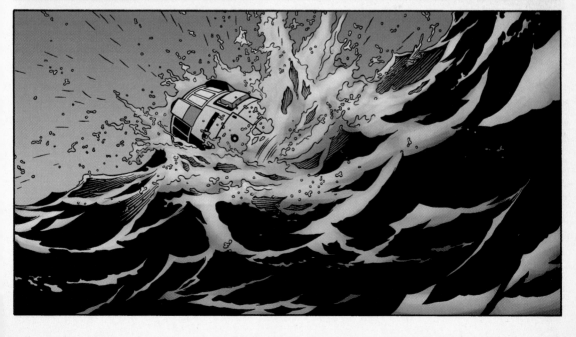

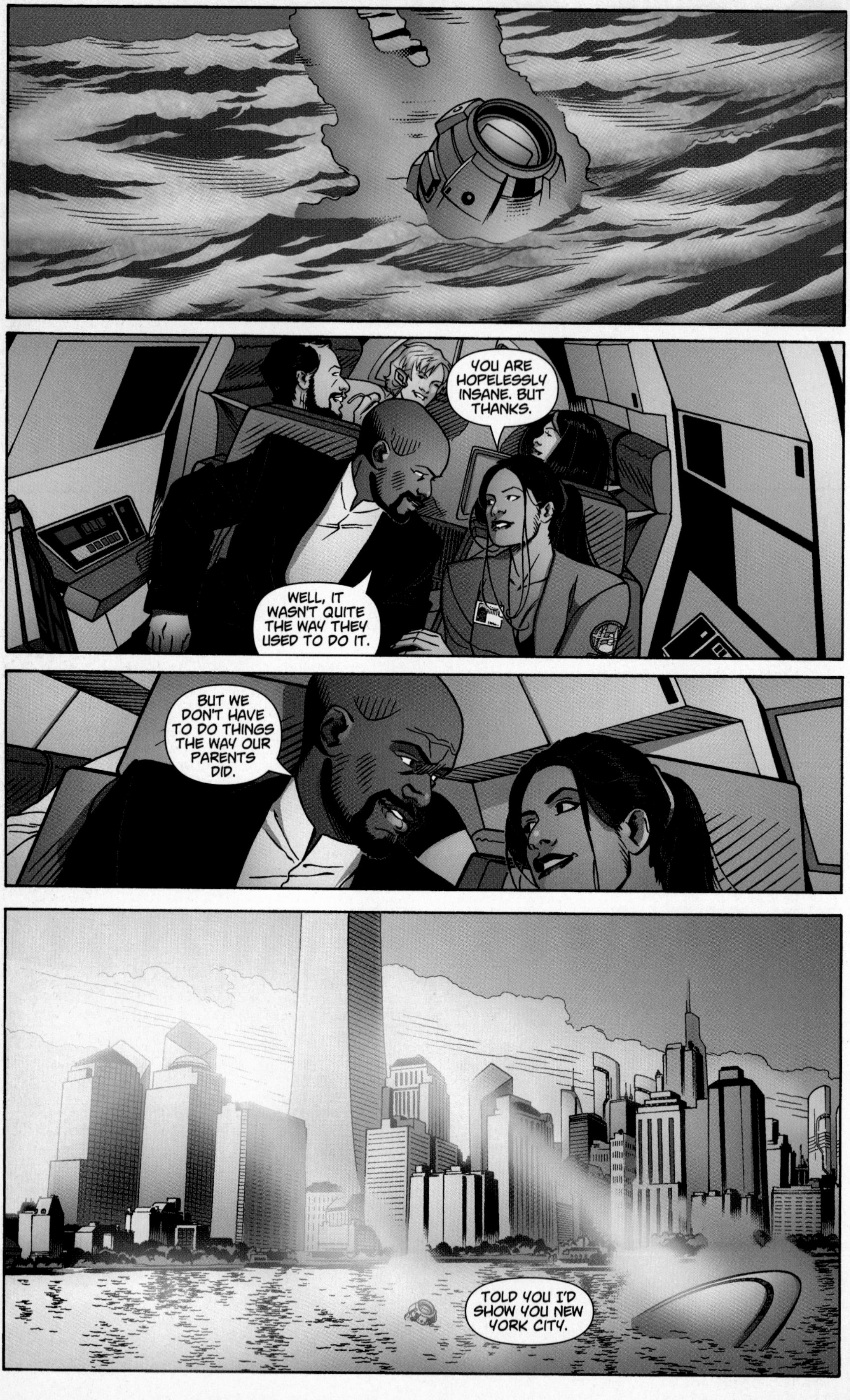
YOU ARE HOPELESSLY INSANE. BUT THANKS.
WELL, IT WASN'T QUITE THE WAY THEY USED TO DO IT.
BUT WE DON'T HAVE TO DO THINGS THE WAY OUR PARENTS DID.
TOLD YOU I'D SHOW YOU NEW YORK CITY.

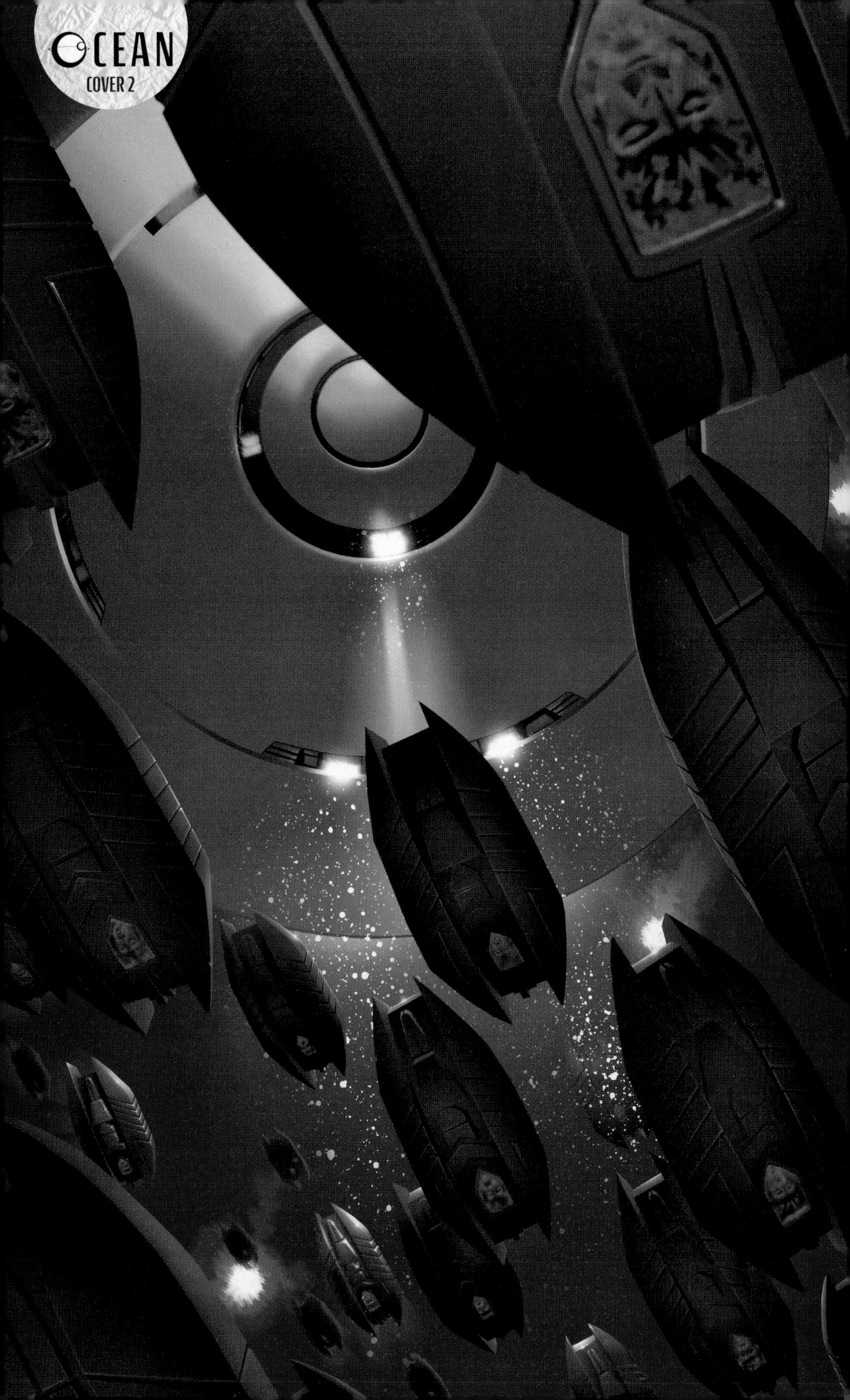
OCEAN
COVER 2

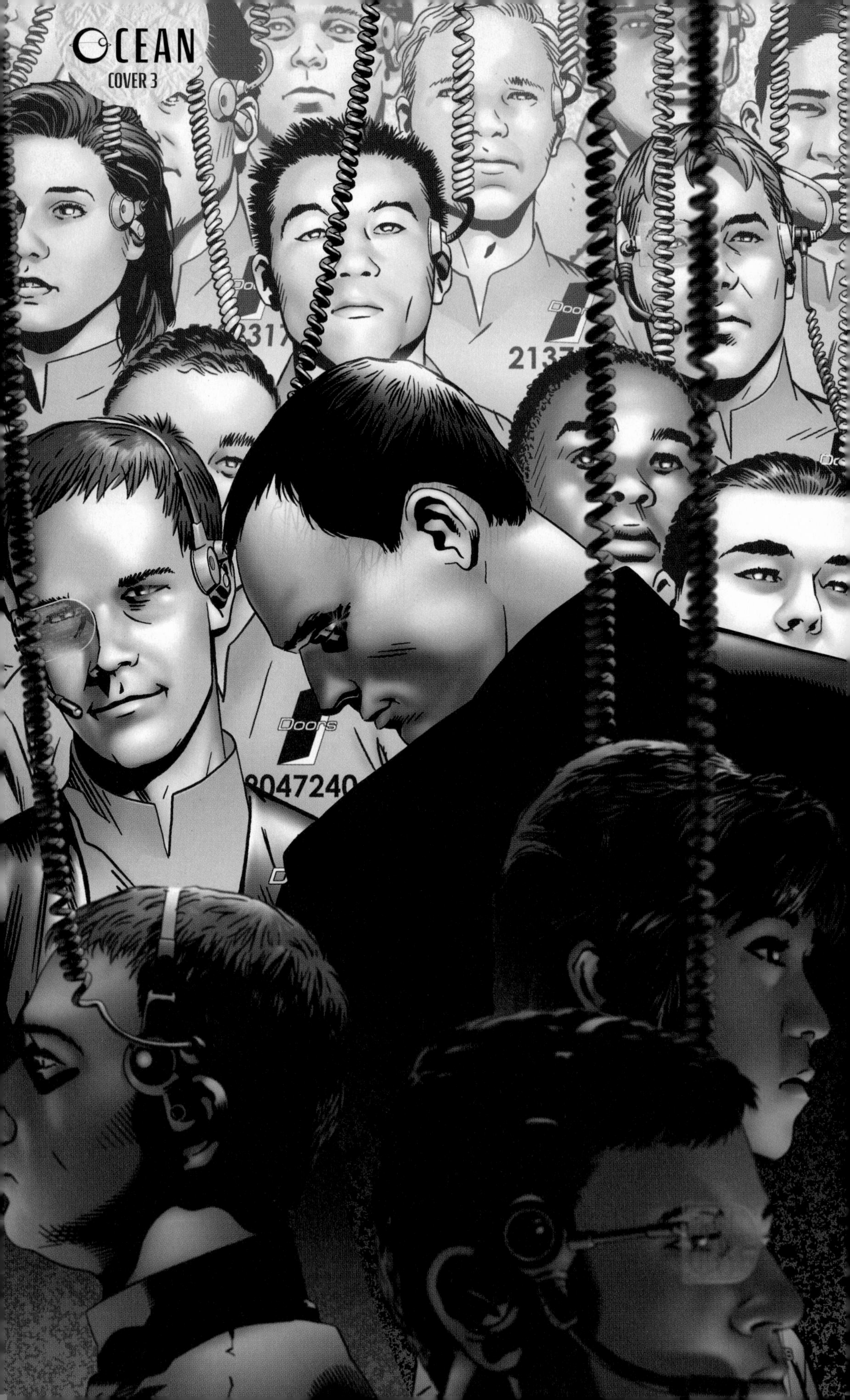
OCEAN
COVER 3
Doors
8047240

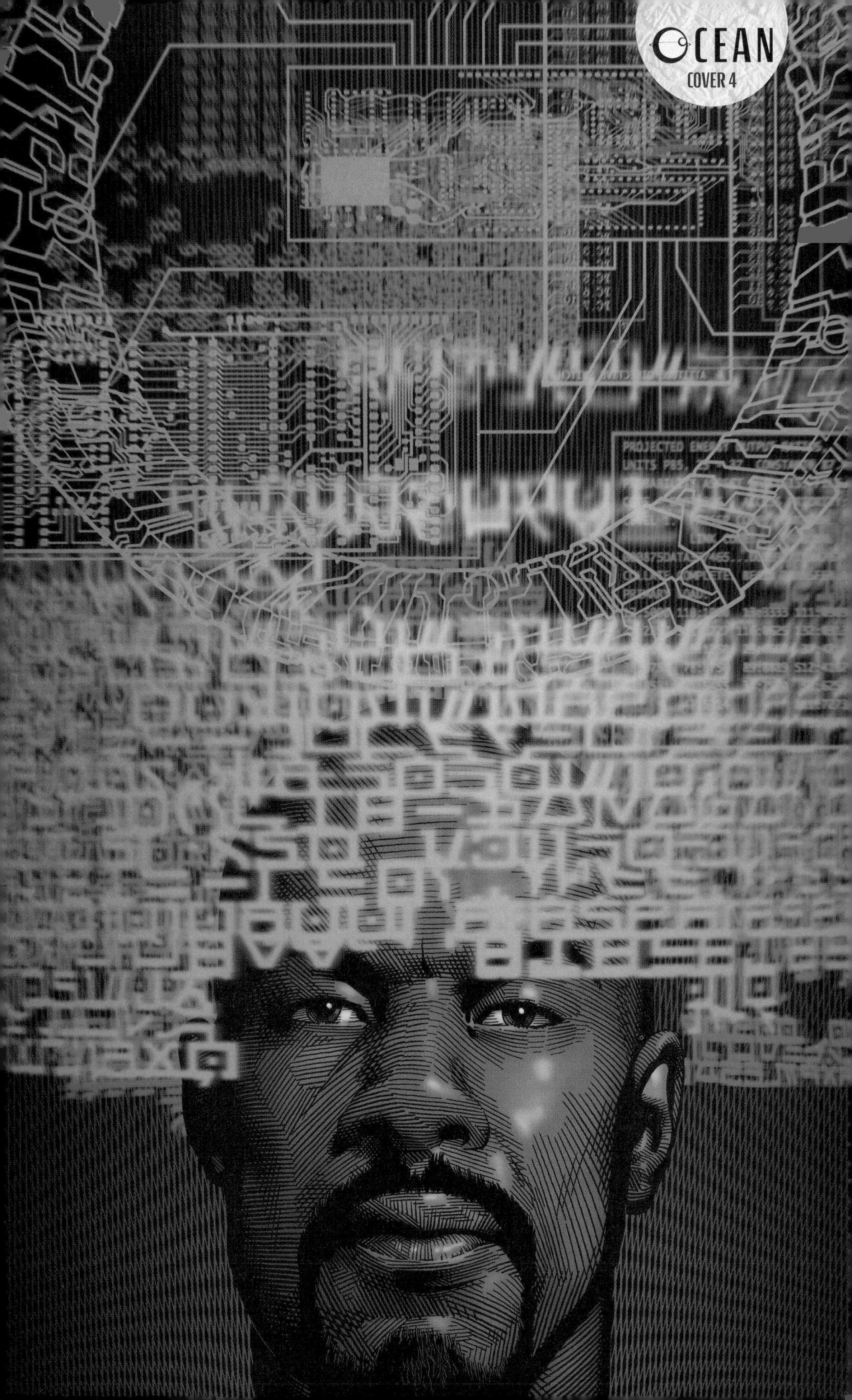
OCEAN
COVER 4

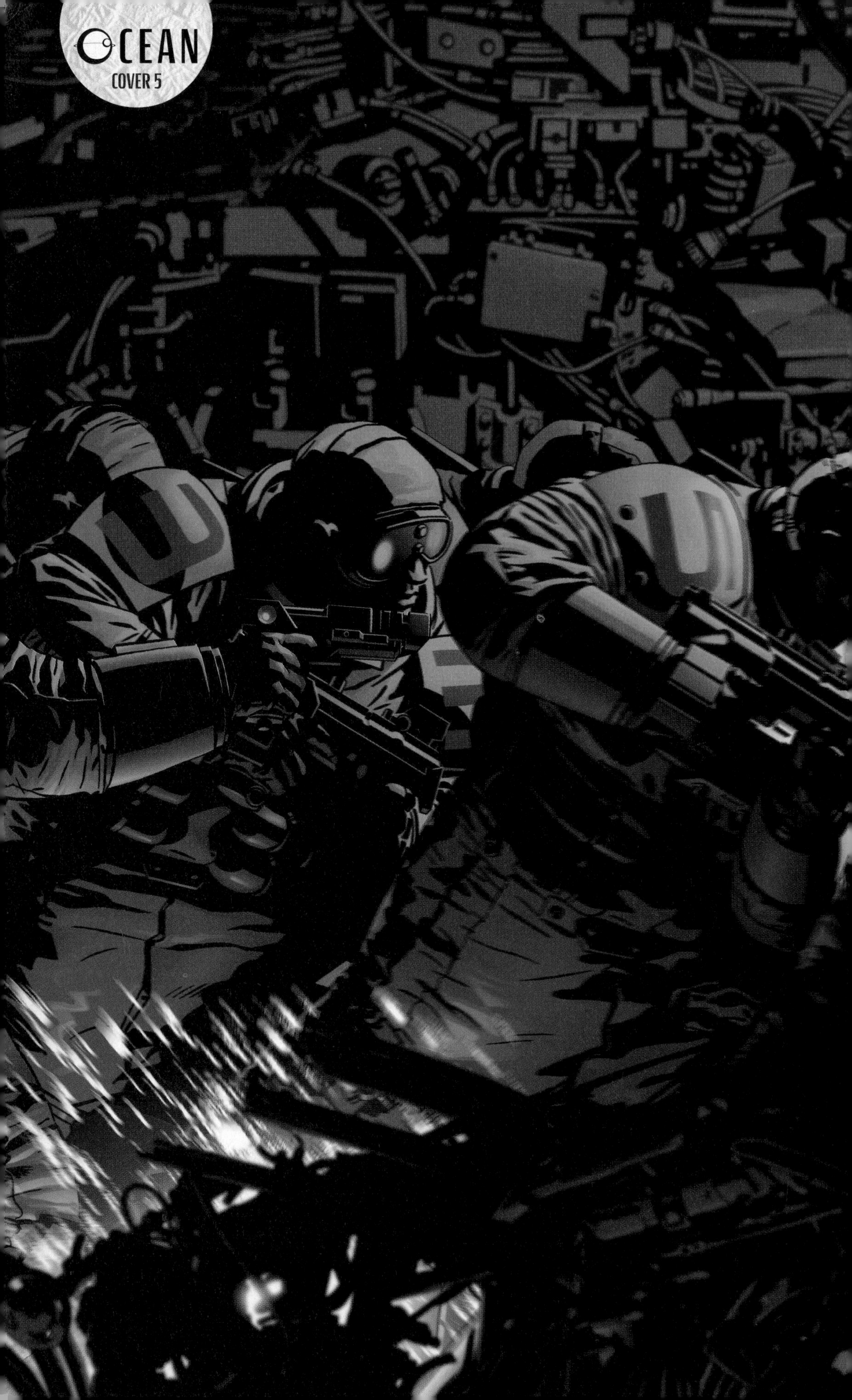
OCEAN
COVER 5

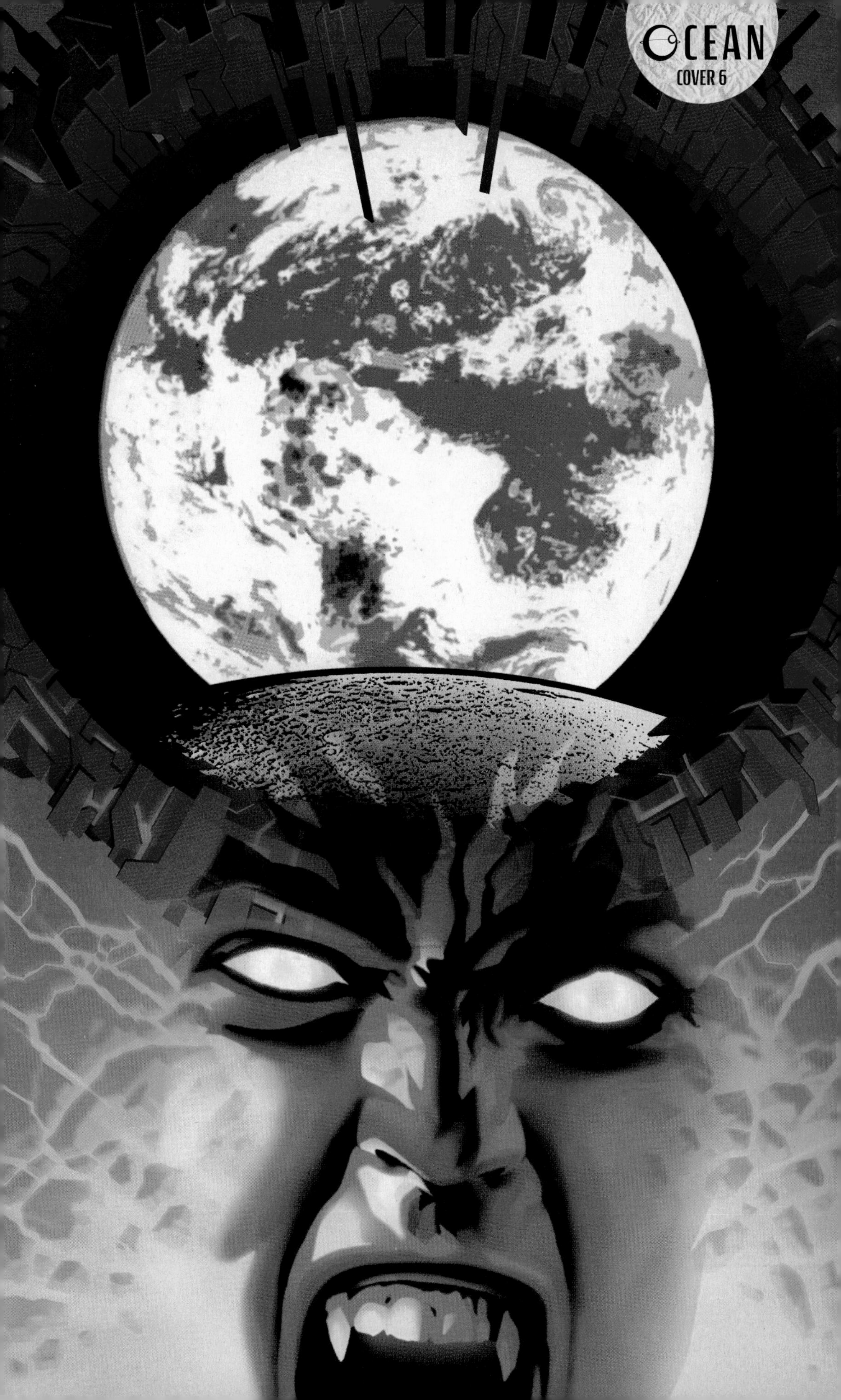
OCEAN
COVER 6

OCEAN

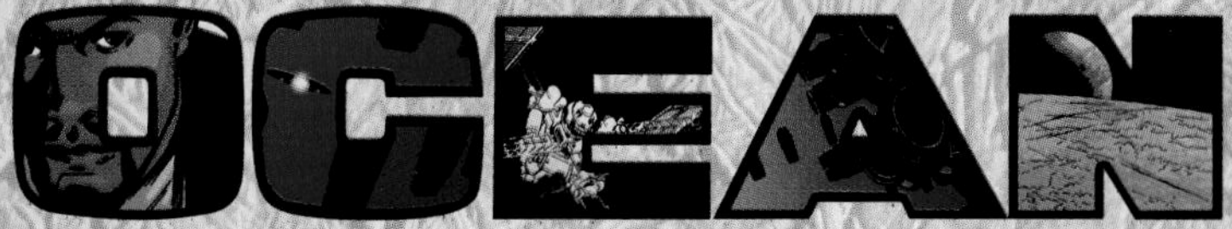

Cold Harbor Descent

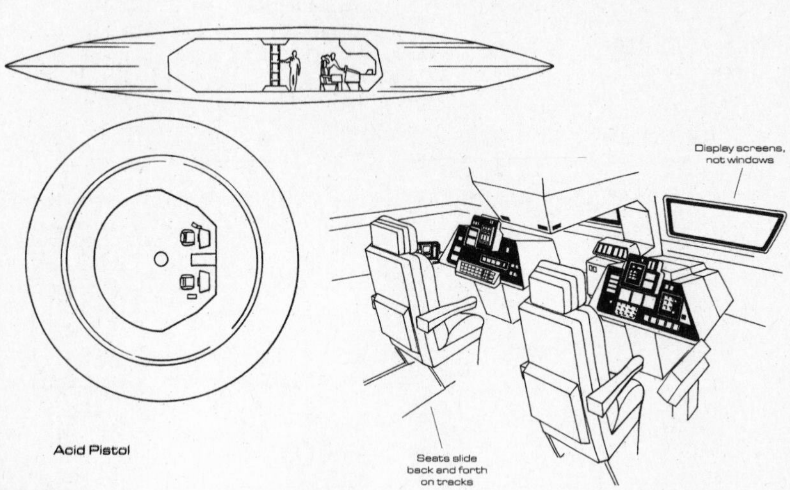
Display screens, not windows
Seats slide back and forth on tracks

Acid Pistol

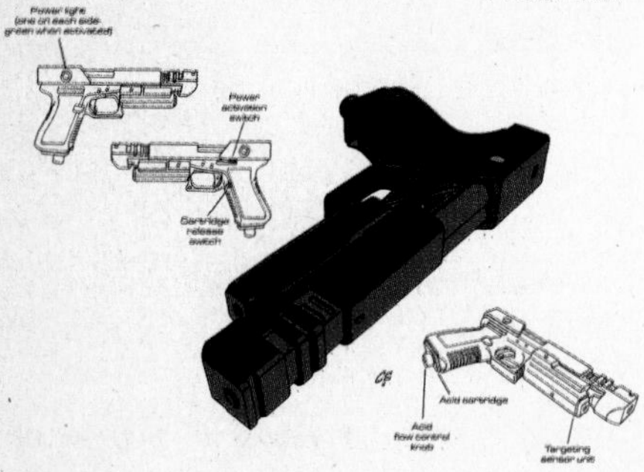
Power light (one on each side-green when activated)
Power activation switch
Cartridge release switch
Acid cartridge
Acid flow control knob
Targeting sensor unit

Cold Harbor Staff

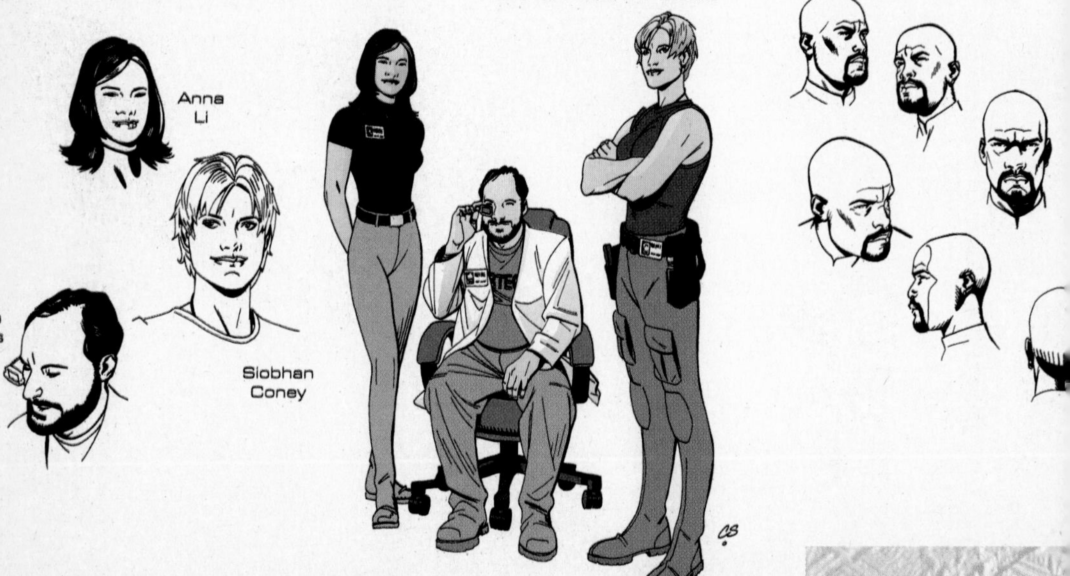
Anna Li
John Wells
Siobhan Coney

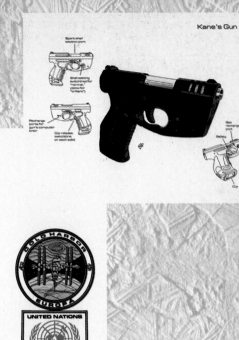

Kane's Gun

Spent shell ejection port
Recharge ports for gun's computer brain
Clip release switch(one on each side)
Gas recharge port
Safety
Clip

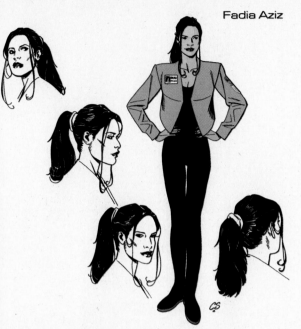

Fadia Aziz

COLD HARBOR
EUROPA
UNITED NATIONS
EXPLORATORY FORCE

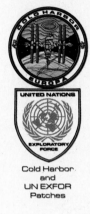

Cold Harbor
and
UN EXFOR
Patches

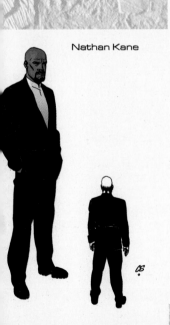

Doors Station Manager

Doors

Doors
Corporate
Logo

Nathan Kane

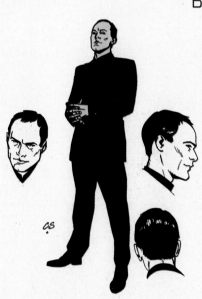

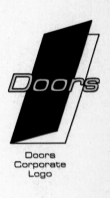

Other books by WARREN ELLIS

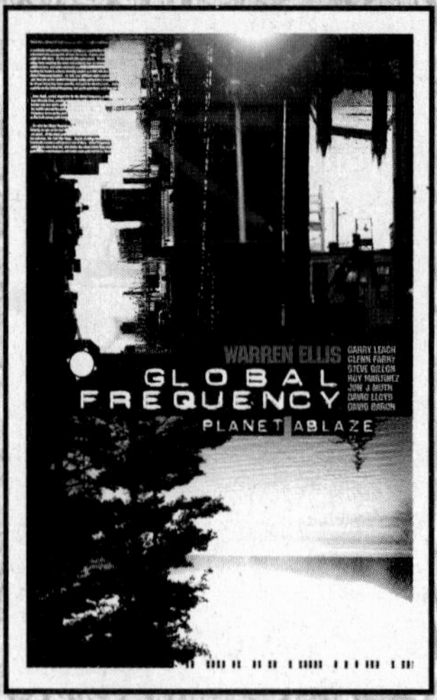
WARREN ELLIS
GLOBAL FREQUENCY
PLANET ABLAZE

GLOBAL FREQUENCY
BOOKS 1 & 2

ELLIS/VARIOUS

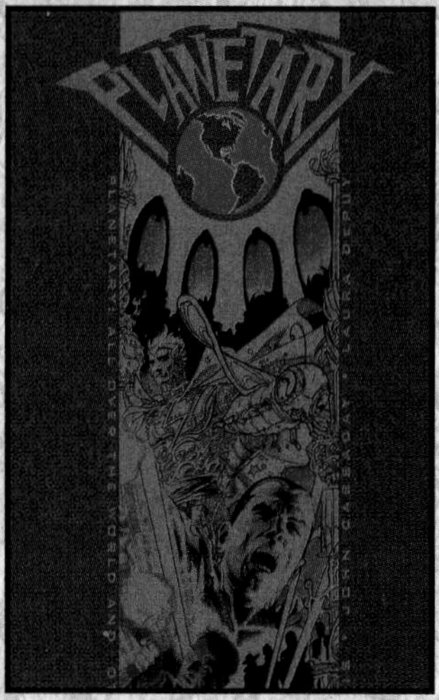
PLANETARY

PLANETARY
VOLUMES 1–3

ELLIS/CASSADAY

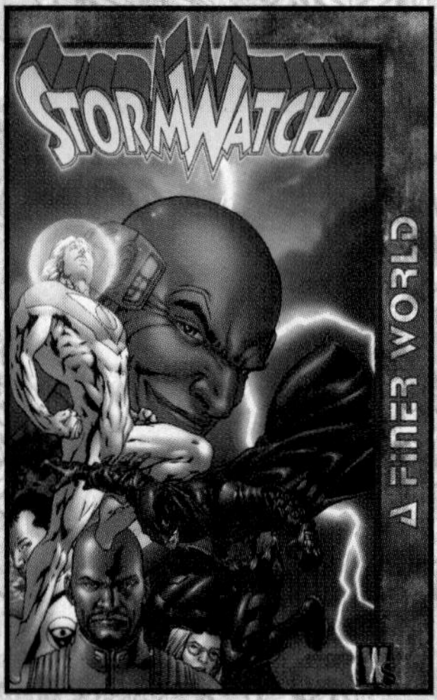
STORMWATCH
A FINER WORLD

STORMWATCH
BOOKS 1–5

ELLIS/RANEY/VARIOUS

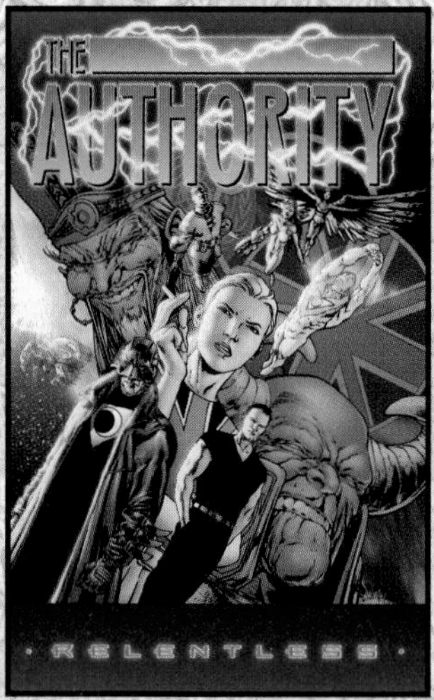
THE AUTHORITY
RELENTLESS

THE AUTHORITY
BOOKS 1–7

ELLIS/HITCH/VARIOUS

Search the Graphic Novels section of wildstorm.com for art and info on every one of our hundreds of books!

TO FIND MORE COLLECTED EDITIONS AND MONTHLY COMIC BOOKS FROM WILDSTORM AND DC COMICS, CALL 1-888-COMIC BOOK FOR THE NEAREST COMICS SHOP OR GO TO YOUR LOCAL BOOK STORE.